Arbeiten und Texte zur Slavistik

Begründet von Wolfgang Kasack
Herausgegeben von Frank Göbler und Rainer Goldt

Band 78

Verlag Otto Sagner
München

Reading for Entertainment in Contemporary Russia:
Post-Soviet Popular Literature in Historical Perspective

edited by
Stephen Lovell and Birgit Menzel

Verlag Otto Sagner · München
2005

Bibliografische Information der Deutschen Bibliothek
Die Deutsche Bibliothek verzeichnet diese Publikation in der Deutschen Nationalbibliografie; detaillierte bibliografische Informationen sind im Internet über <http://dnb.ddb.de> abrufbar.

Bibliographic information published by Die Deutsche Bibliothek
Die Deutsche Bibliothek lists this publication in the DeutscheNationalbibliografie; detailed bibliographic data are available in the Internet at <http://dnb.ddb.de>.

Verlag Otto Sagner
c/o Kubon & Sagner Buchexport-Import GmbH
D-80328 München (Germany)

Telefon 089 / 54 218-106
Telefax 089 / 54 218-226
verlag@kubon-sagner.de

Umschlag- und Reihengestaltung: Christopher Triplett, London
Druck und Bindung: Difo-Druck, Bamberg

Alle Rechte vorbehalten
© 2005 Verlag Otto Sagner
Printed in Germany

ISSN 0173-2307
ISBN 3-87690-912-0

Contents

Introduction (Stephen Lovell/Birgit Menzel)	7
Literature and Entertainment in Russia: A Brief History (Stephen Lovell)	11
Reading the Russian Popular (Stephen Lovell)	29
Writing, Reading and Selling Literature in Russia 1986-2004 (Birgit Menzel)	39
Russian Detective Fiction (Marina Koreneva)	57
The Action Thriller (*Boevik*) in Contemporary Russia (Boris Dubin)	101
Russian Science Fiction and Fantasy Literature (Birgit Menzel)	117
Russian Romantic Fiction (Mariia Cherniak)	151
Russian Historical Fiction (Boris Dubin)	173
A Selected Bibliography of Works on Post-Soviet Popular Literature (Birgit Menzel)	197
Notes on Contributors	201

Stephen Lovell/Birgit Menzel

Introduction

Popular literature has formed the subject of much academic work over the last forty years, but it has not yet made too many inroads into Russian studies. The main reason for this state of affairs is not hard to identify: the Soviet Union was deeply hostile to commercial entertainment literature, tending to see it as the debased cultural product of the West. While it is untrue to say that writing of this kind was eradicated in Soviet Russia, it certainly took extremely specific – and, to a Western sensibility, bizarre – forms: there was a peculiarly Soviet variety of historical novel, a Soviet science fiction, even a Soviet mode of detective fiction. This situation was brought to a remarkably sudden end by the economic reforms of the late 1980s and early 1990s. Book publishing became a true 'business', and all genres of literature were fair game for the emerging literary entrepreneurs. Western thrillers and romantic novels were widely translated, but 'native' authors were soon trying their hand at these new forms – some of them with great commercial success. Russia was assimilating foreign cultural models with extraordinary rapidity, but at the same time giving them a new flavour. The pages of post-Soviet entertainment novels were crammed full of recognisably Russian types and stereotypes: bandits, scoundrels, 'New Russians' (i.e. nouveaux riches), bureaucrats, redemptive heroines and 'positive heroes' distantly related to the protagonists of socialist realism.

The present volume is designed to combine an engaging and informative account of the first ten years of this new mass-appeal literature with a detailed 'prehistory' of Russian popular fiction. Chapters have been specially commissioned from experts in the field so as to cover the main genres of contemporary Russian popular fiction and to trace those genres back to their twentieth- and nineteenth-century roots. A further objective of this book is to combine literary and historical analysis with an account of the social, economic and institutional factors underlying the post-Soviet publishing business. In pursuing these aims we also have the opportunity, in the chapters by Koreneva, Dubin and Cherniak, to put before an anglophone audience some of the most interesting recent Russian scholarship on popular fiction, its publishers and its audiences.

Our intention, however, is not merely to apply to the Russian case research agendas that have been more fully developed by scholars of other European cultures. We also wish to suggest that Russian popular culture deserves the attention even of people with no specialist interest in Slavic studies. Post-Soviet Russia developed a commercial popular culture at amazing speed, and the various genres of popular fiction together constitute a fascinating chapter in the history of the post-Communist transition. They reveal a culture deprived almost overnight of its former authorities and canons – not to mention its economic structures. Writers, journalists and (especially) publishers boldly stepped into the void and set about providing values and narrative models for a 'new' Russia that in some ways had a good deal in common with the 'old' versions but in other ways departed drastically from them. In cultural history, paradigm shifts are rarely as much of a white-knuckle ride as was the case in Russia in the 1990s. For this and other reasons, comparativist students and scholars of popular culture will, we hope, find much to intrigue them in the pages that follow.

The structure of the book is simple and largely self-explanatory. The detailed investigation of individual genres is preceded by three introductory chapters. In the first of these, Stephen Lovell provides a brief outline history of formulaic entertainment literature in Russia, and suggests that fiction of this kind belongs much closer to the centre of Russian literary history than it has conventionally been placed. In Chapter 2, which moves on from the history to the content of popular literature, Lovell sets down a few hypotheses about how Russian literary formulas can be classified and interpreted. In Chapter 3, Birgit Menzel provides the crucial socio-economic background to the story of contemporary Russian popular literature by surveying post-Soviet developments in publishing and the book trade in all their many aspects.

The second half of the book is devoted to a series of genre studies. In Chapter 4, Marina Koreneva provides a detailed and deeply historical account of detective fiction in Russia. By casting her net widely to include tales of adventure, transgression and retribution dating back to the nineteenth century and before, Koreneva is able to present the post-Soviet *detektiv* not just as striking in its own right and revealing of post-Soviet social preoccupations, but also as the latest in a long series of narrative responses to the perennial themes of crime, punishment and justice. In Chapter 5, Boris Dubin investigates the post-Soviet action thriller (*boevik*), a genre with a less elaborate pre-history than the *detektiv*, but a crucial source of mass-cultural responses to the collapse of social order in the 1990s. The *boevik* hero is a strong and undemonstrative loner with right on his side as he battles the corruption and depravity of the world around him. As well as providing plentiful psychological compensation for a largely disempowered and dislocated male readership, this protagonist serves to redefine the notion of 'success' and to redraw the boundaries of legitimate individual action in post-Soviet Russia.

In Chapter 6, the focus shifts from the violation and re-imposition of social norms in the contemporary world to the projection of social norms into other, imagined times and places. Birgit Menzel's account of the fantastic takes an extended look back at the Soviet era, when science fiction enjoyed periods of enormous popularity and public prestige. It also, however, could become a problematic and subversive genre – especially in the post-Stalin era, when the predetermined Future of communist ideology showed few signs of arriving. In her study of post-Soviet developments, Menzel traces an important shift from future-orientated, technologically informed science fiction to the new genre of 'fantasy', which is more likely to take as its subject Slavic mythology. Russian society has not lost its craving for imagined other worlds, but it now seeks them more often in the past than in the future.

In Chapter 7, Mariia Cherniak describes a post-Soviet popular genre that constituted a significant break with Soviet cultural patterns: romance. In the 1990s, women became perhaps the most lucrative of the target audiences for newly commercialised Russian publishers. The book market responded quickly by releasing translations of dozens, and in due course hundreds, of American and British Harlequin romances. While Western authors retained much of their appeal, they were soon joined by Russian authors working in the same vein. But Russian-style romance departed in many ways from the American model, revealing a very different understanding both of gender roles and of the nature of a true 'happy end'; here, in fact, we have one of the most eloquent cases of divergence between Russian and Western popular narrative formulas.

In Chapter 8, Boris Dubin rounds off the collection by discussing an increasingly popular and successful genre of popular fiction: the historical novel. As Dubin shows in some detail, the fictional treatment of the national past fluctuated significantly in twentieth-century Russia, but in the 1990s it came to be permeated by an increasingly strident imperialist and isolationist nationalism. Dubin serves us with a powerful reminder that the interplay between state, society and commerce is not guaranteed to produce the civilised pluralism that we often expect to find in capitalist democracy. Sometimes the interests and values of these various parties may pull in the same illiberal direction. This, at any rate, appears to be the case in Putin's Russia, where statist nationalism has gained a disturbing hegemony in both public discourse and popular opinion and provides the common currency of the 'patriotic historical novel'.

This project was supported by a two-year research grant from the British Council (project number 1154) and the Deutscher Akademischer Austauschdienst (DAAD). We thank those institutions, and we also gratefully acknowledge the valuable contribution made by several colleagues who participated in the project at earlier stages: Annett Jubara, Andrei Rogachevskii, Ekaterina Rogachevskaia, Rosalinde Sartorti and Werner Thiele.

Stephen Lovell

Literature and Entertainment in Russia: A Brief History

There are plenty of reasons to expect the history outlined in this chapter to be 'brief' indeed. Russian literature, for the last one hundred and fifty years, has made its mark on European culture for its deep seriousness, moral and social engagement, and philosophical ambition. Russian writers, it is commonly believed, were concerned with enlightening and edifying their readers, but hardly with entertaining them. The works they created – most notably the 'baggy monsters' of the nineteenth century – subverted or superseded formulas, but never succumbed to them. The Russian classics, it is often assumed, were resistant to the pressures of the literary market and of 'readability' in a way that Dickens and Balzac were not. The reason for this state of affairs is usually sought – and found – in the Russian intelligentsia: a group of literary-minded educated people who first coalesced as a distinct social entity in the 1840s and set the tone for intellectual life all the way through to 1917 (and, according to many accounts, well beyond that). The Russian intelligentsia enjoyed cultural hegemony in an exceptionally polarised society, and for that reason took upon itself a 'civilising mission'. It is charged with (or championed for) having been intransigently hostile to commercial popular culture, convinced of its own prerogative to create a culture of greater value, and committed to transmitting that culture to society at large.

This standard outline history of Russian literary culture has the merit of strongly articulating the distinctiveness of the Russian case. But, like all such outlines, it has limitations. It tends, for example, to rely on a partial understanding of nineteenth-century Russian literature that accords greatest significance to Dostoevskii, Turgenev and Tolstoi, much less to Pushkin or early Chekhov, and none at all to dozens of 'lesser names'. Evidence for the high seriousness of Russian literature is sought from a self-selecting sample; 'high' literature is not shown in its complex interactions with 'popular' and 'middlebrow' forms. Similarly unnuanced treatment is handed out to the 'intelligentsia', a group whose social composition and cultural values changed significantly through the nineteenth century, and whose authority over literary life was in any case always far from absolute. The argument of this chapter, and of this book, will be that entertainment literature (books that aim to please and to sell) do belong in the mainstream history of Russian culture. By attending to Russia's 'formula' genres, to their mutations and their interactions with 'high' literature, we can build a foundation for properly informed comparison of Russia's literature with that of other European cultures; only by taking this synthesising approach can we give an account of Russia's 'distinctiveness' that does not depend on cliché and stereotype.

On closer inspection, received wisdom can prove less than illuminating. Take for example one of the cornerstones of Russian intellectual history: the assumed hostility of the intelligentsia to the market. It is far from clear how exactly this makes Russia different from England or Germany. After all, hostility to commercial popular culture on the part of the educated public was very much the rule in nineteenth-century Europe, not the exception. It pays to look in more detail at how the educated public came into being, and how its existence affected the economic conditions of literature.

In Russia this public was, of course, late to develop. Rulers did not relinquish control over printing until the 1720s, and it was not until the middle of the eighteenth century that book production was truly becoming the domain of civil society rather than that of the Church or the state. In any case, the public was still tiny. The number of active readers (that is to say, regular consumers of journals and books) in the 1750s and 1760s was probably not much in excess of 1,000. *Sankt-Peterburgskie vedomosti* (the court newspaper) had, for example, 150 subscribers in 1751. The subscription editions introduced just afterwards were even less widely read. The first volume of Philipp Dilthey's *Universal History* (published in 1762) attracted only eighty-three subscribers. Over the last few decades of the eighteenth century, however, the public grew dramatically by the standards of the time. The number of active readers at the end of the 1790s is reliably estimated at 12,000-13,000. Most of these came from the nobility (especially its middle ranks), but the clergy and merchantry were also gaining significant representation.[1]

---

[1] The figures cited here are from Iu.A. Samarin, *Chitatel' v Rossii vo vtoroi polovine XVIII*

The reading public continued to grow in the first third of the nineteenth century. More and more people, in other words, were coming to believe that 'literature' might be important and interesting, and that at least some of it might be written by Russians and in Russian. Although literacy statistics are extremely sketchy for most of the nineteenth century, the best estimate holds that somewhere around 2.5 million people (out of an overall population of 50 million) could read in the 1820s, and that, of these, around 50,000 were regular readers. From the mid-1820s to the mid-1840s literature took shape as a social 'institution': the expansion of the reading public increased the commercial possibilities of writing, new periodicals and publishers became established, and writing became less of a pastime or calling and more of a profession.[2]

This 'institutionalisation' of literature was, in and of itself, far from unique to Russia. It is undergone by all societies as they acquire a public sphere and a reading public that can support a book trade. But even so, the Russian case had certain peculiarities. Above all, Russian literature was exposed to commercial pressures when it was still in a somewhat inchoate state. In the 1820s, it was a matter of dispute what the Russian literary language should be. The term *literatura*, first fixed in printed Russian in the Petrine era, still sounded like a foreign import. The range of its potential referents was far from being universally accepted. Some critics, scholars and literary practitioners reserved the homegrown and wholesome word *slovesnost'* for much that we would call 'literature'.[3] Many others, however, felt that *literatura* opened exciting new cultural possibilities: not least, the opportunity to enter the European cultural mainstream. And the complications did not end there. Russia was acquiring not only a literature and a national culture in the 1820s and 1830s but also an urbanised elite culture. Nobles were flocking to St Petersburg as never before, the central bureaucracy was swelling, and these new urbanites were receiving a better edu-

---

    veka (po spiskam podpischikov), M, 2000. A more rounded account of reading and publishing in the eighteenth century can be found in G. Marker, *Publishing, Printing and the Origins of Intellectual Life in Russia, 1700-1800*, Princeton, 1985.

[2] A.I. Reitblat, *Kak Pushkin vyshel v genii: Istoriko-sotsiologicheskie ocherki o knizhnoi kul'ture Pushkinskoi epokhi*, M, 2001 (the estimate of literacy rate is on p. 14).

[3] The distinction between *literatura* and *slovesnost'* has something in common with the Kultur/Zivilisation divide in German culture. The parallel is not exact, however: the word *literatura*, though it did not connote *narodnost'* and was not normally used for folk or 'traditional' culture, was not considered necessarily antithetical to the national spirit. Rather, it lent itself to a concept of nationhood centred on educated 'civil society' (*obshchestvo*). *Literatura* remained a fluid, and for the most part positively construed, concept throughout the nineteenth century. I am grateful to Andy Byford for elucidation of this point.

cation as they prepared to make their careers. Everyone could agree that the 'public' was expanding rapidly, but much less clear was whom it comprised. Nobles, bureaucrats of all levels, merchants and other townsfolk were all making demands on print culture.

All this meant that writers of the generation of Aleksandr Pushkin (1799-1837), far from being loftily indifferent to the market and the demands of the public, were constantly debating questions such as: Should the writer take money for his poetry? What and where is the public? Should the writer aim to please the public? If so, how? Pushkin himself was by no means the least adept writer of his time in finding answers to these questions. He enjoyed renown tinged with scandal in his youth, and on his return to Moscow in September 1826 after several years of exile was fêted by the beau monde. He was also granted an audience with Nicholas I where the recently installed emperor offered to be his personal censor. This meeting is usually interpreted as dismal evidence of state interference in the life and work of Russia's national poet, but at the time Pushkin reacted to it very differently: with elation. To receive this mark of individual attention was in fact a guarantee that Pushkin would return straight to the centre of Russian literary life.

At the same time as working within the old patronage system, Pushkin was able to develop an acute sense of his own commercial worth. When in southern exile and nominally employed in state service, he turned down an assignment to investigate a plague of locusts in the surrounding area, arguing that poetry, not pest control, was his 'trade'. By the standards of his day, he was extremely well rewarded for his writing.

Yet there was undeniably tension between Pushkin's several literary personae: he was court artist, salon poet, professional writer, lonely genius, and member of elite literary coterie.[4] Much as he might have liked to combine commercial success with personal independence and the appreciation of connoisseurs, in practice this was not always possible. And, as he switched between his various roles, he did not necessarily take the reading public along with him. His prose works of the 1830s were, for example, much less celebrated in their time than his 'novel in verse' *Evgenii Onegin* had been in the previous decade. From the late 1820s onwards, Pushkin found himself in demeaning competition with writers who reckoned to keep much more smartly in step with changing tastes. Foremost

---

[4] An interesting exploration of these complexities can be found in W.M. Todd, *Fiction and Society in the Age of Pushkin: Ideology, Institutions, and Narrative*, Cambridge, MA, 1986.

among these was Faddei Bulgarin, detested by his literary contemporaries as a police spy and unscrupulous hack, but also the most talented journalist of his time and an extremely popular author in his own right. Bulgarin founded and edited *Severnaia pchela* (The Northern Bee), the first newspaper in Russia to aim at an urban 'middle-class' audience. He devoted much thought to the emerging reading public, in the mid-1820s dividing it into four main sections. First, the wealthy and aristocratic elite, who read mainly foreign books. Second, the 'middle estate', who read mainly in Russian. Third, the 'lower estate', whose taste was mainly for devotional literature and for simple and moralising tales of adventure. Finally, there were the 'scholars and writers', who were not numerous enough for a newspaper editor to concern himself with them greatly.[5] Bulgarin's target audience was the middle estate of educated but non-elite urbanites: these people he saw as the true backbone of the Russian reading public. He laid claim to this audience by a variety of means – fair and foul. He designed his newspaper so as to draw in the reader with up-to-the-minute accounts of Petersburg life. He publicly disparaged his competitors – including notably Pushkin – as literary 'aristocrats' who were incapable of writing for anything more than a public of salon dilettantes. At the same time, he promoted himself as a down-to-earth and straight-talking type of littérateur.[6] He wrote an entertaining picaresque novel, *Ivan Vyzhigin*, that was an instant and huge success on its first publication in 1829. And this was no fluke. Bulgarin had not only written the nearest thing to a bestseller in early nineteenth-century Russia, he had also created a winning formula. His manner of narration was intimate and chatty, and he addressed the reader as his silent partner in an entertaining conversation. *Ivan Vyzhigin* had another important component of popular literature besides entertainment: it offered the reader satisfying solidarity with the narrator's values. Although the next twist in the plot might be unpredictable, the narrator was morally stable and reliable, and the reader's complicity in his view of the world could be complete. In the 1830s, Russian literature was experimenting with a number of more sophisticated narrative techniques (such as those employed in the stories of Nikolai Gogol'). For this reason, Bulgarin's *Vyzhigin* soon lost whatever interest

---

[5] A.I. Reitblat, *Ot Bovy k Bal'montu: Ocherki po istorii chteniia v Rossii vo vtoroi polovine XIX veka*, M, 1991, pp. 10-11.
[6] On which see N.N. Akimova, 'Bulgarin i Gogol' (literaturnaia biografiia i literaturnaia reputatsiia)', *Russkaia literatura*, 3, 1996, pp. 3-18.

it had initially held for the literary elite. But among the author's beloved 'middle estate' it retained its appeal for some while longer.[7]

Bulgarin, then, may be seen as a pioneering creator of literature that entertained readers, confirmed their view of the world, yet did not patronise them. He had discovered a formula that worked. But such formulas are liable to lose their force rather quickly as the character of the audience changes. In the middle third of the nineteenth century, the Russian reading public(s) continued to expand and to make new demands on writers. Urbanisation continued, literacy rates improved further (especially in the cities), and new printing technologies appeared that made publishing for the 'mass' market a distinct possibility. By the 1860s Russia's 'active readers' numbered in the hundreds of thousands, and they could not remotely be seen as a single homogeneous 'public'. They included, as always, an elite of 'serious' readers, but also a sub-elite that depended on digests and surveys to make sense of new literary and scholarly developments. More numerous still were readers who required from books and periodicals that blend of entertainment, escape, and practical and moral guidance that tends to be characteristic of modern 'popular' literature.

So what did the literate common people – peasants, shopkeepers, traders, servants, clerks, workers – have on offer? As Bulgarin bore witness in the 1820s, a 'lower estate' of readers had existed much earlier in the century, and its main reading matter was the Russian equivalent of chap-books (known as *lubki* or *lubochnaia literatura*).[8] Until the 1870s, these tended to be dominated by religious and folkloric subjects and styles (though war and travel stories, and humorous tales from everyday life, also figured). But the second half of the nineteenth century saw a distinct secular turn. New subjects such as crime, science and romance gained in popularity. Even where folkloric subjects were used, they were written up in more 'realistic' style, with fewer fantastic or supernatural touches and more details to supply plausible motivation.[9]

---

[7] For more on the stylistic and narrative features of *Vyzhigin*, see N.N. Akimova, 'Bulgarin i Gogol'' (massovoe i elitarnoe v russkoi literature: problema avtora i chitatelia)', *Russkaia literatura*, 2, 1996, pp. 3-22.

[8] The term *lubok* (pl. *lubki*) strictly speaking denotes a kind of popular print, and so belongs to the realm of visual culture rather than that of popular verbal narrative. But the word by extension attached itself to literature for the lower classes (and even, for many intellectuals, to all literature that they considered low-grade). For a history of the *lubok*, see W. Koschmal, *Der russische Volksbilderbogen: von der Religion zum Theater*, München, 1989.

[9] See J. Brooks, *When Russia Learned to Read: Literacy and Popular Literature, 1861-1917*, Princeton, 1985, chapter 3.

Lubki continued to be produced until – and even during – the First World War, but by the end of the nineteenth century they were not the only, or even the main, source of reading matter for the urban lower classes. People might now buy adventure novels in instalments from a kiosk or bookshop. They might also subscribe to one of the several periodicals that now catered to the 'popular' market. 'Boulevard' newspapers offered serialised novels, as well as keeping up an engaging and entertaining commentary on urban life (in which respect they differed fundamentally from *lubki*). The early twentieth century saw further innovations, as the first 'kopeck newspapers' appeared: by offering extensive coverage of crime, scandal, and national and international news, these addressed themselves to a reader even more deeply immersed in the modern world. The increased consumption by the lower classes of periodicals and instalment novels, as opposed to isolated *lubki*, signified a move towards more 'modern' and urbanised habits: now reading was not a one-off affair, but involved a more regular and informed commitment to a set of formula genres. A representative case was Semen Ivanovich Kanatchikov, a peasant-turned-worker who arrived in Moscow in 1895: his work cooperative (*artel'*) had a collective subscription to *Moskovskii listok* and were avid readers of both the paper's crime reports and its serialised fiction.[10]

But the formulas of popular fiction themselves changed in interesting ways in the last few prerevolutionary decades. *Moskovskii listok*, for example, was truly innovative in providing material that was potentially appealing to all of the urban lower classes. But it also showed continuity with earlier popular culture. Its most sensationally successful feuilleton novel (published from 1882 to 1885) was the latest in a long line of specifically Russian 'bandit' tales. The hero, Vasilii Churkin, had much in common with all his predecessors in the genre. This was no Robin Hood figure, and no chivalrous knight driven outside the law by wrongs inflicted on him. Rather, Churkin was the embodiment of elemental and often violent freedom. He conformed to a long-standing 'Russian myth about the contradiction between freedom and the orderly world, and the individual's imperative to choose between them'.[11] For all its pioneering impact on urban popular culture, then, *Moskovskii listok* still maintained a traditional view of the world as governed by authority that could be overridden only very temporarily and that allowed little room for individual initiative.

---

[10] *A Radical Worker in Tsarist Russia: The Autobiography of Semen Ivanovich Kanatchikov*, trans. and ed. R. Zelnik, Stanford, 1986.
[11] Brooks, *When Russia Learned to Read*, p. 182.

In the early twentieth century *Moskovskii listok* was overtaken by publications that offered lower-class readers a more modern and individualistic set of formula narratives. Where bandit heroes figured, they were likely to be more 'cultured' and less indiscriminately violent than Churkin; their activities beyond the law did not necessarily lead to their ruin or to their moral surrender. Even more significantly, the bandit tales were now joined – and largely supplanted – by adventure and crime stories that were set in modern times and often outside Russia, and figured self-willed heroes whose activities did not place them in opposition to authority but rather made them the embodiment of authority. In other words, Russia acquired its own detective stories. The best-known of these told the adventures of Nat Pinkerton, a character borrowed from American popular fiction but one who acquired a peculiarly Russian flavour in the serials of the 1900s and 1910s. The Russian Pinkerton was less an ingenious sleuth than a hard-boiled cop who pursued criminals relentlessly, caught them by a mixture of energy, experience, astuteness, courage and sheer luck, and then saw that they were shown no mercy. In 1908, the influential literary critic Kornei Chukovskii (subsequently, in Soviet times, a celebrated children's writer) contrasted Pinkerton unfavourably with Sherlock Holmes, claiming that the violence of the former had displaced the brainwork of the former in contemporary popular fiction; Holmes had mutated into a gorilla with a pistol.[12] Even if some allowances need to be made for Chukovskii's typical intellectual's contempt for commercial popular culture, he was pointing to features of Pinkerton that distinguished the detective both from *lubok* protagonists and from the slightly more cerebral sleuths of Western popular fiction of the same period. A sample Pinkerton plot has the hero investigating an abduction in New York's Chinatown, coming across a fortunate lead in another part of the city, and then infiltrating the Chinese community. The story ends with a bloody shootout that saves the kidnapped American just before he becomes the victim of a ritual sacrifice. As the tale concludes, 'Nat Pinkerton proved once again that a detective needs not only a calling, but also a broad education'. Besides strong nerves and sharpshooting skills, Pinkerton had know-how and a thorough mastery of the language and culture of the most threatening of New York's immigrant communities. The fact that he did not have to show brilliant powers of observation and deduction mattered not at all, since he had so many attributes that were likely to be prised

---

[12] K.I. Chukovskii, 'Nat Pinkerton', in idem, *Sobranie sochinenii v shesti tomakh*, M, 1965-69, vol. 6, pp. 117-147.

more highly by Russia's lower-class 'popular' readers: energy, experience, and education and (self-)training that equipped him to achieve spectacular practical success.[13]

So far I have described how market principles entered Russian literature in the first half of the nineteenth century, and how they encouraged a dynamic and diverse culture of popular print in the second half of the century. By the 1880s, non-elite urbanites had on offer a much greater range of material that catered explicitly to their interests: old-style chap-books, instalment novels, the 'boulevard' press. Lower-class tastes and values were themselves moving in new directions: away from the religious and the folkloric and towards more secular genres – such as adventure, romance, and the detective story – that placed much more emphasis on individual agency and on success and gratification without retribution. By the early twentieth century, as Jeffrey Brooks argued in his pathbreaking study *When Russia Learned to Read*, Russia was acquiring a modern and urbanised reading culture that made it broadly comparable with Western Europe (even if there were, as we have seen, striking differences in the way that Russians used formula genres such as the detective story).

All this would be a good enough reason by itself to make a serious study of prerevolutionary Russian potboilers. But it is also important to note that urban popular literature is not the exclusive property of the lower classes: although it played a crucial role, for example, in conditioning the adaptation of peasant migrants to life in the big city, it had impact in other areas too. The authors of Russia's literary mainstream were far from being impervious to the 'mass' fiction that was being produced around them. Nikolai Chernyshevskii began his *What Is to Be Done?*, a novel that served as the Bible of radical youth in the 1860s, with a first chapter that affected the manner and the narrative technique of a potboiler so as to seize the reader's attention. Dostoevskii's *Crime and Punishment* contains perhaps the most suspenseful scene in the whole of Russian literature: a scene that could not have been written without the author's close acquaintance with the boulevard press of the time. Anton Chekhov began his writing career working within the narrow constraints of the humorous sketch popular in the newspapers and magazines of the 1880s, and the episodic quality of this form left a definite mark on his later literary development (even if his narrative techniques

---

[13] 'The Bloody Talisman', in J. von Geldern and L. McReynolds, *Entertaining Tsarist Russia: Tales, Songs, Plays, Movies, Jokes, Ads, and Images from Russian Urban Life 1779-1917*, Bloomington, 1998. This anthology contains many other useful illustrations of popular urban genres mentioned in this chapter.

moved on and became more subtle and sophisticated).[14] Maksim Gor'kii, championed by many members of the elite literary intelligentsia in the late 1890s and 1900s, was also a huge popular celebrity whose works were astutely marketed by creating an image of the author as Romantic outsider. Even the severe and puritantical sexagenerian Lev Tolstoi wrote a novella, *The Kreutzer Sonata*, that offered a sensational account of a marriage gone terribly wrong. The narrator's finishing touch is to recall, in gruesome detail, how he stabbed and fatally wounded his wife: his dagger first met the resistance of her corset, but then plunged into soft flesh. Tolstoi apparently meant his work as a serious polemic against what he saw as the destructive moral effect of sexual relationships, but his contemporaries, with much justification, saw it very differently: as a compelling and fast-paced account of pathological jealousy and violence.

The introduction of 'popular' themes and devices into 'elite' literature is not the only way in which the degree of their separation is reduced. Although late imperial Russia was an extremely polarised society by wider European standards, there was no simple opposition between literary intelligentsia and lower-class readers. By the 1880s, and even more so by the 1900s, there were many other, intermediate, groups of readers: moderately educated, socially aspirational, curious but non-intellectual types. While these people might willingly partake of 'serious' literature and of 'mass' fiction, they also had available for their consumption a range of texts that did not quite fit either of these models. Russia was, in other words, acquiring a 'middlebrow' fiction of its own.[15] Perhaps the most successful work in this vein was Anastasiia Verbitskaia's *The Keys to Happiness* (*Kliuchi schast'ia*, 1908-13), a multi-volume romance that was a sensation on its first publication. Literary critics were not slow to disparage Verbitskaia and all she stood for. Kornei Chukovskii intervened in print after reading only the second of the novel's six volumes. He took the author to task for an overblown style that he found to be characteristic of the traditions and 'unwritten aesthetics' of 'boulevard literature'. He also mocked what he saw as Verbitskaia's moral pretensions and her immodest public pronouncements (she had, for example, mentioned herself in the same breath as Gor'kii, Andreev and Kuprin). But Chukovskii failed to notice that the implausible combination of a popular literary

---

[14] On Chekhov and the popular humorous genres of his time, see A. Chudakov, *Mir Chekhova: Vozniknovenie i utverzhdenie*, M, 1986, pp. 69-140.

[15] This is the principal argument of B. Holmgren, *Rewriting Capitalism: Literature and the Market in Late Tsarist Russia and the Kingdom of Poland*, Pittsburgh, 1998.

form (the romance) and a certain literary seriousness made *The Keys to Happiness* not ridiculous but rather symptomatic of an intriguing new mode of literary production: one that met the contrasting imperatives of entertainment, social engagement, and moral and practical guidance. If we treat Chukovskii as a sociologist rather than as a moralist or a literary 'gatekeeper', then we find many telling observations in his article on Verbitskaia. Although she wrote in the style favoured by 'army clerks, hairdressers, market traders and young manservants', she was in fact read by students and members of the intelligentsia as well as by workers and ordinary townspeople.[16] She was, in other words, a leading practitioner of the kind of literature that could overcome several of the deep cultural divides of Russian urban society.

Here too we find evidence that Russia in the early twentieth century was developing a range of popular entertainment genres that would be more recognisable to a Western European reader. To be sure, Russia's 'middlebrow' fiction bore the imprint of a specific kind of moral seriousness; it was less 'westernised' even than the commercially successful literature of the neighbouring Kingdom of Poland.[17] But the very existence of urban novel-length fiction that was not folksy or recherché or philosophically overburdened represented a striking innovation of the last few prerevolutionary decades.

The start of the Soviet period arrested this diversification of urban print culture (including entertainment literature). For all the violence they did to sections of the intelligentsia, the Bolsheviks quickly made common cause with the many literary intellectuals who despised the market.[18] They poured scarce funds into publishing approved Russian classics and started a campaign against decadent and 'bourgeois' entertainment genres. *Lubok* and *Pinkerton* became thoroughly dirty words, and purges of library collections made prerevolutionary popular fiction one of their first targets. The spirit of the times is indicated by a recommended scenario for an evening of cultural propaganda in 1920s youth clubs where God, Nat Pinkerton, Anastasiia Verbitskaia and Tarzan appeared on stage as enemies of Soviet culture.[19]

---

[16] Chukovskii, 'Verbitskaia' (1910), in *Sobranie sochinenii*, vol. 6, quotation on p. 13.
[17] See Holmgren, *Rewriting Capitalism*.
[18] For an account of the 'romantic anti-capitalism' of the Soviet Russian intelligentsia, see K. Clark, *Petersburg: Crucible of Cultural Revolution*, Cambridge, MA, 1995.
[19] V. Zhemchuzhny, 'Evening of Books for Youth Clubs' (1924), in J. von Geldern and R. Stites (eds), *Mass Culture in Soviet Russia: Tales, Poems, Songs, Movies, Plays, and Folklore 1917-1953*, Bloomington, 1995.

In the 1920s there were still attempts to use the forms of Western-style or prerevolutionary popular culture to make Soviet-style sentiments palatable to the postrevolutionary reader. The 'Red Pinkerton' was a recognised literary phenomenon of the time.[20] Marietta Shaginian and Il'ia Erenburg were among the well-known novelists who used suspense and adventure to enliven their writings. Il'ia Il'f and Evgenii Petrov wrote *The Twelve Chairs* (*Dvenadtsat' stul'ev*), perhaps the nearest to a popular Soviet 'cult' novel, by returning to one of the oldest kinds of popular literary protagonist: the energetic and charismatic rogue. But by 1927, the year that *The Twelve Chairs* was first published, such allusions to popular culture were very much the exception rather than the rule. The audience for fiction was still highly unstable, and included many people who had received their education and/or arrived in the city very recently, but Soviet publishing policy increasingly began to impose on readers a kind of literature that purported to speak to all of them. The one thing that Soviet culture could not tolerate was diversity. In those modern societies where a commercial print culture exists, writers adopt many different literary forms and cater to many different (though often overlapping) audiences. Soviet writers, by contrast, were required to write for a single but enormous audience. They were to produce literature that was 'popular' in the sense of being for the whole people.

The main ingredient of this recipe for Soviet literature was an idealised model of the 'people' for whom this literature was to be written. The image of the 'new Soviet reader' took shape in the first half of the 1930s and represented a creative synthesis of the desires of three interested parties. First, and most importantly, the regime, which insisted on a literature that was ideologically correct and formative. Second, the writers, whose belief in their own importance and in literature's high moral seriousness was easily compatible with the Party's political agenda. Third, the newly formed Soviet readers, many of whom had been introduced to the printed word very recently and required of literature things that the writers and political leaders were all too happy to give them: a straightforward narrative, practical 'usefulness', a clear and simple message. They did *not* want modernist experimentation, bad language, or lurid sex scenes; once again, the masters of Soviet culture were delighted to oblige.[21]

---

[20] On which see R. Russell, 'Red Pinktertonism: An Aspect of Soviet Literature', *The Slavonic and East European Review,* 60, 1982, pp. 390-413.

[21] See E. Dobrenko, *The Making of the State Reader: Social and Aesthetic Contexts of the Reception of Soviet Literature*, Stanford, 1997.

This synthetic image of the 'mass Soviet reader' proved to be a great practical success. No literary institution was in a position to put forward an alternative model, given absolute state control over publishing. Very few writers had an interest in writing for any other audience. And Soviet readers in the 1930s consumed more or less willingly what they were given. As can easily be imagined, Soviet literature – with its newly enshrined aesthetic, socialist realism – left no room for the genres of popular literature as they were understood in Western Europe at the time, or as they had been understood in Russia in the 1900s. Genres such as the thriller, the romance and the detective story disappeared from view, while themes such as the occult, magic and religion had been entirely taboo from the beginning of the Soviet period. Science fiction had an early Soviet flowering in the 1920s, but after that lost much of its prominence. Historical fiction came to the fore in Soviet literature of the 1930s, but it was informed by a Great Russian Marxism that differentiated it from the more adventure-orientated popular historical fiction of the nineteenth century.

All this did not mean that Soviet readers did not want to be entertained or to receive the practical emotional guidance that is usually dispensed by popular literature. Reliable evidence on reader response in the Stalin era is patchy, but it does suggest that many Soviet people found the formula narratives of socialist realism to be inspiring and/or satisfying. The function of the romance passed to novels of the 'boy meets girl meets tractor' variety, while the narratives of individual success that commonly underpin Western popular fiction had the biographies of Soviet 'positive heroes' as their Soviet counterparts.

It is easy to forget, moreover, that the socialist realist classics of the 1930s and 1940s made certain concessions to popular taste. In the polemical 1920s, and during the period of 'cultural revolution' from 1928 to 1932, many writers had been addicted to plotlessness and smaller forms such as the sketch and the short story; some advocated an astringent 'literature of the fact' that negated conventional forms such as the novel and offered unvarnished and energetic 'truthfulness'. Facticity, according to this view, was the guarantee of authenticity. What it did not guarantee, however, was an engaging and morally coherent narrative. This was increasingly seen as a failing by Soviet critics and publishers, who by the mid-1930s were actively trying to find a recipe for a popular literature that could be accessible, inspiring and politically correct.

The shift from 'revolutionary' and 'proletarian' styles of writing to a new, 'socialist realist', aesthetic was exemplified by the genesis of the most famous canonical novel of the 1930s, Nikolai Ostrovskii's *How the Steel Was Tempered* (*Kak zakalialas' stal'*). Inspired and empowered by the proletarian writing movement and by the cultural revolution announced in the late 1920s, Ostrovskii set out to write a 'simple story about facts'. The work followed faithfully the pattern of the author's autobiography: his difficult childhood and adolescence, his experiences as a combatant in the civil war, his rise to revolutionary 'consciousness', his struggle to overcome all obstacles (including his own failing health) through feats of Bolshevik willpower, and even his decision to become a writer. So great was Ostrovskii's commitment to truth unmediated by literary form that he strongly opposed the genre designation of 'novel', which to him smacked of cliché and of stale convention. His intentions and wishes counted for little, however, when his work entered Soviet literary life. The manuscript was subjected to 'collective authorship' in the Young Guard publishing house, which meant that inappropriate episodes such as the hero's flirtation with the Workers' Opposition were written out. Soon after the work's first appearance, critics began to downplay its autobiographical character and to emphasise its qualities as a socialist realist classic. Even without such strong intervention by publishers and critics, however, it is hard to imagine how Ostrovskii could have remained true to his original conception while addressing the Soviet 'mass reader'. As he packaged his own autobiography for mass consumption he could not avoid the established formula genres of popular fiction. The ideological superstructure of *How the Steel Was Tempered* is based on many of the formal elements of the adventure novel. The hero's political development is the result not of abstract reflection but of action; it is driven not by philosophy but by plot.[22]

The case of Ostrovskii illustrates how certain traditions of popular literature could serve socialist realist purposes. To be sure, the resulting product differed profoundly from entertainment fiction as encountered in Western Europe at the same time, but it shared part of its genealogy, and some of its functions, with non-socialist formula literature. The same point could be made with respect to the historical novel, a genre that gained much prestige in the Stalin era. Far from subscribing to a theory of history informed by grand impersonal forces (such as Historical Necessity), Soviet historical authors tended to bring Russia's Great Men to the fore. Ivan the Terrible and Peter the Great, not bourgeoisie and socio-economic crisis, were the principal protagonists. History was personalised in

---

[22] See A. Guski, 'N. Ostrovkijs "Kak zakaljalas' stal'" – biographisches Dokument oder sozialistisch-realistisches Romanepos?', *Zeitschrift für slavische Philologie*, 42, 1981, pp. 116-145.

much the same way as it had been in thoroughly un-Marxist prerevolutionary textbooks.[23]
The synthesising of popular appeal and ideological acceptability was never, however, a straightforward matter. Ostrovskii and others, supported by the efforts of Soviet publishers and critics, had shown that socialist realism was a workable aesthetic, even if it did not conform to the standards of popular literature elsewhere. But over the next twenty years socialist realist formulas were modified in slight and significant ways, and each new canonical work required careful editorial preparation followed by huge but controlled publicity.[24] The socialist realist aesthetic depended on achieving an equilibrium between Party, writers and readers that could not be maintained without constant effort and supervision. The equilibrium was upset in the mid-1950s, when a group of Soviet writers, encouraged by the regime's de-Stalinising policies, began to question the formulas of Soviet literature. This period in Soviet literary life, usually called the Thaw, is usually associated with political reform and the reassessment of Soviet society that followed Khrushchev's 'secret speech' to the Twentieth Party Congress in 1956. But it was also bound up with the raised expectations of Soviet writers and their readers, who now wanted more 'human' heroes and more engaging treatments of social issues. Their objection to socialist realism as it had ossified in the late 1940s was not only that it had been tainted by its association with High Stalinism but also, quite simply, that it was boring. Soviet readers were now better educated and more sophisticated than in the 1930s, and were starting to gain increased exposure to Western literature; their expectations could hardly fail to be raised.
The spirit of the age was reflected in a slight loosening of publishing policy. In 1956, for example, 920 works of fiction by foreign authors were published in the Soviet Union, this representing an increase of nearly 300 per cent over 1950. In the same period the average print-run of these books had risen by a factor of five. The newly established favourites of the Soviet reading public included Mayne Reid's *Headless Horseman*, Dumas's *Three Musketeers*, E.A. Burroughs's *Tarzan*, and various Sherlock Holmes stories. This was hardly racy fare by the standards of Western popular fiction, but it represented a striking new development in Soviet culture. It also overstepped the limits set by the political

---

[23] E. Dobrenko, '"Zanimatel'naia istoriia": Istoricheskii roman i sotsialisticheskii realizm', in H. Günther and E. Dobrenko (eds), *Sotsrealisticheskii kanon*, SPb, 2000.

[24] For an example from the late 1940s, see T. Lahusen, *How Life Writes the Book: Real Socialism and Socialist Realism in Stalin's Russia*, Ithaca and London, 1997.

masters of Soviet culture. In January 1958, the Department of Culture of the Communist Party of the Soviet Union reported in detail on recent publishing and found that it accorded excessive prominence to 'books of a light entertainment genre that have no serious ideological-artistic value'. The chosen authors paid little or no attention to 'the growth and strengthening of the socialist camp, the collapse of colonialism, the inexorable decline of the whole capitalist system, and the disastrous effect of imperialism on people's lives'. The profit motive in publishing was taking over to a disturbing extent.[25]

Documents such as this are remarkable for what they reveal of the Soviet regime's extreme hostility to commercially successful, entertainment-orientated popular literature, but they also suggest that official hostility is not the full story. Publishers and journals were sometimes able to act in partial defiance, or in feigned ignorance, of ideological proscriptions. They had begun to sense the changing needs of the reading public, even if their recognition of these needs took only highly attenuated forms. Soviet culture in the last three decades of its existence still doggedly resisted the incursion of market principles and deemed certain genres and styles of writing to be beyond the pale, but Russians were nonetheless able to find a number of ways of satisfying their thirst for entertaining reading matter. Some might turn to mainstream novels – many of them historical epics – that were published in enormous print-runs and continued to be the staple of Soviet literary culture. Research into reader reception in the 1960s and 1970s suggests that the more widely disseminated socialist realist novels, like popular fiction in the West, met an unsophisticated response: their heroes and plots were almost interchangeable, but this very conformity to formula made the books engrossing and enjoyable for many Soviet people (often the less educated and culturally ambitious members of the reading public). These books – by such Soviet luminaries as Mikhail Alekseev, Anatolii Ivanov and Georgii Markov – dated very quickly in the glasnost era and became the object of only ironic attention. Oblivion – the fate of most formula literature – was in their case accelerated by the social and cultural upheaval of the late 1980s. But their cultural impact in their heyday – the 1970s – had been considerable.[26] More sophisticated readers might take pleasure in 'elite' literature, using it for

---

[25] *Ideologicheskie komissii TsK KPSS 1958-1964: Dokumenty*, M, 1998, p. 34.
[26] The best analysis of this phenomenon is S. Shvedov, 'Knigi, kotorye my vybirali (Vcherashnie bestsellery i segodniashnie chitateli)', in *Pogruzhenie v triasinu (Anatomiia zastoia)*, M, 1991, pp. 389-408. In English, see K. Mehnert, *The Russians and Their Favorite Books*, Stanford, 1983.

enjoyment rather than intellectual or moral engagement. The most striking example of this kind was Mikhail Bulgakov's *The Master and Margarita* (1928-40), which was first published in the Soviet Union in 1966-67 in two issues of the literary journal *Moskva*, and quickly became the biggest 'cult' novel of its time. Still another option was to search out those few items of 'pure' entertainment literature that were made available to the Soviet reading public. In the 1960s and afterwards some Western detective authors (none of them contemporary or socially engaged) were published; it was in this era, for example, that Agatha Christie became well known to the Soviet reading public. At the same time, home-grown authors were able to try their hand at crime fiction: the resulting 'Soviet *detektiv*' was profoundly different from the Western detective story, but it represented an important attempt to synthesise ideological correctness with a popular cultural form. The 'adventure' novel was another genre with which authors might experiment: here they faced, and often fudged, the challenge of showing how violence, intrigue and subterfuge could be compatible with the doctrine of literary 'heroism'. The difficulty of their task is indicated by their failure to dislodge the greatest favourites of the Soviet reading public in the 1970s: the French historical novelists Maurice Druon and Alexandre Dumas, whose works were published in 'series' with large but still insufficient print-runs, and became the 'hard currency' of the unofficial market in books.

For all that the Soviet reading culture was becoming somewhat more diverse in the 1960s and 1970s, the fact that it performed the function of entertainment and diversion was hardly ever discussed. The Soviet regime, and the Soviet intelligentsia, remained committed to the idea that literature should be morally uplifting and help people to become properly 'cultured'. Even when the Soviet Union was finally acknowledged to have social and economic problems, its culture was still exalted: Soviet literature, unlike Western literature, had shown that mass audiences were not incompatible with moral and intellectual value. Popular entertainment culture still existed under very serious constraints.

This situation began to change fast in the late 1980s, when the policy of 'openness' (glasnost) led to the publication of many forgotten and forbidden works. First to receive official sanction were novels and histories that exposed the horrors of the Stalin era. Somewhat later came works that fundamentally reassessed Lenin, the early Bolsheviks, and the Revolution itself. These ideologically controversial works were joined by modern classics that had been taboo for a range of less obviously political reasons: for their formal experimentation, their lewdness, or their foreignness. The sudden appearance of all these 'rediscovered' treasures brought a huge reading boom: a mass reading public with enormous curiosity and pent-up demand came into contact with an entire century of literary heritage over a period of two or three years. In the last years of the Soviet Union, elite literary journals (which were often the first to publish authors such as Pasternak, Solzhenitsyn and Nabokov) could, for the first and last time, attract an audience of several million.

This was an extraordinary situation, and it could not last. Elite intellectual readers retained their fascination with Solzhenitsyn and Nabokov, but the rest of society moved on. The 'rediscoveries' of the late 1980s, for all that they had brought to light dozens of important works, had done nothing to introduce to the Russian reading public the many genres of popular literature that had been intensively cultivated in Western Europe and America throughout the twentieth century, but that had been considered beyond the pale for much of the Soviet period. In the early 1990s, publishing houses finally gained full autonomy and were able to make highly profitable experiments with detective novels, fantasy writing, romances, and many other genres.

In the first post-Soviet decade, then, Russian readers were able to gorge themselves on formerly forbidden fictional fruit. But we should not assume from this that they were undiscriminating consumers or the dupes of Western mass culture. Although translated fiction was popular in the early days of post-Soviet publishing, it was not long before Russian authors were trying their hand at the formula genres, and in some cases their sales quickly outstripped those of the Western authors. As in the early twentieth century, Russia was acquiring a popular literature that clearly owed much to Western models and, in its broad outlines, conformed to patterns of urbanisation and consumerism elsewhere. But even more striking were the ways in which this literature differed from Western models. It existed in a society unaccustomed to thinking of mass culture in anything but a pejorative sense, was produced in conditions of acute sociocultural uncertainty, and amply reflected the difficulties of a society struggling to position itself between a Soviet past and an ill-defined future. To give an account of this remarkable interaction between mass-cultural forms and post-Soviet conditions and values is one of the main tasks of the chapters to follow.

Stephen Lovell

Reading the Russian Popular

In the previous chapter I argued that entertainment and formula can be seen as significant elements in the history of Russian literature. Now it is time to sharpen the analytical focus: to begin to inquire how Russian formulas can be categorised and what they can tell us.

It seems clear that all cultures take pleasure in their own familiar stories. It may also be that certain archetypal stories are found fulfilling in many different cultures. Narratives that centre on love, adventure and crime (or some combination of the three) have had extraordinarily wide application in Western civilisation. But, as John G. Cawelti pointed out in a pioneering study of formula stories, 'in order for these patterns to work, they must be embodied in figures, settings, and situations that have appropriate meanings for the culture which produces them'.[1] Formulas can be pushed only so far. Each culture sets its own limits of plausibility; there are points beyond which the reader's credulity or unselfconscious engagement can be strained no further. For an Anglo-American audience it is hard to imagine a politician serving as the hero of a romantic novel, or a woman as a hard-boiled police officer. The aim of this chapter is to provide a tentative typology (and glossary) of popular genres in Russia, and to sketch out the conventions and patterns that govern their production and reception, and that make them 'readable'.

This task has certain complicating circumstances. While it is true that formula literature was widely condemned by intellectuals everywhere in Europe in the nineteenth and twentieth centuries, the difficulties it faced in Russia were extreme in ways both quantitative and qualitative. This was partly a question of the intensity of vituperation expended on commercial popular literature, but it also

---

[1] J. Cawelti, Adventure, *Mystery, and Romance: Formula Stories as Art and Popular Culture*, Chicago, 1976, p. 6.

had to do with simple lack of understanding, with the absence of concepts and institutional structures that might define popular forms more sharply. Although the Russian print market was developing fast in the post-emancipation decades, it was still trailing in the wake of Western Europe. The relationship between imported literary formulas and 'native' popular literature was often ambiguous.[2] And literary scholars in the late imperial period had little motivation to delve too deeply into these matters, as their concern was above all to build a national canon and thereby legitimate their own field of study.[3]

Yet, surprisingly enough, a group of Russian critics and scholars in the 1920s did begin to take popular literature seriously as a topic for investigation, and in the process they gave important new impetus to the study of modern European formula fiction. These men (usually known as the Formalists) made a pioneering contribution by recognizing that their formal method could be extended to a broader range of material than canonical imaginative literature. In a 1928 manual for novice writers, the redoubtable critic and theorist Viktor Shklovskii noted that the 'mystery story' (*novella tain*) had a considerable literary pedigree and should not be ignored by writers seeking to work their material into engaging form.[4] He then devoted two chapters of his treatise *On the Theory of Prose* (1929) to 'mystery' as a device in plot construction. In his view, the appeal of this device could explain the fact that detective stories had by and large come to supplant 'bandit' fiction in European literature. He gave detailed analysis of Conan Doyle stories, and even extracted from them a plot archetype. More speculatively, Shklovskii wondered what would become of the private detective (invariably more successful than the plodding representatives of the state police and judiciary) if he were exported to the Soviet Union: 'if these stories were being written by someone in a proletarian state, who was himself a proletarian writer, one of the detectives would still be unsuccessful. In all probability, the state detective would be successful and the private one would get involved in vain.' In Shklovskii's view, Sherlock Holmes would now 'find himself in the service of the state', but the basic construction of the story would not change.[5]

---

[2] So Beth Holmgren, in her study of late imperial entertainment fiction (*Rewriting Capitalism: Literature and the Market in Late Tsarist Russia and the Kingdom of Poland*, Pittsburgh, 1998), is left with the catch-all 'middlebrow'.
[3] On which see Andy Byford's D. Phil. thesis *Literary Academia in Late Imperial Russia (1870s-1910s): Rituals of Self-Representation*, University of Oxford, 2004.
[4] V. Shklovskii, *Tekhnika pisatel'skogo remesla*, M/L, 1928, pp. 38-40.
[5] V. Shklovskii, *O teorii prozy*, M, 1929, p. 136.

The Formalists were forced to rein in their activities at the end of the 1920s. When their insights were finally taken up and developed by Russian intellectuals later in the Soviet period, they were used to illuminate areas of inquiry far removed from modern popular culture. Semioticians and structuralists from the 1960s onwards applied the formal method far more widely than their intellectual progenitors had done: not just to novels and poems but also to behaviour, social rituals, ethnography, cybernetics, and much else besides. But adventure, mystery and romance were not subjects they touched – partly because their scholarly disposition and cultural background did not dispose them to do so, partly because research on such topics would have been almost impossible to justify in Soviet academe. In the post-Stalin era, as throughout modern Russian history, public discourse had great difficulties with the concept of 'the popular'. One major problem, in a vast multi-ethnic state, lay in determining precisely which 'people' the 'popular' could be said to represent. Another was the huge challenge – greater even than in Western Europe – that the popular culture of modernity posed both to intellectuals and to governing elites. Even in the 1980s, the Russian language still had no adequate equivalent for 'popular culture'. The old word, *narodnost'*, coined around 1820 as the Russian Romantic counterpart to the French *nationalité*, by now had connotations of folksiness and of state-supervised patriotism that made it wholly inadequate to an era of global mass communications.[6] The simple borrowing from English, *populiarnyi*, sounded like an ungainly neologism to the Russian ear. And, in the context of the Cold War on the cultural front, the phrase *massovaia kul'tura* could never shake off negative associations with Western decadence.

In post-Soviet times, although some of these problems and uncertainties persist, Russian journalists and intellectuals are finally getting down to writing on popular culture in an idiom not too far removed from that of their Western counterparts. From 1997 the prominent daily *Nezavisimaia gazeta* has published a regular supplement on mass literature. Several of the weighty literary journals, those mainstays of Russian intellectual life over the last two hundred years, have also carried articles on post-Soviet popular fiction. *Novoe literaturnoe obozrenie* (*New Literary Review*), the most intellectually ambitious, and best, of current Russian scholarly journals in the humanities, has given mass literature sustained

---

[6] For a good brief history of the term, see M. Perrie, '*Narodnost'*: Notions of National Identity', in C. Kelly/D. Shepherd (eds), *Constructing Russian Culture in the Age of Revolution: 1881-1940*, Oxford, 1998, pp. 28-36.

attention in several of its issues, as well as publishing numerous other articles and reviews on the subject.

Many of these studies seek to digest work done on popular literary forms by Western scholars, who have been active in this field for much longer. What guidance can their insights offer students of Russian culture? John Cawelti identified five basic types of literary formula, each one representing a kind of 'moral fantasy'. First was adventure, whose main theme is the overcoming of obstacles by a hero. Second was romance, which centres on the development of a love relationship. Third, mystery: 'the investigation and discovery of hidden secrets, the discovery usually leading to some benefit for the character(s) with whom the reader identifies'. Fourth, melodrama: 'narratives of a complex of actions in a world that is purportedly full of the violence and tragedy we associate with the "real world" but that in this case seems to be governed by some benevolent moral principle'. Fifth, 'alien being or states', a type most commonly exemplified in the modern imagination by horror stories.[7]

This typology is not complete (it has no place for comedy, as Cawelti himself acknowledges), but these five types, in isolation and in combination, cover most of the popular formula narratives of modern societies. What they do not do, of course, is provide a foolproof recipe for writerly success. In Cawelti's words, 'conventional story patterns work because they bring into an effective conventional order a large variety of existing cultural and artistic interests and concerns'; and these interests and concerns are liable to vary enormously from one cultural setting, or era, to another. Practitioners of formula genres have to achieve a sometimes precarious balance between affirming a moral order that the audience can wholeheartedly endorse and offering readers stimulation and excitement by depicting plausible, if ultimately controllable, threats to that order. The main example considered in detail by Cawelti is the Anglo-American crime story, whose values and narrative techniques have moved on many times: from the 'classical' to the 'hard-boiled' detective story (and beyond). One category of value change to which Cawelti and other scholars justifiably attach much importance is a shift in the symbols of moral and social authority. Broadly speaking, they argue that the emergence of the modern crime genres became possible only when the Church ceded much of its moral authority to the family in the first half of the nineteenth century. On the one hand, the weakening of the religious/moral framework left the way open for the 'aestheticisation' of crime.

---

[7] Quotations from Cawelti, pp. 42, 44-5.

On the other hand, fictionalised crime could find a niche in the family circle, a setting that was bound to engage the attention, interest and anxieties of the reading public. Later in the nineteenth century, and even more so in the twentieth, symbolic authority came to reside less in the family than in the individual, a phenomenon that goes some way to explaining the appeal of the hard-boiled detective.

The question of the relationship between literary form and the social and cultural environment that brings it alive for a reading public is exceptionally stark and fascinating in the Russian case. The whole history of Russia from the eighteenth century to the present may be regarded as the struggle of alien cultures to survive transplantation to, and then to flower in, Russian soil. The very word 'literature', as we saw in Chapter 1, was a foreign import. Yet, as this last example suggests, Russia has been much more than the slavish recipient of humanist (or classical, or romantic) aid. By the end of the nineteenth century, a century it had begun without its own *literatura*, Russian literature was renowned across Europe as nationally distinctive and uniquely valuable. The interaction of Western 'forms' and Russian social and cultural 'content' had been astonishingly intense and productive.

By now it should be clear that the distinction between form and content is an artificial one. Ideas and concepts cannot be imported into Russia like Ecuadorean bananas or Scandinavian kitchen appliances. For Petersburg intellectuals in the 1840s *literatura* was already not *literature* or *littérature*; in the late nineteenth century, or the mid-twentieth, there was just as much clear water between these concepts.

If we have problems of cultural translation even with a general term such as 'literature', how much greater must they be when we move on to more specific genres and formulas. We saw in Chapter 1 what variations are possible even in a genre delimited by a single hero and setting: the Russian Pinkerton was profoundly different from his authentically American counterpart. Similarly, what Russian literary critics of the early twentieth century regarded as slushy 'boulevard' fiction often showed greater social engagement and intellectual ambition than an English or American reader would expect from the formula archetype of romance. Even so, there are good reasons to argue that Russian popular literature was beginning to converge with other popular literatures of modernity. The value of individual achievement, especially, was becoming much more prominent in the 1900s than ever previously. But the Soviet period brought divergence, not to say total disjuncture. Popular entertainment literature in a Western sense was simply not acknowledged as existing. Soviet culture sought to eliminate the distinction between 'high' and 'low', 'popular' and 'elite': from now on, writing was to be both popular and serious. Intellectuals and other opinion formers declared that culture could – indeed must – be both 'popular' (i.e. accessible, authentic, of the people) and 'serious' (morally improving, intellectually challenging, and of high literary quality). They did not allow for the dialectic of 'high' and 'low', 'popular' and 'elite', that proved so culturally productive elsewhere in the twentieth century. The result of their efforts was not a unified and harmonious culture, but rather enduring ambiguity and ambivalence: even in the post-Soviet period, 'popular literature' was a difficult and controversial concept in Russia.[8]

That said, the Soviet period did not bring total rupture with earlier patterns of popular culture. In some ways, it may be seen as having reinstituted popular cultural archetypes from the middle of the nineteenth century or even before. Most Western formula genres in the nineteenth and twentieth centuries have depended to a large extent on the strong, successful, self-reliant, self-motivated, but morally sound hero. Formula stories present the legitimacy of actions as residing in the individual's will, or reason, or conscience. For many Russian formula stories of the prerevolutionary period the moral universe had a very different constellation of values. As Jeffrey Brooks showed, life outside the collective was difficult even for a hero endowed with exceptional qualities of physical strength, energy and cunning. To be a self-willed loner was not normally compatible with eventual success and happiness. The group was the ultimate arbiter of truth and right (or, in Russian, *pravda*). This assumption was shared by both traditional culture and the radical movement. A revolutionary agitator of the time recalled appealing to his worker audience by establishing a connection between banditry and the revolutionary cause: 'Churkin has got his band organised and lives in freedom, but we don't know how to organise even the smallest circle to defend ourselves'.[9]

If we now fast-forward to the mature Soviet formula genres of the 1960s and 1970s – the social epics produced by luminaries of the Writers' Union and promoted assiduously by the Soviet publishing system – the resemblances to much

---

[8] See for example B. Menzel, 'Chto takoe „populiarnaia literatura"? Zapadnye kontseptsii „vysokogo" i „nizkogo" v sovetskom i postsovetskom kontekste,' *Novoe literaturnoe obozrenie*, 40, 1999, pp. 391-407.

[9] P.A. Moiseenko, *Vospominaniia 1873-1923*, M, 1924, p. 58.

older Russian formulas are striking. As before, the will of the individual was subordinate to the ethos of the collective: only if an individual's will acted in harmony with this ethos could he be considered a hero. Individual achievement was correspondingly downplayed. Positive characters were expected to work hard, but the result of the labours was relatively insignificant: the effort they expended, not the outcome they achieved, was the main criterion for judging the worth of their activities. Kindness and generosity were generally viewed as positive qualities, and as attributes of the Russian national character. But on closer inspection they could also be seen to stand for support of one's own, as means of ensuring group cohesion. Firm criteria for distinguishing right from wrong did not exist outside the moral universe of the collective. Crimes and misdemeanours could be forgiven if a character remained 'one of us'. As this last example begins to suggest, the 'collective' of socialist realist epics could not be equated with the Soviet state. It was quite possible to envisage a conflict between the law (as defined by the state) and *pravda* (as defined by the collective). The primary loyalty of Soviet man lay with a community close at hand that, while it certainly provided an idealised model for Soviet society as a whole, was far from being identical with that society.[10]

Soviet mass fiction, then, can be seen to have differed from Western popular fiction in several fundamental ways. First, it remained committed to the goal of moral improvement through reading, and for this reason excluded types of writing that have been enormously successful and influential in the West. A Soviet Harlequin romance would, for example, have been unthinkable even in the 1980s. Second, Soviet writers were not operating in a market, and so had no interest in developing certain kinds of mass appeal. Third, the Soviet mass genres were underpinned by a moral structure that was thoroughly alien to the Western reader. Western fiction generally relied on a charismatic, high-achieving hero who actions, however, had to conform to certain rather clear-cut moral standards. In the Soviet case, by contrast, good and evil were not particularly significant categories. Much more important for the hero's viability was the extent to which he could demonstrate group allegiance through enlightened and purposeful action.

The post-Soviet period, the main catalyst for this book's investigations, has undeniably done much to narrow the gap, or bridge the chasm, between Russian

---

[10] S. Shvedov, 'Knigi, kotorye my vybirali (Vcherashnie bestsellery i segodniashnie chitateli)', in *Pogruzhenie v triasinu (Anatomiia zastoia)*, M, 1991, pp. 389-408.

and Western popular literatures. In the early 1990s Russian publishers suddenly became free to import whichever authors or genres of 'mass' literature they thought would achieve commercial success. The rigidly planned system of state book production collapsed, and a market of the most cut-throat and competitive variety was established. Romantic novels, hard-boiled detective stories, thrillers and fantasy could all take their place on the bookstalls.

But this book will show that, although post-Soviet popular literature may seem to share many of its genres with the West, the resemblances are to a great extent illusory. This has been another great collision between Western cultural 'forms' and Russian sociocultural 'content', and it has resulted in a remarkable synthesis. Previously taboo formula genres have exercised enormous fascination over post-Soviet readers, but they have also been adapted to respond to acute social stresses and tensions, and to meet the expectations of a public raised on a Soviet reading culture.

The complexities of the situation are well illustrated by the case of crime fiction (discussed in much more detail by Marina Koreneva in Chapter 4). The Soviet *detektiv*, as has been convincingly argued by Anthony Olcott, cannot easily be classified according to Western genre designations. It was not a 'murder mystery', both because it did not always involve a murder and because there was usually little 'mystery' regarding the identity of the criminal. Like Dostoevskii's *Crime and Punishment*, it was a 'whydunnit' rather than a 'whodunnit'. Nor was the *detektiv* a detective story, because Russian crime fighters were above all members of investigative teams rather than individual agents. Their actions were, moreover, informed by a distinctive Soviet legal consciousness that attached relatively little importance to the abstract definition of a crime and rather more to its effects and social meaning.[11] As Olcott and Koreneva both show, the legacy of the Soviet *detektiv* can be felt in contemporary Russian crime fiction – in a reluctance to view the law as a reliable or definitive arbiter of right and wrong, in a tendency to see a distinction (and often incompatibility) between 'law' (*zakon*) and 'justice' (*spravedlivost'*). Russian and Western notions of transgression continue to differ in fundamental ways. But at the same time, the narrative possibilities of the detective story, and the scope for cross-fertilisation with other formulas, have expanded significantly. Now authors are not bound by the unwritten rule that the number of murders in a crime novel should not exceed

---

[11] A. Olcott, *Russian Pulp: The Detektiv and the Way of Russian Crime*, Lanham, Maryland, 2001, chapter 1.

one; on the contrary, the bloodier a book is, the better its prospects. Russian crime fiction is no longer restricted to the genre of *detektiv* but has been extended to include the violent thriller (*boevik*) examined by Boris Dubin in Chapter 5. Crime-fighting heroes are now more likely to be self-willed loners than dedicated members of a *kollektiv*. Whether in the *detektiv* or in the *boevik*, writers do not feel obliged to explore the motivations of the criminal at any length, or to reveal the identity of the criminal any sooner than the final page. Often, in fact, plots are extraordinarily convoluted and pile intrigue upon conspiracy upon coincidence. A few of the main detective authors and protagonists are now women, which has led scholars and critics to speak of the subgenre of the 'women's *detektiv*' (*zhenskii detektiv*).[12] The locus of crime has switched from isolated unsoviet individuals such as spies, murderers and black marketeers to figures much closer to the mainsprings of power and wealth. Politicians, media magnates, 'New Russians' and (of course) *mafiozniki* all feature regularly as the instigators, executants or victims of crime. These themes and preoccupations very obviously reflect post-Soviet realia, but they also betray moral and social disorientation, along with a yearning for the mixture of entertainment and moral cohesion and certainty that is so abundantly available in Western popular culture and so miserably lacking in Russian fiction (both Soviet and post-Soviet). Yet the crime genre in post-Soviet Russia is also polymorphous enough to include an intelligentsia *detektiv*. One of the greatest publishing phenomena of recent years has been Boris Akunin (pseudonym of Grigorii Chkhartishvili), whose novels are set in the late tsarist period, published with covers that eschew the customary gaudiness of post-Soviet book promotion, and written in a 'filigree' Russian language and according to the 'classical' standards of the genre.[13]

One potential source of moral certainty, if not of cohesion, is Russian nationhood. Quite apart from the socio-economic trauma of the last fifteen years, Russia has been going through the difficult process of shedding its imperial identity: an identity that has been central to Russian culture for several centuries. Questions of national self-affirmation have for this reason been extremely prominent in post-Soviet popular literature. As Boris Dubin shows in Chapter 8,

---

[12] See H. Trepper, 'Philip Marlowe in Seidenstrümpfen oder Misogynie im russischen Frauenkrimi? Zur Figur der Privatdetektivin bei Marina Serova', in E. Cheauré (ed.), *Kunstmarkt und Kanonbildung: Tendenzen in der russischen Kultur heute*, Berlin, 2000, pp. 243-260.

[13] On Akunin, see K. Kasper, 'BAkunin und andere: Fiction, Semi-Fiction, Non-Fiction oder Pulp-Fiction?', *Zeitschrift für Slawistik*, 47, 2002, 2, pp. 193-201.

they have all but taken over historical fiction, and they also provide the *idées fixes* of the 'Slavic fantasy' discussed by Birgit Menzel in Chapter 6.

In short, the genres of popular fiction delineated and analysed in the chapters to follow have much to tell us about contemporary Russian culture in a broad sense: the ideas, concepts and assumptions that Russians use to try to make sense of their current predicament. They also provide the latest chapter in the long and difficult history of modern Russian attempts to grapple with 'the popular'. 'Mass culture' is not remotely as disreputable a term as it used to be in Soviet times, but it is still not a stable concept. It is only to be expected that the picture we draw in this book will seem out of date in ten or twenty years time, as the formula genres continue to reconfigure themselves. But the doomed effort to grasp a fluid situation is worthwhile, as it will help to establish the parameters within which Russian popular culture has developed and hence to open up that culture to a broader comparativist audience than it has enjoyed hitherto.

Birgit Menzel

Writing, Reading and Selling Literature in Russia 1986-2004

All the great hopes of the Russian intelligentsia that after the fall of censorship and political control the masses would joyfully turn to the hitherto suppressed legacy of Great Russian Literature, from Nabokov to Solzhenitsyn, as their preferred reading matter, had by 1991 turned out to be an illusion. The Great Russian Writer – *Velikii Pisatel' Russkoi Zemli*, VPRZ, as postmodern critics, wickedly parodying a Soviet type of abbreviation, dubbed the symbolic embodiment of literary value – ran out of time after some 150 years. The Great Writer had been the highest authority in Russian culture ever since the early nineteenth century for both the government and the people, whether in official or unofficial culture, and had helped to maintain a notion of literature as an institution of enlightenment and moral education, as the conscience of the nation. By the end of the 1990s, this key figure in literary life had been replaced by the publisher – the PR face of literature – in a radically more commercial environment.

Russian readers, when asked about the current state of books and literature in Russia, tend to express two opposed opinions. Some say that even if the bookstores and street stalls are groaning under the weight of printed matter, there is nothing 'real' to read, there is no true literature any more. Others say that there are just too many interesting new books, so that only a tiny proportion of them can be read. Both opinions have their own logic and plausibility, once they are viewed within the context of wider cultural changes and put into historical perspective. Four main changes have occurred in the basic conditions of culture: the massive *erosion of the intelligentsia*; the *dissolution of all the state institutions* that had ruled literary life since 1917; the *commercialisation of culture* since 1991; and the changing *impact of new/mass media* (TV, video and, since 1996, the electronic media and the Russian internet (runet)).[1] This chapter will give a

---

[1] Boris Dubin, 'Televizionnaia epokha: zhizn' posle', in idem, *Intellektual'nye gruppy i sim-*

survey of these major changes from the beginning of perestroika and describe their effects on literary communication in its institutional, sociological, economic and symbolic aspects.

Both the *erosion of the intelligentsia* and the *decline of state-governed literary institutions* can be exemplified by the fate of the *thick monthly journals*.[2] By their combination of fiction and criticism, as well as through the social and political journalism they offered, these publications had shaped literary life in Russia and the Soviet Union ever since the early nineteenth century.[3] Most literary texts were published first in journals, and by no means all later appeared as books. The journals had linked the two metropolitan cultures with the vast periphery of the country, and played a major role in focusing the attention and identity of the intelligentsia on publications and public discussions, which were construed as 'cultural events' involving the majority of the educated readership. After 1986, thanks to the courageous efforts of intellectuals, artists, writers, editors — most of them from the older Thaw generation of the sixties — numerous formerly suppressed works of literature, philosophy, film and music were published, censorship and ideological control were lifted, nonconformist intellectuals were championed and in many cases brought back to positions of cultural prestige and authority.[4] The thick monthly journals experienced an unprecedented boom, which brought the leading journals *Novyi mir*, *Druzhba narodov* and *Znamia* average monthly circulations of more than a million. *Novyi mir* even reached a figure as high as 2.7 million.

---

volicheskie formy. Ocherki sotsiologii sovremennoi kul'tury, M, 2004, pp. 185-208.

[2] On the situation of the thick journals since the 1990s see B. Dubin, 'Zhurnal'naia kul'tura postsovetskoi epokhi', *Novoe literaturnoe obozrenie*, 4, 1993, pp. 304-311, and idem, *Slovo – pis'mo – literatura*, M, 2001, pp. 135-147.

[3] D. Martinsen (ed.), *Literary Journals in Imperial Russia*, Cambridge, 1997. On monthly journals in Soviet Russia, see L. Gudkov/B. Dubin, 'Konets kharizmaticheskoi epokhi. Pechat'' i izmeneniia v sisteme tsennostei obshchestva', *Svobodnaia mysl'*, 5, 1993, pp. 32-44, and L. Gudkov/B. Dubin/N. Zorkaia, 'Zhurnal'naia struktura i sotsial'nye protsessy', in Gudkov/Dubin, *Literatura kak sotsial'nyi institut*, M, 1994, pp. 288-345.

[4] Grigorii Baklanov became chief editor of Znamia, Sergei Zalygin of Novii mir and Vitalii Korotich took over the weekly magazine Ogonek. All three of these men had been popular writers since the 1960s.

Writing, Reading and Selling Literature in Russia 41

	1985	1986	1987	1988	1989	1990	1991	1992	1993
Nm	430,000	415,000	495,000	1,150,000	1,550,000	2,700,000	200,000	241,300	60,000
Dn	156,000	160,000	150,000	800,000	1,100,000	800,000	200,000	100,000	45,000
Zn	175,000	250,000	270,000	500,000	980,000	1,000,000	419,000	192,000	73,000
Zv	120,000	120,000	140,000	150,000	310,000	340,000	130,000	70,000	35,000
Mo	500,000	500,000	430,000	750,000	770,000	450,000	150,000	85,000	35,000
Ns	200,000	220,000	220,000	240,000	313,000	488,000	311,000	163,000	92,000
Ok	156,000	175,000	185,000	252,000	385,000	335,000	242,000	114,000	60,000
Lg						4,200,000		1,200,000	
Vl	15,000	15,000	15,000	16,000	16,000	26,000	13,000	8,800	4-17,000

Nm = *Novyi mir*; Dn = *Druzhba narodov*; Zn = *Znamia*; Zv = *Zvezda*; Mo = *Moskva*; Ns = *Nash sovremennik*; Ok = *Ogonek*; Lg = *Literaturnaia gazeta*; Vl = *Voprosy literatury*.[5]

This historical peak of the thick journals was, however, quickly followed by crisis and decline as the intelligentsia lost its cultural status. In the first period of perestroika the journals had admirably served the purpose of politicising and mobilising a mass audience: they had joined the cause of reform-communist intellectuals as they struggled for power against the defenders of the old regime. The overwhelming interest of the population in all the revelations served up in the journals raised the hopes of the reformist intelligentsia, the *shestidesiatniki*, that the utopian goals of the Thaw period, and even those of the 1920s, could be achieved: these intellectuals set their sights on a renewal of socialism and the unification not only of the intelligentsia with the newly enlightened political leadership, but also with the masses who, by assimilating the moral values of classical and more recent unofficial Russian high culture, would raise themselves to the challenge of creating a civilised modern society.

History, however, took a different path. In 1991, with the end of the communist system, state financial support came to an end, and culture was exposed almost overnight to the laws of the market. The process of commercialisation brought a massive decline of the thick journals along with the high-speed privatisation of publishing and a radical differentiation of society and the reading public. A new law on the press, promulgated in June 1990, permitted the founding of private companies, and from this moment the number of private publishing enterprises

---

[5] Birgit Menzel, *Bürgerkrieg um Worte. Die russische Literaturkritik der Perestrojka*, Köln-Wien, 2001, p. 46.

increased rapidly. By 2000 Russia had more than 5,000 publishing houses.[6] Until the early 1980s there had been only about 100 publishing houses in the entire Soviet Union, half of them situated in Moscow. In 1991 only 8 per cent of all book titles and 21 per cent of total copies were released by private publishing houses; by 2002 these figures had risen to 66 per cent and 87 per cent respectively. Commercialisation brought about the end of the book shortage, and the variety of available material increased massively – between 1990 and 1996 there was a rise of 126-136 per cent in the number of titles published. However, these figures appear rather differently when put into historical perspective. In 2000, the number of titles printed in the Russian Federation was altogether 50,085: about the same as in the mid-eighties. In 1994-96, under the pressures of price liberalisation, this figure had fallen as low 33,623, which was about the same number as in the year of 1913, when most of Russia was still illiterate. True recovery seems to have begun only in the early twenty-first century: in 2001, for example, 70,332 titles were published. Most telling is a comparison of the number of titles with the total number of copies printed. Total copies of printed books fell from 1,725 million in 1985 to 542.3 million in 2001, i.e. by more than two-thirds. While in 1985 the average number of copies of a book publication was 33,000, in 1994 it was only 14,000, and by 2002 only 7,710 copies.[7]

Not only book production but also periodicals began to follow the rules of the market instead of the interests of the intelligentsia. While in 1985 across Russia 3,869 periodicals (not including newspapers) were published with an annual total of 2,726 million copies, in 1994 there were 3,007 periodicals with only 306 million copies and, in 1999, 3,358 periodicals with 601 million copies. The figure for 1999 represented only 12 per cent of the total for 1985.[8] Once prices

---

[6] Between 1991 and 1992 licenses were given to 456 new publishers, and by April 1994 6,551 publishers were registered and actually working. By 2000 the number of officially registered licenses was as high as 15,000, though many of these firms were either tiny or ceased to function after a short time. See Petra Becker, *Verlagspolitik und Buchmarkt in Russland (1985 bis 2002)*, Wiesbaden, 2003, p. 154; idem, 'Russische Verlage und ihr Auftritt im Netz', *Osteuropa*, 10, 2001, pp. 1185-1197. Concerning the law on the press, see Becker, *Verlagspolitik*, pp. 140-151, and Andrei M. Il'nitskii, *Knigoizdanie sovremennoi Rossii*, M, 2002.

[7] B. Dubin, 'Chitat' nechego?', *Itogi*, 6 October, 1998, pp. 52-53; L. Gudkov, *Chitaiushchii mir i chteniia*, *Sbornik statei*, M, 2003; L. Gudkov/B. Dubin, 'Institutsional'nye izmeneniia v literaturnoi kul'ture Rossii (1990-2001gg.)', *Monitoring obshchestvennogo mneniia*, 6, 2002, pp. 43-50.

[8] In 2001 Dar'ia Dontsova published 5,393,000 copies of her books (a total of 40 novels), Aleksandr Bushkov 2,085,000 (altogether 49 novels), B. Akunin published 1,485,000 cop-

went up and everyday concerns took over most people's lives, once the reforms lost their dynamic speed, and once people had satisfied their initial craving for suppressed art and information, the majority of society reverted to political indifference. The boom was over, the mass reader turned partly to mass literature, and partly away from literature entirely. What followed was an avalanche in the quantity of publishing accompanied by a radical devaluation of the intelligentsia's status, activities and values.

Newspapers, a growing number of smaller journals, the so-called 'glossy magazines' (*gliantsevye zhurnaly*), and the more recent internet journals became the main venues for journalism and criticism. On the book market, pulp fiction elbowed aside 'artistic' literature. Although in 2003 almost all of the former thick journals still existed, their print-runs ranged from 3,000 to 10,000, and all of them had to struggle hard for survival, heavily dependent on private funding that was by no means guaranteed for the longer term.[9] This shift of the mode of publishing from a slow rhythm of four months between submission and publication of a text – for the monthly journals – to a weekly or even daily basis reflects the accelerated speed of literary life in post-Soviet Russia. Especially since the second half of the 1990s, the members of the older *shestidesiatniki* generation – the former activists of the unofficial culture and the opinion leaders of perestroika – have almost disappeared from the public stage, due to disillusionment, resignation and despair. They were not prepared for the challenges and dynamics of cultural life in the new Russia: it did not come naturally for them to market literature, to compete with foreign or domestic bestsellers, to advertise their literary works through TV appearances or internet publications. Their place has been taken by ambitious professionals of the younger generation, with language skills and international know-how, whose concerns are often less moral than material.

Another state institution that shaped Soviet literary culture and that declined radically in the 1990s is the system of *libraries*. Different from those of Western countries in several aspects, libraries had a high status and great importance for Soviet Russian readers. The Soviet literary system, founded in the 1930s and basically preserved until the late 1980s, was based on planned centralised publishing and distribution according to long-term programmes. Print-runs were determined with no reference to likely reader demand or market research. Pub-

---

ies of 24 different novels, Aleksandra Marinina sold 1,132,500 copies of 16 novels and Polina Dashkova 1,077,200 copies of 21 novels.

[9] Gudkov/Dubin, 'Institutsional'nye izmeneniia'.

lishing policy followed the goal and principle of educating a homogenised society through the controlled publication of a clearly shaped canon of literature. Subscriptions of multivolume editions formed part of this project, as did the preference for a centralised delivery system over less predictable retail sales in bookstores.[10] After the Thaw period, however, the rising level of education of the Soviet population meant that more people wanted to read books that did not fit the demands of production plans and censorship. Accordingly, the publishing system became notorious for the book shortage it created. Since shortage books became precious objects for private collection and informal distribution, home libraries constituted a special kind of symbolic capital for the intelligentsia in both the humanities and the technical professions. Officially the low print-runs of readers' favourite books were justified by reference to a chronic paper shortage, but in reality they were also a political strategy to channel and control the reading process without engaging in overt censorship. Readers without access to samizdat or domestic libraries, especially those in provincial towns and rural areas, were mostly supplied by mass periodical editions such as the *roman-gazeta*, which were delivered along with the ordinary mail, or (more often) by the mass libraries. Right up to the early 1980s, 91 per cent of the population outside the two capitals could be considered to frequent these public libraries.[11] In the 1990s, however, the end of state subsidies, the explosion of prices for paper and books, along with the extension of the electronic media with their global reach and the shift to mass production of pulp fiction, brought a devastating decline in the system of public libraries. Only 15 per cent of all former public libraries are still open, and they are frequented by only 3 per cent of the former readers.[12] Most libraries, both in the two major cities and throughout the country, have ceased to buy new books, so that they are much less intensively frequented and will be doomed in the near future without a renewal of state provision. Altogether, the trend towards the regionalisation of Russian literary culture is clear; and the decline of the centre has left large areas deprived of their previous means

---

[10] L. Gudkov/B. Dubin, 'Literaturnaia kul'tura. Protsess i ratsion, *Druzhba narodov*, 2, 1988, pp. 168-189; also idem, *Intelligentsiia. Zametki o literaturno-politicheskikh illiuziiakh*, M, 1995, pp. 8-41. On the Soviet system of libraries see *Kniga i chtenie v zerkale sotsiologii*, M, 1990.

[11] Dubin, *Kniga i chtenie*, p. 89; Stephen Lovell, *The Russian Reading Revolution. Print Culture in the Soviet and Post-Soviet Eras*, London, 2000, pp. 45-72.

[12] B. Dubin, 'Obzhivanie raspada, ili ritualizatsiia kak priem. Sotsial'nye formy, znakovye figury, simvolichnye obraztsy v literaturnoi kul'ture postsovetskogo perioda', *Chitaiushchii mir*, 2003; idem, 'Chitatel'' v obshchestve zritelei', *Znamia*, 5, 2004, pp. 168-178.

of connection with the national literary culture (the mass libraries and the thick journals).

However, new audiovisual and electronic media have begun to fill this gap – if only for certain age and educational groups – and exert an ever growing influence on writing, reading and selling Russian literature. Although TV even in the 1970s accounted for a much greater proportion of the population's leisure time than was admitted either by the authorities or by the intelligentsia, in the 1990s Russia advanced to become one of the most TV-addicted countries in the world. According to 2001 survey data, 91 per cent of the population watched TV daily, only 24 per cent read a newspaper, and only 4 per cent read magazines. Nevertheless, among the population aged from 25 to 49, 82 per cent of females and 68 per cent of males answered that they read on a regular basis.[13] The sociologists Boris Dubin and Lev Gudkov have argued that today it is only on TV that Russia experiences itself as a nation. TV creates the illusion of community and of a wholeness that does not exist outside this medium. The price one has to pay for this illusion, however, is the reduction of society to a society of 'spectators' instead of participants and active members. As a nation of collective spectators – as distinct from an individualised reading public – the Russian people can find reassurance only in ritualised shows and endless repetition, the eternal return of sameness.[14]

The spread of personal computers, as well as of the Russian internet, has been much less impressive than in the United States or some countries in Western Europe, and has only begun to grow significantly since 1999. In 2000, only 5 per cent of the population (15.6 million out of 103.9 million adults in Russia) had access to a computer and to the internet. But in the past few years, the young urban generation in particular has massively transferred to this new medium, which for certain genres of literary expression, like popular fantastic literature and criticism, has changed the system of communication altogether.[15]

After this brief survey of basic changes in the social and economic conditions of literature, a closer look will now be taken at the traditionally defined elements in literary communication – writing, reading, distributing – as well as at the very notion and status of literature in society. Both the working conditions and the

---

[13] Ellen Mickiewicz, *Changing Channels. Television and the Struggle for Power in Russia*, Durham/London, 1999; Mariia Levina, 'Chitateli massovoi literatury v 1994-2000gg. – ot paternalizma k individualizmu?' *Monitoring obshchestvennogo mneniia*, 4, 2001, p. 31.

[14] Gudkov/Dubin, 'Obschchestvo telezritelei'.

[15] On the Runet see Ia.I. Zdorovets, *Politicheskii runet. Chto est' chto*, M, 2004, pp. 9-48.

image of the author have changed. The traditional image of the writer as a teacher and prophet, as the moral or social conscience of the nation, reached the end of its natural life in the late perestroika era. It had been embodied both by officially approved writers, like Iurii Trifonov or Valentin Rasputin, and by expelled dissidents like Alexander Solzhenitsyn or Andrei Siniavskii. The end of the myth of the writer, which the critic Natal'ia Ivanova called the 'Twilight of the Gods',[16] is perhaps best indicated by the reception of Solzhenitsyn in the 1990s. Even if he stirred up some political debates through his journalistic writings and was given an orator's platform in the Duma, he still remained a controversial and rather marginal figure in the contemporary cultural field. The centre of public interest moved from the charismatic 'creator' (*tvorets*) of master works to the more mundane 'composer' of books (*sochinitel' knig*) in the sense of a professional author supported and promoted by editors, publishing houses and public relations managers.

The formerly separated émigré and domestic literatures have now been united. Russian writers living abroad (like for instance Fridrikh Neznanskii, who writes very popular detective novels in Germany, where he emigrated in 1977), writers living both in and outside of Russia (like Vasilii Aksenov) and non-Russian writers living within the Russian federation (like the Uzbek detective author Chingiz Abdulaev) all coexist within one market and together compete for the readers' consumer choice and wallet.

An excellent example of a New Russian authorial persona is provided by Grigorii Chkhartishvili, alias Boris Akunin or B. Akunin – an allusion to the nineteenth-century Russian anarchist Mikhail Bakunin. His detective novels became bestsellers in 1998. In a personal statement about culture and commerce in 2001, Chkhartishvili, a highly sophisticated scholar of Japanese literature and ex-editor of the journal *Inostrannaia literatura*, observed that a writer in Russia currently has three ways of adapting to reality: first, to change his profession, become a politician, journalist or literary manager; second, to insist on his poetic and mental autonomy, to remain the 'tsar of his own work, but without readers', the most dignified, but also materially unrewarding role; and third, to follow a double strategy by aiming to write and publish good-quality prose and at the same time make money from it. 'In this way, you serve the readers' interest in entertainment, while at the same time following your own artistic designs.'[17]

---

[16] Natal'ia Ivanova, 'Gibel' bogov (O slome literaturnoi epokhi)', *Nezavisimaia gazeta*, 10 August 1991.

[17] "1) Smetenie professii, 2) samyi trudnyi, no i samyi dostoinyi: bud'te tsarem i zhivite odin,

Akunin, by taking the third option, created what critics called the first mainstream entertainment literature in post-Soviet Russia. The new Russian writer has three characteristic elements: first, *professionalisation*; second, and deliberately connected with this, an orientation towards commercial *success*; third, a *playful and parodic authorial persona* that makes use of pseudonyms, plays with genre expectations, and is concerned to project a public image (which is often ironic). When the assumed name of one female writer, Marina Serova, in fact conceals a whole collective of authors producing by the dozen bestselling 'women's detectives', pseudonyms come to seem nothing other than a sales strategy. Since the late 1990s, this has become a new way to use and exploit qualified intellectuals on a large scale for cheap and anonymous labour. Literary toilers of this kind have received the ironic nickname 'negro-writers'. The creation of and play with different names have a long tradition in Russian literature and have been employed to different ends. Practices include the theft of a different identity, as in the vast phenomenon of literary usurpation (*samozvanstvo*), the artful self-mystification of authors that dates back to romanticism, as with Osip Senkovskii (alias Baron Brambeus), and, in Soviet times, the risky game played with Soviet censorship, as in the case of Abram Terts (alias Andrei Siniavskii).[18] Now all this has become a stock technique to deconstruct traditional images of the writer and basic literary norms, for example in the output of Akunin and in the work of some other bestselling members of the postmodern elite, like Viktor Pelevin.

In this light, it is hardly surprising that the relationship between the authorial persona and the biographical writer has undergone fundamental changes. In Russia there has traditionally been a strong link between these two levels of authorial existence. Ethics and aesthetics have been conflated: a good writer is considered or required to be a good person with a noble character and an immaculate biography. This set of assumptions has been challenged only in a few periods: by Symbolism at the turn of the twentieth century and by the Avantgarde in the 1920s. In the post-Soviet decade not only the biographies themselves but also the very notion of biography is in flux. Various biographical patterns can be found: Akunin constructs his own life as a trajectory of success, while Pelevin

---

3) tretii variant, promezhutochnyi: strukturiruite svoe sochinitel'stvo". See Grigorii Chkhartishvili, 'Kul'tura i rynok', *Znamia*, 6, 2000, pp. 189f.

[18] Vsevolod Bagno/Tat'iana Novichkova, *Chuzhoe imia*, 6, SPb, 2001, pp. 4-14; Boris Uspenskii, 'Mena imen v Rossii v istoricheskoi i semioticheskoi perspektive', in *Izbrannye trudy II, Iazyk i kul'tura*, M, 1994, pp. 151-163.

reduces his biography to a 'virtual' existence, rejecting personal interviews and avoiding public appearances. To his readers he is accessible only on the net – in this way, he constructs his own biography as mystification and riddle. Some female authors, like Aleksandra Marinina, the detective novelist, and Svetlana Alekseeva, the writer of documentary novels on topics from Chernobyl' to women and the war experience, present autobiographical information to support their claim that their fiction is based on real personal experience. Others, like some of the postmodernist writers from the former underground, Dmitrii Prigov and Vladimir Sorokin, ironically present themselves as victims of their own success and suggest that fame is a curse.[19]

For decades, Soviet literary life had maintained a stable hierarchy of leading writers among readers in both the official and unofficial spheres. The canon stood firm. But reader requests in the 1990s have shown that there is no longer an established pantheon of favourite writers. A survey on the ten greatest Russian writers of the twentieth century revealed such a diversity of preferences and levels of literary quality that no homogenous imagined author can be discerned any more.[20]

Along with the image of the author, the *reading public*, its roles, habits and interests have changed considerably since 1986. First of all, the quantity of reading, especially reading of fiction, has fallen dramatically, as the reduced print-runs of literary journals begin to indicate. In a 1994 survey, 23 per cent of the adult

---

[19] This is a pattern, which can equally be traced back to Russian literature in the nineteenth century – as in the conflict between Nikolai Gogol' and his popular rival Faddei Bulgarin – and in other literary cultures. See Irina Kaspe, 'Soedinennye s upekhom (Biografiia 'massovykh' pisatelei)', *Novoe literaturnoe obozrenie*, 56, 2002, pp. 329-339.

[20] Reader response research in the late Soviet era was highly manipulated, but after 1985 VTsIOM (the All Russian Centre for the Study of Public Opinion) in Moscow has regularly conducted reliable reader surveys. B. Menzel, 'Der sowjetische Leser als Thema der Forschung. Probleme, Methoden und Ergebnisse der empirischen Literatursoziologie', in *Sprache-Text-Geschichte. Festschrift für Klaus-Dieter Seemann*, München, 1997, pp. 184-200; idem, *Bürgerkrieg um Worte*.
In 1994, the five writers with the highest reputation were Lev Tolstoi, Mikhail Sholokhov, John Chase, Valentin Pikul' and Aleksandr Pushkin (Dubin, *Knizhnoe obozrenie*, 10, 1994); in 2001 the five bestselling writers in Russia were Chingiz Abdulaev, Marina Serova, Barbara Cartland, Daniela Steele and Ioanna Chmielewska. In 1998, the five best Russian novels of the twentieth century were considered to be Mikhail Sholokhov's *Tikhii Don*, Anatolii Ivanov's *Vechnyi zov*, Mikhail Bulgakov's *Master i Margarita*, Il'ia Il'f and Evgenii Petrov's *Dvenadtsat' stul'ev*, and Konstantin Simonov's *Zhivye i mertvye*. See B. Dubin, 'Veshchi veka, Roman veka v kontse stoletiia, prorochivshego konets romana', *Nezavisimaia gazeta*, 30 December 1998; also idem, 'Rossiiskaia intelligentsiia mezhdu klassikoi i massovoi kul'turoi', in his *Slovo – pis'mo – literatura*.

population replied that they did not read books at all, and 53 per cent did not read journals and magazines; by 2002 as many as 40 per cent did not read any books and the same 53 per cent read no journals.[21] Even though higher prices and wider economic problems have been mostly responsible for keeping people from buying books, a great number of readers also turned away from books to other media, first of all TV.

Russian mass readership was transformed from the mass mobilisation of the late 1980s to mass consumption and entertainment in the 1990s. If in the Stalin era readers had been infantilised,[22] and in late Soviet times they had been socialised as collectors of shortage cultural material, in the 1990s they underwent a period of socialisation as consumers. They were no longer inclined to idolise uncritically any Russian writers from abroad and any foreign writers, or to welcome blindly a wave of second- and third-rate Western popular authors and soap operas in mostly bad translations.[23] They became more discriminating and developed more of a taste for home produce. All this has taken only a few years. In Western countries, we should not forget, the emergence of different literary levels from high art to pulp fiction, and the development of multifunctional reading habits, was a process which took many decades (not to say centuries).

Reading preferences also changed, but in ways that varied according to the age, gender and educational level of readers. Habits were modified by the new reading matter on offer, as well as by the prominence of new media: while the intellectual-artistic elite of the older generation almost gave up reading fiction in the 1990s and preferred theoretical, philosophical, and other humanities literature, the majority of people who read fiction preferred the popular genres, which they read very often not at home, but on the road, in between private or work commitments, or at work. The favourite genres of popular literature range from the undoubted champion, detective fiction (preferred by 26 per cent of readers in 1994 and by 29 per cent in 2000), to historical novels (23 per cent in 1994 and 24 per cent in 2000), romance (23 per cent in 1994 and 24 per cent in 2000), and science fiction/fantasy (11 per cent in 1994 and 15 per cent in 2000).[24] Alongside

---

[21] *Russian Public Opinion. Annual 2002*, ed. VTsIOM, 2003, p. 42.

[22] About the infantilisation of the Soviet reader, see Evgeny Dobrenko, *The Making of the State Reader. Social and Aesthetic Contexts of the Reception of Soviet Literature*, Stanford, 1997, pp. 282-306; in Russian, *Formovka sovetskogo chitatelia*, M, 1997; idem, 'Vse luchshee – detiam (Totalitarnaia kul'tura i mir detstva)', *Wiener Slawistischer Almanach*, 29, 1992, pp. 159-174.

[23] N. Ivanova, 'Vot pridet barin', *Ogonek*, 16, 1988, pp. 27-29.

[24] Levina, 'Chitateli massovoi literatury'; *Delovoi Peterburg*, 15 July 2002, p. 29.

popular fiction, the majority of readers tended to opt for advice books, a category of literature hugely under-represented in Soviet publishing, for the information they provided on problems of everyday life. Academic readers of the younger generation tended to choose non-canonical genres and marginalised areas of literature outside the classical mainstream. These include science fiction, fantasy and memoirs as well as the literatures of smaller nations, peripheral or formerly colonised regions, such as Africa, Siberia or the Far East, the Baltic and the Balkans, and Israel. Well-educated younger readers also pay close attention to the latest literary publications on the internet. More generally, large genres like the epic novel have increasingly given way to shorter prose, a trend typical for all transitional periods of history. Another 'transitional' aspect of post-Soviet reading culture is a heightened interest in formerly inaccessible sources of knowledge and belief-systems: 36 per cent of all publications in the humanities in the late 1990s were connected with esoteric and occult topics.[25]

Distribution, which includes the publishing, promoting and selling of books, has been the most fundamental problem in literary culture ever since the state-monopolised system collapsed, subsidies stopped flowing, and publishing was put on the track of privatisation. Literary culture became less controlled and more anarchic as former hierarchies collapsed or lost their authority. Private publishers accordingly found themselves in a powerful position to steer the book market by adopting clever promotional strategies. 'PR' became a loan-word firmly entrenched in the Russian language (pronounced PE-AR with numerous derived neologisms such as *piarshchina* and *piarshchik*). The *piarshchik* has become the central figure in literary life. Some of the leading publishers, like Maksim Kriuchenko from the Petersburg-based Azbuka publishing house and Andrei Gertsev of the Moscow AST-trust, but also smaller, though prestigious figures like Ivan Limbakh and Mark Zakharov or Alexander Ivanov (Ad Marginem), are treated like stars in the media. While in the first half of the 1990s new private and cooperative publishing houses, both commercial and subsidised, mushroomed all over the country, after the devaluation crisis of 1998 the number of publishing houses for literature fell considerably, and firm monopolies were established on the book market. Sociologists see these monopolising pressure groups as operating within informal networks even stronger than those that obtained in the Soviet past.[26]

---

[25] B. Dubin, 'Kul'turnaia reproduktsiia i kul'turnaia dinamika v segodniashnei Rossii', *Monitoring obshchestvennogo mneniia*, 4, 1998, pp. 22-32.

[26] B. Menzel, 'Generationswechsel – Autoritätenwechsel. Buchmarkt und literarisches Leben

In 2002, the biggest publishing houses for literature in Russia – not including the two giants for teaching material Drofa and Tsentropoligraf – were AST, Eksmo, Olma-Press and Terra, all founded between 1990 and 1992 and situated in Moscow. They put out between 1,000 and 1,800 popular titles per year with total copies ranging from 23 to 38 million. While the numbers of titles and copies have radically increased for AST and Eksmo (1991/1997/1999 = 42/ 1,039/ 1,530 with 3.8/19.5/23.5 million for AST and 1997/1999 = 1,032/1,854 for Eksmo with 30.1/38 million copies), Terra Fantastika and other publishers from St. Petersburg fell behind in conditions of increasing monopolisation (1997/ 1999 = 665/430 with 12.6/4.5 million copies).[27]

Let us take a closer look at the production of 'mass' literature. In 2001 only 2.3 per cent of all newly published titles were published in more than 50,000 copies, while 35.5 per cent of all titles were published in print-runs ranging only between 500 and 5,000 copies. The bestselling authors of detective novels publish several million books a year. About one third of all fiction titles (36 per cent counted by titles; 47 per cent counted by copies) are still of foreign origin (most of all English, followed by French and German), which indicates that the process of catching up still continues. In the mid 1990s, three out of five new published books were translations. The balance between Russian and foreign authors did, however, vary according to genre in the second half of the 1990s. Romance literature was still dominated almost exclusively by English writers: several of the new Russian authors of romance novels used English pseudonyms. Russia did not seem to offer favourable conditions for generating images of beautiful and happy lives. As for the still heavily favoured detective genre, there was a clear turn to novels set in Russian everyday life written by Russian authors (many of them women). The same re-nationalisation can be observed in science fiction, fantasy and children's literature.

As already mentioned, books took over from journals as the main medium of literature in the newly commercial environment of the 1990s. However, the publishing houses did not focus their attention on individual books but instead worked to shape these books into *series*. The number of publishing series rose

---

in Russland seit den 1990er Jahren', in Menzel (ed.), *Kulturelle Konstanten Russlands im Wandel. Zur Situation der russischen Kultur heute*, Bochum, 2004, pp. 113-123.

[27] Sources: *Knizhnii biznes, Knizhnoe delo, Knizhnoe obozrenie, Delovoi Peterburg, Izdatel'stva Rossii* (1999), publishers' websites. It should be taken into account that, while in the Soviet past official statistics on numbers of copies tended to exceed reality, today publishers tend to reduce official numbers in order to save on taxes.

from 220 in 1993 to 1,200 in 1997.[28] As a result, even writers with an eye for commercial success do not write single books any more, but build a profile through evolving series or 'projects'. Aleksandra Marinina and B. Akunin have become exemplary for this strategy. Chkhartishvili/Akunin's 'Fandorin project' wittily ran the full gamut of the detective genre, since it announced the publication of sequels in all conceivable subgenres of the 'classical crime novel' (the spy novel, the political detective novel, the conspiracy novel, and so on) before they were even written.[29] For the first twelve volumes the strategy worked very well. According to statistics, Akunin reached the upper end of the bestseller charts with all thirteen of the novels he published between 2001 and 2004.[30]

In 2002, the new promotional strategies of post-Soviet publishing gave rise to major literary scandals involving the writers Eduard Limonov, Vladimir Sorokin and Aleksandr Prokhanov, who were arrested, sued and charged for illegal writings and/or activities. The small highbrow publishing house Ad marginem, which had established its profile through the publication of French philosophers and postmodern literature, published Vladimir Sorokin's novel *Blue Lard* (*Goluboe salo*), for which the writer was charged with pornography and gained enormous international media attention. Ad Marginem then, quite unexpectedly, published the demagogic and anti-Semitic pamphlet-novel *Mr. Hexogen* (*Gospodin Geksogen*) by Aleksandr Prokhanov, a writer well known since the 1970s as an officially approved Soviet author of war novels who during the 1990s had become an extreme right-wing nationalist activist.[31] Whatever the reason for the publishing house's policy, whether it was the political motive of supporting a novel on terrorism that was supposedly directed against the policies of President

---

[28] Il'nitskii, *Knigoizdanie*, p. 36
[29] *Azazel'* (1876) – konspirologicheskii detektiv; *Turetskii gambit* (1877) – shpionskii detektiv; *Leviafan* (1878) – germetichnyi detektiv; *Smert' Akhillesa* (1882) – detektiv o naemnom ubiitse; *Osobye porucheniia* (1886, 1889) – povest' o moshennikakh i povest' o man'iake; *Statskii sovetnik* (1891) – politicheskii detektiv. See B. Akunin, *Azazel'*, M, 2000.
[30] Statistical material by VTsIOM drawn from periodicals and newspapers June 2001-June 2002; see also Karlheinz Kasper, 'BAkunin und andere: Fiction, Semi-Fiction, Non-Fiction oder Pulp-Fiction', *Zeitschrift für Slawistik*, 47, 2002, 2, pp. 193-201.
[31] For further information on these literary scandals see B. Menzel, 'Blick durch ein deutsches Teleskop. Russische Literaturkritik im Wandel', *Osteuropa*, 9-10, 2003, pp. 1295-1306; in Russian, *Neprikosnovennyi zapas*, 4, 2003, 30, pp. 145-153; on the case of Limonov, see Olga Matich, 'Edward Limonov: Making Love and War', in *The Post Communist Condition, vol, 3, Zurück aus der Zukunft. Osteuropäische Kulturen im Zeitalter des Postkommunismus*, Frankfurt, 2005.

Putin, or simply the commercial motive of creating a bestseller through pure controversy, these scandals reflect the unstable nature of literary and cultural value in post-Soviet Russia. Where else would the same elite publisher release two such contrasting novels in such quick succession? Nevertheless, some commercial publishing houses have recently shown awareness of their responsibility to foster a reading culture and developed new strategies to promote publications of high artistic literature along with pulp fiction.[32]

How did these changes in publishing affect *literary criticism* and other expressions of informed opinion? Did they help to liberate people's minds and enable them to re-evaluate the past? Did they encourage more pluralistic notions by putting forward alternative concepts of literature, by widening the corpus of books reviewed and by reshaping aesthetic tastes? The extensive growth of the book market and the disappearance of a clearly defined literary field make significant new demands on professional critics. Literary criticism, however, although it had been one of the most authoritative institutions of Soviet literary culture, has become marginal and rather meaningless over the past decade. Instead of relinquishing its edificatory role and instead helping to orientate the reader in a new cultural situation, criticism itself seems disorientated, concerned above all to reaffirm its own importance. With its traditional didactic style, with its sprawling review articles discussing texts already known to the readers, criticism was closely tied to the thick journals, and its traditions were bound to decline along with those of its principal medium. Since the early 1990s, criticism has shifted to newspapers and, more recently, to the internet. Almost all critics of the older Thaw generation, like Igor' Dedkov, Iurii Burtin, Vladimir Turbin and Lev Anninskii, have retreated from the public domain or died. The major critical genre has become the short book review, whose role is to inform readers succinctly. The monthly journals have played a relatively minor role in the process of reconstructing literary life in the post-Soviet era. An analysis of the books reviewed in 1997-98 in the monthly journals has shown that the subjects of preference were mostly authors of the past, classics of the nineteenth and twentieth centuries from Dostoevskii to Nabokov, but very little contemporary literature, few foreign works and even fewer popular titles.[33] Critics of the

---

[32] Thus the SPb publisher Azbuka has founded a special award for bestselling quality fiction, advertises 'serious' fiction in TV-magazines and offers books as prizes in literary crossword puzzles in mass magazines.

[33] B. Dubin/A. Reitblat, 'Literaturnye orientiry sovremennykh zhurnal'nykh retsenzentov', *Novoe literaturnoe obozrenie*, 59, 2003, pp. 557-570.

intermediate generation, like Sergei Chuprinin, Natal'ia Ivanova or Aleksandr Ageev, and of the younger generation, like Andrei Nemzer, Viacheslav Kuritsyn, Aleksandr Arkhangel'skii, Vladimir Berezin and Sergei Kostyrko, shot to prominence in the 1990s and became opinion-leaders as journalists in newspapers, illustrated magazines like *Profil'*, *Kar'era* or *Russkii zhurnal*, or as internet correspondents. A small number of literary experts make regular appearances in the media, often on the internet, and at public events such as book awards. In Soviet times volumes of literary criticism were a standard type of publication, and as late as 1993 a print-run of 30,000 copies was considered a rather low figure for Sergei Chuprinin's monograph *Kritika – eto kritiki*.

One way in which critics can hope to reach a broader public and determine the status of new literature is through the distribution of *literary prizes*. Since 1991, more than 100 awards have been re-established or newly founded. Some are international joint-venture awards, like the supremely prestigious Booker Prize and the Pushkin Prize; others are private and commercial or private and non-commercial (as in the cases of the Solzhenitsyn, Astaf'ev and Okudzhava prizes). In addition the state offers prizes both old and new: the Russian State Prize and the National Bestseller (Natsbest) Prize, which was first established in 2000 as the literary equivalent of the 'national idea' that Yeltsin set out to formulate in 1998.[34]

In 2002 the extreme nationalist writer Prokhanov was awarded the Natsbest. His novel *Mr. Hexogen* was not a bestseller until it acquired a scandalous renown. The controversy was further stoked when several young critics with the reputation of being eccentric liberals lent fierce support both to the writer and to his novel. The result was a paradoxical and divisive set of alliances between parties from the extreme anti-establishment camp to the radical nationalists.[35] The scandal surrounding Prokhanov's novel and the Natsbest Prize once more reveals some of the basic problems of literary life in today's Russia: in the absence of common parameters to describe and evaluate different types of literature. Writers, publishers and critics are inclined to engage in eccentric acts of provocation in order to gain the media spotlight at any cost. Once literary professionals were deprived of state benefits and public authority, some of them rejected supposed political correctness at the cost of political or moral responsibility. The common

---

[34] 'Kritiki o premii. Kruglyi stol', *Znamia*, 1, 1998, pp. 190-208.
[35] On Prokhanov and this literary scandal see W. Eismann, 'Repressive Toleranz im Kulturleben. Prochanov, ein Literaturpreis und das binäre russische Kulturmodell', *Osteuropa*, 6, 2003, pp. 821-838.

quest for a single book to connect the literary public as a national community also betrayed an anachronistic desire on the part of political leaders, critics and other intellectuals to re-establish cultural homogeneity and a stable sense of literary value. Nevertheless, the era of stable hierarchies, whether officially or unofficial, seems to be over.

Ever since the 1960s, Russian literature had been much more diverse than the monolithic concept of socialist realism had officially presented it. But it was only during and after perestroika that this variety became publicly perceptible. The changing conditions, roles and discourses of literary communication were accompanied by a transformation in the *concept, status, and symbolic meaning of literature*. As politics and postmodernism blurred the boundaries between cultural spheres, diasporas, and official and unofficial cultures, so too boundaries within literary works have themselves dissolved. Writers experiment with non-canonical genres, postmodernists use pulp genres and topics to create virtual language-worlds, and fantasy writers simulate modern poetry. Since eclecticism, recycling and retro-styles have displaced the conventional emphasis on innovation and originality as indicators of literary quality, so high art and popular genres have been blended, with the result that irony, satire and parody have become popular literary strategies. The values of homogeneity and unity, so long hegemonic in Russian literary culture, have been subject to dissolution in the post-Soviet era. The homogenising and unifying function seems now to have been transferred to TV. Literature, by contrast, has become polarised as a rapidly widening gap opens up between the sophisticated metropolitan elite and the peripheral mass readers: a small literary-minded section of the population gets to read a growing number of new titles, while mass readers turn to an ever more homogenised pulp fiction. The realm in between, which in other countries is filled by a multifunctional mainstream literature, is still almost unoccupied.

All that has been stated here does not by any means indicate the end of literature as a meaningful cultural institution in Russia. The amazing energy and idealism with which a great number of new publishing houses try to translate, edit and print literature of all kinds, the great variety of books available on the market now – a diversity unthinkable even 15 years ago –, even the dissolution of hierarchies and former authorities, all this can be seen as signifying a period of transition towards a pluralist reading culture. Recent debates on certain novels, even the trials of certain writers for ideological or aesthetic reasons, but especially the enormous popularity of certain genres like fantasy and the historical novel, indicate that literature will continue to play a major role in reflecting and reinterpreting the past. Only the future will show whether and how far this process will be one of assimilation to global patterns and to what extent it will be shaped by Russia's own specific cultural traditions.

Marina Koreneva

Russian Detective Fiction

In post-Soviet times the detective novel has shown itself to be a dynamic and self-assertive genre. It has gained a position of supremacy in the book market and attracted constant attention from journalists and literary critics (even if the latter adopt a somewhat condescending attitude to it). But it is still ignored by Russian scholarship in much the same way as it was ignored in the Soviet period. As a consequence, one of the most resilient genres of Russian literature does not even have the kind of outline history that must precede any attempt at theoretical investigation. But empirical description is in turn made difficult by the absence of a suitable conceptual vocabulary in Russian literary scholarship. Conversely, Western concepts are often not applicable to the kind of texts that are classified by Russian publishers and authors as detective novels. Whatever differences of opinion may exist between them, Western literary scholars are unanimous on the basics of definition: a detective novel contains a crime that is not so much the centre of the narrative as a pretext for the construction of a plot, which in turn leads to the criminal being exposed and punished.[1] The presence of these characteristics cannot be disputed, but they do not provide an exhaustive definition either. Although they allow us to isolate all literary plots connected in some way with murder (from the Biblical story of Cain and Abel to *Macbeth*), they do not help us to understand where to draw the line between the stories of Conan Doyle and Dostoevskii's *Crime and Punishment*. Nor do they explain how to classify narratives where the crime is 'committed' by external forces, or where the identity of the criminal is known from the start and the main focus of the action is the attempt to foil and punish him. Back in the 1970s, German

---

[1] For theoretical conceptions and a review of theoretical literature see Peter Nusser, *Der Kriminalroman*, Stuttgart, 1980, Ulrich Suerbaum, *Krimi: Eine Analyse der Gattung*, Stuttgart, 1984, and Jochen Vogt (ed.), *Der Kriminalroman. Zur Geschichte und Theorie einer Gattung*, 2 vols., München, 1971.

scholarship found a way out of this difficulty by constructing an opposition between *Verbrechensliteratur* and *Kriminalliteratur*. The first of these terms denotes works where crime is examined in its social, psychological or existential aspects, while the second refers to works that do not entertain such ambitions and are focused exclusively on the solution of the crime.[2] But this opposition cannot be transplanted to Russian soil, and in any case it does not really work, because it is never clear-cut. Even if a novel is concerned mainly with the quest to solve the crime, it is unlikely to leave moral and psychological matters out of consideration. Indeed, a detective novel, precisely because it has no particular philosophical agenda, may give us a more searching social or psychological portrait of an era than a piece of fiction that is explicitly subordinated to the author's interpretative design.

The problem of definition can, I think, be solved if we bear in mind that the detective novel is a formula genre and has to include a number of structural and compositional elements that work together to meet the reader's expectations. The first element is an action or event that contravenes the norms of a given community, and is thus usually called a crime. The second is a counteraction or 'counterevent' whose consequence is a reversion to the norms in question. The interaction of these two elements forms the basis of the plot. It is also important to note that the action and the counteraction must have different agents. The norm-breaking action does not necessarily have to be a 'mystery'. All that is required is for the reader to be confronted with various unknowns as the action is gradually uncovered.

A History of the Russian Detective Novel

Even the briefest history of the Russian detective novel has to resolve the question of where to begin. Some scholars have started their account in ancient times, selecting from the corpus of surviving texts those plots that in some way or other are bound up with crime and its resolution.[3] Others – the majority – start with the stories of Edgar Allan Poe, and, more specifically, with the first publication in 1841 of his novella 'Murder on the Rue Morgue', a work that seems to include

---

[2] Nusser, *Der Kriminalroman*, pp. 1-7; Norbert Franz, *Moskauer Mordgeschichten. Der russisch-sowjetische Krimi 1953-1983*, Mainz, 1988, pp. 20-21.
[3] See for example R. Messac, *Le 'Detective Novel' et l'influence de la pensée scientifique*, Paris, 1929, and V. Ladenthin, 'Aufklärung vor der Aufklärung: Literarische Detektive im Mittelalter', in Werner G. Schmidtke/Armin Arnold (eds), *Sherlock Holmes auf der Hintertreppe. Aufsätze zur Kriminalliteratur*, Bonn, 1981, pp. 82-113.

all the basic plot elements of the detective novel. But to focus on a single text in this way does not do justice to the variations in national literary traditions. The development of the genre depends greatly on the cultural context of its adoption. We can hardly claim that Poe exerted a large influence in the Russian case, as this writer was known to Russian readers mainly as the author of fantastic stories with elements of the demonic, and not as the author of crime stories. The latter were first translated into Russian only in the 1870s, by which time Russia had crime novels of its own.[4] These novels relied less on direct borrowings than on the steady accumulation of formal elements necessary for the detective genre.

We can divide the history of the detective novel into 'latent' and 'explicit' phases. The signal for the onset of the second phase is usually the appearance in a given language of a stable term to denote the detective genre. In Russia the concept of 'crime novel' (*ugolovnyi roman*) took hold in the second half of the nineteenth century; in the twentieth it was displaced by 'detective novel' (*detektiv*). The emergence of the crime novel as a genre of its own was preceded by a long period when appropriate plots and motifs were developed in literary forms with different aims. If we take crime (or non-normative action) as a defining characteristic of the genre, then we should start tracing the 'latent' history of the detective novel by referring back to folklore. Russian folk tales contain much relevant material, including plot structures that later become staples of the detective genre. In folkloric depiction the crimes in question are not actions against the lives of human beings or living creatures, since life is not the ultimate value in this cultural universe. Instead, great importance is attached to offences against customary norms: these are always punished, especially if they concern property. Many narratives concern animals. For example, in the tale 'The Peasant and the Bear', the bear demands half the harvest from the peasant, but is then tricked by him: this is nothing less than a story about racketeering. In 'The Fox and the Hare', the fox takes away the hare's hut (i.e. living space), and the hare, finding himself on the street, seeks retribution for this lawless behaviour by appealing to higher authority (the bear, the bull, and so on). In the end he is saved by a brave cockerel. The resemblance of this story to more recent property disputes is only too clear. Russian folk epics (*byliny*) are also full of 'criminal' content that in many ways prefigures the post-Soviet crime thriller. In the tale

---

[4] For more on Poe's influence in Russia, see Joan D. Grossman, *Edgar Allan Poe in Russia: A Study in Legend and Literary Influence*, *Colloquium Slavicum* 3, Würzburg, 1973.

'The Nightingale Brigand', the criminal is not only made one of the main characters, but his very name indicates his status as norm-breaker.

Both tales and epics were intended for a wide audience. They were recited orally for entertainment at markets, fairs and other gathering places. A similar entertainment function was performed by the first adventure romances and stories that circulated widely in the seventeenth century. These were required less to edify than to 'stagger' and 'amaze', as is well attested by the epithets 'miraculous' and 'worthy of wonder' that tend to recur in the titles of Russian translations of Western European chivalric romances. Having arrived on Russian soil, these texts were transformed into folk tales (*skazaniia* or *skazki*), which put them in the same category as indigenous folkloric texts with larger-than-life heroes. Seventeenth-century Russia was taking on board not the classical models of the courtly romance but its popular versions as they existed in the chapbooks printed in large numbers and sold to the lower orders at fairs or hawked by pedlars. What this meant was that the chivalric hero was brought firmly down to earth and pursued worldly goals, but also that the adventure itself became the meaning and the goal of the narrative. A good example is *The Tale of Bova Korolevich*, a story that had a long life in Russian popular culture. More than seventy versions have come down to us. Right up to the early twentieth century the story was distributed in *lubok* publications and actively russified.[5] The Russian adventure story was a crucial forerunner of the *detektiv* not only because it contained appropriate plot elements but also because it shaped readers' taste for fiction without lofty pretensions. Many examples in this genre focus not on the central character and the logic of his actions but on the story or event and its resolution; they frequently concern a crime (theft, murder, kidnap) and its punishment. The most significant examples are *The Tale of the Peasant Son* (of which the oldest fragment dates back to 1620), *The Tale of Karp Sutulov*, and *The Tale of Frol Skobeev*. Another interesting case is *Shemiaka's Judgment*, usually considered the most popular tale of the seventeenth century, which was subsequently adapted many times in the eighteenth and nineteenth centuries. This story is particularly worthy of attention because, as well as preserving ancient mythic elements, it made explicit reference to the present day and was read as a 'contemporary' work. Its specific target was the judicial practice of that time.

---

[5] For more detail, see V.D. Kuz'mina, *Rytsarskii roman na Rusi: Bova, Petr Zlatykh kliuchei*, M, 1964.

Example 1: *Shemiaka's Judgment (Povest' o Shemiakinom sude)*
Shemiaka's Judgment tells of the tragicomic misadventures that befall a poor peasant, who in the end has to answer for his unintended misdeeds in court. His rich brother gives him a horse but no collar. The peasant has to attach the horse to the cart by its tail, which in the end is torn off. He then spends the night at a priest's, but is not invited to have supper. Looking ravenously at the food laid out on the table, the poor man falls from his bunk on to the table and kills the priest's child. Then, reaching the town to stand trial, the peasant tries to kill himself by jumping off the bridge, but another person happens to be passing by under the bridge taking his father to the bath-house on a sledge. The peasant falls on the sledge and kills the father. Then comes a sequence of anecdotes that leads into the scene of the judgment. The sentencing is a mirror image of the peasant's adventures: the owner of the horse is ordered by the judge to wait for the tail to grow back; the priest is ordered to give the poor peasant his wife and wait for them to have a child so he can kill it in exactly the same way; and the son of the old man is ordered to jump off the same bridge and strike down the peasant. All these sentences were a kind of parody of the Law Code (Ulozhenie) of 1649, according to which retribution for a crime was to be identical to the deed that had been committed: death for murder, burning for arson, swallowing molten metal for forgery, and so on.

In the eighteenth century the Russian adventure novel and story developed in the direction of greater specialisation. According to one prominent type, adventures involved the revelation of some kind of secret (be it a secret of birth, a treasure, or an act committed in the past). Here we can identify several categories. First, novels of mystery and horror in the style of Anne Radcliffe (who was exceptionally popular in Russia): in these stories, if a mystery was revealed, this was not usually the result of conscious, planned efforts, but rather of circumstance. Second, novels of discovery (of treasure, for example), where the plot was propelled forward by chance in combination with the strategy adopted by the hero. Third, mystery novels containing a puzzle which the hero could solve by using his analytical abilities to escape from a difficult situation (as in Voltaire's *Zadig*, which had numerous Russian imitations). A separate group was made up of works devoted to the biographies of famous 'bandits', which drew on the English tradition of the 'noble criminal'. These were not the 'noble bandits' who became common literary currency in the first quarter of the nineteenth century, and represented conscious flight into a different social environment in the service of a particular idea (be it revenge, retribution or some other lofty motive). In the eighteenth century, by contrast, fictional bandits were generally real-life criminals about whom many different legends had come into being. Just such a legendary figure was Van'ka Kain (1718-1760), a Moscow thief and robber.

Example 2: *Van'ka Kain, the Marvellous Thief and Swindler*
(O Van'ke Kaine, slavnom vore i moshennike)
The story is based on a real person. Van'ka Kain, a peasant's son, was sent into service in Moscow at the age of thirteen. After robbing his boss and having all kinds of adventures, he heads for the Volga and joins up with the gang of Mikhail Zaria. Then he returns to Moscow and voluntarily enters service in the department of criminal investigation, where he gains command of a team of soldiers. He then starts hunting down petty thieves and swindlers while protecting the major thieves. He persecutes Old Believers while extorting money from them for all kinds of 'concessions'; he opens a gambling den in his home and robs the participants. Using a combination of bribery, blackmail and force, Van'ka gains control over the whole department. He turns into an all-powerful secret governor of Moscow; he gives protection to a large number of fugitives, thieves, swindlers and murderers who bring terror to the city's inhabitants. Arson and robbery become constant occurrences. A whole investigative commission is sent from Petersburg, but it is powerless because the Moscow investigative department is in Van'ka's pocket. Only three years later, after a purge of police personnel, is it possible to catch Van'ka red-handed and bring him to trial. The court sentences the bandit to death, which is then commuted to exile in Siberia.

This anonymous story was subsequently reworked and published in various versions. There was even an 'autobiography' by the (illiterate) Van'ka, first published in 1764 and then reprinted many times over the nineteenth century. Curiously enough, in this publication Van'ka is called the 'Russian Cartouche' even though there was a fundamental difference between the famous French bandit and his Russian 'imitation': the Moscow thief entered state service and was a kind of 'double agent', which is why he might be called both a swindler and a detective. His biography is striking not just for its content but also for the style in which this content is presented: for the first time in the history of Russian literature a story offers an unvarnished and comprehensive portrait of contemporary society. It has all the elements of post-Soviet crime fiction: corruption, bribery, lawlessness, general contempt for the law among the population, absence of moral principles at all levels of society. Yet in spite of all this the roguish hero still gained the reader's sympathy. The story of the legendary bandit kept its place in the book market for almost a century and a half, and in the early twentieth century it entered the cinema: in the 1900s several well-promoted films were made about this popular hero. However, Van'ka Kain stories were located at the very bottom of the literary hierarchy. The heroine of Orest Somov's story 'Mother and Son', who 'reads without omission all novels and stories translated or composed in Russia', rejects Van'ka Kain when offered it by a pedlar, preferring instead the Gothic novels which were a much more prominent phenomenon in the early nineteenth century than bandit tales.[6]

Most adventure stories of the eighteenth century were translations that had undergone significant Russian adaptation and become widely imitated.[7] These texts have the following general characteristics:

- their heroes have an ethical code that reflects contemporary understandings of good and evil, of right and wrong, of the boundaries of transgression against property or human life

- they maintain a clear opposition between characters who are 'one of us' and those who are 'outsiders'; this explains a character's course of action and determines its ethical value

- they provide no explicit evaluation of the characters' actions: the hero is always a positive character, regardless of what actions he commits

- the characters are individually responsible for the deeds they have committed: the 'positive' hero himself determines the extent of the guilt of the negative character and resolves the conflict between them by committing acts of 'individual retribution'

- 'institutional' characters such as representatives of the government or the state, who might take upon themselves the defence of individual rights and the meting out of punishment, are absent; if such characters do appear, they usually have only a comic role

- death and horror have an aesthetic value

- situations are emphasised as being unusual or extraordinary, and thus unique and unrepeatable; for this reason, a distance is preserved between the text and the reader, who cannot make a direct connection between literary experience and real-life experience

---

[6] Orest Somov, 'Matushka i synok' (1833), in idem *Kupalov vecher. Izbrannye proizvedeniia*, Kiev, 1991, pp. 471-494.
[7] For more detail, see *Istoriia russkoi perevodnoi literatury. Drevniaia Rus'. XVIII vek*, vol. 1, *Proza*, SPb, 1995, pp. 142-280.

- one way such distance is achieved is by placing the action in an exotic location: either in a foreign country (an adventure novel was often a travel novel as well) or, less often, in social strata other than that of the implied reader
- the author/translator remains anonymous, which gives the text a marked 'fictitious' quality

In the first quarter of the nineteenth century the adventure novel was vulgarised, which had an inevitable impact on the literary reputation of the novel in general. The old countess in Pushkin's *The Queen of Spades* (1833) is typical in her assessment. As a representative of a former age, she asks her grandson to bring her something to read, specifying that she wants 'a new novel, but not one of those modern-day ones'. Instead, she requires 'the kind of novel where the hero strangles neither his father nor his mother, and where there are no drowned corpses'.

Along with the vulgarisation of the adventure novel went the emergence of the so-called novel of sentiment, which was part of the active appropriation of Romantic aesthetics. The result was an infusion of Romantic values: above all, the themes of freedom and the strong, free individual personality. When they were added to the adventure narrative, these values produced a particular kind of text centred on a Romantic crime, as in Ludwig Tieck's *Abdallah* (1796) and *William Lovell* (1795-96).

The main result of this period was to make readers accustomed to literary 'horror' (death, murder, kidnap, violence), but also to raise their affective threshold. Although violent phenomena were presented as exceptional and unusual, they were at the same time not terrifying, because, on the one hand, they were distanced from everyday reality, and, on the other, were overcome by a hero endowed with exceptional abilities.

In the middle of the nineteenth century the adventure novel gradually moved to the city. Eugène Sue's *Mystères de Paris*, which enjoyed exceptional popularity with Russian readers, was a special stimulus to the development of an urban literature.[8] The young Dostoevskii, still an engineering student, set to work translating one part of this novel, but ended up destroying his work before he had

---

[8] Sue's work was revived in the perestroika period, when publishers made it available in the old nineteenth-century translations; there was also a TV adaptation with many episodes. Vsevolod Krestovskii's *Petersburg Slums*, another publishing phenomenon of the mid-nineteenth century, was similarly revived in the 1980s. See *Peterburgskie trushcheby. Kniga o sytykh i golodnykh: roman v 2-kh knigakh* (1862), which had more than 55 reprinted publications, only 12 between 1990 and 2002.

completed it. The influx of such texts into Russian literature was accompanied by significant changes in the media culture of the time. In the middle of the nineteenth century the range of periodicals expanded significantly, and newspapers published notices of crimes committed and short reports on trials, which were often used subsequently as the basis for the plots of crime stories. Dostoevskii was far from unique in his reliance on this kind of source. At the same time so-called 'physiological sketches' were coming into fashion: these formed an important context both for the emerging genre of crime novel and for the psychological novel, which examined the individual causes of anti-social behaviour and the social roots of crime. The physiological sketch tended to be based on real material from the lives of the urban lower orders (typical titles included *The Underbelly of Petersburg*, *Petersburg Claws*, *Women Murderers*, *The World of the Swindlers*), which served as the basis for literary texts where crime lost its Romantic aura and ceased to be something unique and heroic.

The emergence of this new genre helped to revive the 'old' form of the adventure novel, which now turned its attention to the secret life of the big city. The native Russian adventure novel of the 'lower depths', which took its lead in many ways from Western models such as Sue, began with Vsevolod Krestovskii, who between 1864 and 1867 published the four volumes of *The Slums of Petersburg*. This epic tells the story of two generations of a princely family in decline made up of 'civilised rascals', whose heroic deeds are bound up with the activities of a band of criminals. This work brought its author scandalous renown, shocking the reading public not so much for its naturalistic details (such as descriptions of doss-houses, brothels and prisons) as for its artistic pathos (its convincing demonstration of the triumph of the 'kingdom of sin' in all strata of society). From this moment on Russian literature was gripped by 'slummania', as one literary critic of the time wrote in an article devoted to Krestovskii's many epigones.[9]

Besides physiological sketches of an ethnographic kind, sketches from a 'professional' viewpoint were also common in this period. They bore titles such as *Notes of a Detective*, *Notes of a Doctor*, *Notes of a Teacher*, and so on. Especially prominent were texts written by well-known lawyers, judges or investigators. Although these sketches had humanist aspirations – their broad aim was to draw public attention to social problems and human rights issues – as a whole they tended to create a romanticised image of representatives of the state.

---

[9] K. Golovin, *Russkii roman i russkoe obshchestvo*, SPb, 1897, p. 241.

Members of judicial institutions came across as zealous defenders of the legal order and of the interests of individual citizens; their professional life was rendered as selfless service in the cause of human rights. At the same time fiction began to develop the image of the 'noble detective', who became the central figure in the detective literature produced in Russia between the 1860s and the 1880s under the influence of the French writer Emile Gaboriau (1832-1873). Gaboriau's novels were all translated into Russian. Especially popular was the novel *Monsieur Lecocq* and its hero, a police detective. One of the first Russian equivalents of Gaboriau was Aleksandr A. Shkliarevskii (1837-1883), a prolific writer of the 1870s, who is now almost forgotten, like the other Russian authors working in this genre.[10] Another was Sergei Ladyzhenskii, who created the retro-detective, a genre recently rediscovered by Boris Akunin.[11]

Detective fiction gained a strong position on the book market in the last quarter of the nineteenth century, but in the longer term Russian literary detectives were out of luck. By the end of the century the first translations of Conan Doyle were appearing, as were the first Nat Pinkerton stories. The Russian detective was forced into the shadows of Western counterparts who proved extremely appealing to Russian readers. Some foreign fiction was already popular: *The Adventures of Buffalo Bill*, the Nick Carter stories, endless novels featuring *Antonio Porro, the terrible avenger* and the already mentioned Cartouche; a *Gallery of World Famous Detective Geniuses* also sold like hot cakes. Cheap editions of the adventures of the brave and unbeatable 'king of detectives' Nat Pinkerton came out in enormous print-runs: 200,000 copies was the maximum, while a normal print-run was 2-3,000. The popularity of this character was so enormous that the educational authorities sounded the alarm and tried to impose a prohibition. A circular forbade pupils of high schools (*gimnazii*) and institutes to read this kind of book.[12] No more forgiving was the response of literary critics, who saw in Nat Pinkerton not only a symbol of the degradation of culture but a reflection of the vices of high literature, which had just experienced a Nietzsche craze. In the

---

[10] See Aleksandr Britikov, 'Detektivnaia povest'' v kontekste prikliuchencheskikh zhanrov', in *Russkaia sovetskaia povest' 20-30-kh godov*, L, 1976, pp. 408-453; Franz, *Moskauer Mordgeschichten*, pp. 67-68.

[11] Note for example his story *Syshchiki. Istoricheskaia povest' iz bivonovskogo vremeni*, SPb, 1868.

[12] See A. Suvorovskii, 'Nat Pinkerton v detskom ponimanii', *Vestnik vospitaniia*, 1, 1909, pp. 157-167; N. Verigin, 'Literatura syska v otsenke uchenikov srednikh klassov gimnazii', *Pedagogicheskii sbornik*, 10, 1909; K. Sivkov, 'Idealy uchashcheisia molodezhi', *Vestnik vospitaniia*, 11, 1909, pp. 117-158.

person of Pinkerton, the superman had landed on the streets of the contemporary world, where he threatened to barbarise culture and to send morals (not to mention taste) into steep decline. But the phenomenal popularity of Nat Pinkerton was not due to the public losing its sense of taste: this public had always read 'low' literature. Nor was his success due to any innovation in narrative form, since these tales of the clever detective were no different from traditional adventure novels with their rapid succession of plot manoeuvres (chases, traps, secrets, and so on). The novelty of Pinkerton lay rather in marketing strategy: the gigantic print-runs, the continuity of the central character through all the stories, the tendency of the plots to touch on the sensations of the day (the triumphs of aviation, current military developments, the fashionable occult movement and so on), and – remarkably – the faith in technical progress. The hero achieves his successes not just because of his exceptional cleverness, strength, quickness, and so on, but also because he makes use of all the latest inventions of science and technology (telegraph, telephone, courier trains, inventions in chemistry, physics, biology and so on). In this sense he stands out from his forerunners and 'colleagues', with the exception of Sherlock Holmes, who has a similar taste for scientific and technological novelties (though in all other respects he is different from Pinkerton).

Unlike the Pinkerton stories, which exploited old narrative forms, the Sherlock Holmes stories constituted a turning point in the development of the detective genre. Conan Doyle brought into literature a fundamentally new type of hero: the main character was an amateur detective whose analytical abilities enabled him to solve even the most mysterious crimes. The form of the genre changed accordingly – from the novel to the short story, which allowed the author to treat specific 'case studies'. So did the structure of the narrative, which tended to work back retrospectively from the completion of the crime to its origins. Also new was the mechanism by which narrative suspense was created and maintained: the reader has just as much information as Holmes, but always lags behind him. Consequently, the process of investigation gains an aesthetic charge, as does the figure of the investigator, who is endowed with heroic, exceptional characteristics. Holmes is presented as a thinking hero who can stand up to sheer force. A defining feature of this type of literary detective is his lack of self-interest: he does not pursue any material goals in his investigations – the important thing for him is the intellectual challenge, for which he is prepared to risk his own life.

Sherlock Holmes stories were extraordinarily popular in Russia: they were not only actively translated and adapted for productions in the imperial theatres but also reworked using Russian material. Whereas Nat Pinkerton always held appeal for undiscriminating readers (including the 'youth' who wanted to be like him), Sherlock Holmes could aspire to a more elevated reading public (even if members of this public were still embarrassed to admit their enthusiasm for this character). As the eccentric philosopher of everyday life and social chronicler Vasilii Rozanov observed: 'Children, it's bad for you to read "Sherlock Holmes". And after confiscating a bundle of stories I get sucked into reading them myself. Each one has forty-eight pages. Now Siverskaia to Petersburg [a commuter rail journey] flies by in a flash. But I offend before bed as well, sometimes beyond three in the morning. They're terrible stories.'[13]

Detective stories were not the only literary form that grew out of the adventure novel. Another variety of literature that emerged from this source in the last quarter of the nineteenth century was the military adventure, which drew also on the tradition of war fiction that had taken off in the early nineteenth century, largely as a response to the campaign of 1812. But whereas these earlier texts were motivated primarily by patriotic principles of which the plots were merely illustrative, at the end of the century stories readily imported spies and secret agents to make their plots more gripping. One subgroup of spy literature was the 'military-utopian' novel, the fictional projection of a future world war, which was a well-known phenomenon in Europe but barely caught on in Russia, although many Western novels of this type were translated into Russian and even re-issued under the Soviet regime in the 1930s.[14] This genre developed further during the First World War. Its basic pattern was an opposition between 'us' and 'them'; the a priori justification of any illegal measures taken against the 'enemy'; and the ideological thrust of actions committed on both sides (something that had previously been absent from narratives of this kind).[15]

By the October Revolution, then, Russian literature contained several types of narrative connected in a broad sense to crime. First, the adventure novel with plots centring on the search for treasure, struggles with pirates, and so on; works

---

[13] Vasilii Rozanov, *Opavshie list'ia*, SPb, 1913, p. 341.
[14] See for example V. Zeeshtern, *Krakh starogo mira*, no place, 1906 (it is likely that this novel was written by Wilhelm II or his brother); A. Nimann, *Mirovaia voina*, no place, 1904/1932; L. Vikonte, *Evropeiskaia voina 1913 g.*, no place, 1901/1929, and others.
[15] Note the popular spy novels of that time by N. Breshko-Breshkovskii, *Gadiny tyla* (1915), *V setiakh predatel'stva* (1916), *Remeslo satany* (1916).

of this kind had shifted to the realm of children's entertainment literature and were published mainly in children's journals such as *Vokrug sveta* and *Na sushe i na more*. Then came the crime novel, the detective novel, and the spy novel. All of these genres were located in the category 'entertainment literature' and were regarded as low-grade (with the possible exception of Conan Doyle).

The Post-Revolutionary Period

The prerevolutionary Russian detective story has been described only sketchily and clearly needs further study, but its post-revolutionary counterpart has received much more thorough attention.[16] This makes it unnecessary to dwell in any great detail on specific periods, but it is still important to attempt a periodisation and a general sketch of the Soviet era. Western studies often claim that the history of the Soviet detective novel can be divided into two periods: from 1917 to the 1930s, and then from 1951 to the start of perestroika. The twenty years between these two periods are considered to be a 'detective-free time'. This claim seems to be not entirely accurate or fair, because no-one has ever attempted a full description, even of a basic bibliographical kind, of the vast numbers of works that appeared in the Stalin era without making more than a passing impression and certainly without leaving any trace in the history of literature. Literary critics had little to say about detective writing. They merely noted the existence of poor-quality texts that did not meet general ideological or aesthetic criteria, or else passed them over in complete silence (which, however, did not prevent these books from finding willing readers).

Detective fiction can be sought above all in the series, or 'libraries', of thin brochure-type books that publishing houses put out for the benefit of various groups of Soviet readers. Examples include *The Library of the Red Army Man*, *The Library of the Young Soldier*, *The Library of the Village Correspondent*, *The Library of the Worker Correspondent*, *The Village Library*, and so on. In the 1930s alone there were dozens of such series, and each one contained among other things various kinds of detective stories - both classics (such as Sherlock Holmes stories) and new works based on current Soviet events. It is true, however, that the genre itself had no stable name in the 'detective-free' era (as, in

---

[16] Extensive literature on the subject is given in the monograph by Norbert Franz cited above. This work also contains a short historical survey of the Russian/Soviet detective novel, although the post-Stalin period receives most attention (it is described in some detail, though a few important names and literary developments are left out).

fact, in the first few years of the Soviet period): the concepts of 'crime novel' or 'investigator novel/story' were losing their currency, but the concept of *detektiv* had yet to arrive. As a result detective stories were diluted in the general pool of adventure literature, where they would remain (for various reasons) right up to the start of perestroika. As early as the 1960s, however, the *detektiv* was gaining some degree of formal independence (while reserving the right to hide behind the term 'adventure' if danger were to loom again in the form of another ideological campaign). The thesis that the detective novel continued to exist without difficulty in the Stalin period can be supported by the following indirect evidence: in 1942, in the thick of the war, when you would think writers had plenty to keep them busy, the Union of Writers established a special commission on adventure literature. A number of significant people sat on this body: Marietta Shaginian, the author of the first Soviet detective novel about 'Red Pinkertons';[17] Lev Sheinin, who worked in the Soviet security organs and in 1938 published his famous *Notes of an Investigator*, which in the postwar period would go through more than thirty editions; Lev Nikulin, famous at that time for adventure novels which (in current terminology) were typical political detective novels;[18] and Nikolai Shpanov, whose combat experience in the Civil War gave him in the 1930s material for gripping adventure stories on the struggle with White Guardists (in the postwar era he would concentrate fully on the detective genre).[19] We also know that Shaginian gave a paper on detective literature in May 1945, while Sheinin, who during the war wrote the novel *A Military Secret* (*Voennaia taina*, 1942), a month later published in *Literaturnaia gazeta* a response to Shaginian's lecture with his reflections on the tasks facing adventure literature in general and detective writing specifically.

Today it is unclear whether the commission had many practical results and what real difference these declarations of principle and exhortations made. It is also questionable whether Soviet literary criticism can serve as a reliable source of information for describing literary reality, which, as is well known, was much more varied than it might seem from published surveys or discussions of literary problems. A striking example is the 'conversations about the *detektiv*' that were heard in the press of the Thaw period.[20] Writers and critics spoke with one voice

---

[17] Marietta Shaginian, *Mess-Mend, ili ianki v Petrograde*, M/ L, 1924.
[18] Nikulin's most popular works were *Nikakikh sluchainostei* (1924) and *Taina seifa* (1925).
[19] His first major works of this kind were *Podzhigateli* (1949) and *Zagovorshchiki* (1951). Both novels were re-issued many times in the Soviet period.
[20] See for example: V. Koroteev, 'Chto meshaet razvitiiu prikliuchencheskoi literatury?', *Lit-*

about the educative function of adventure literature and the importance of developing further the detective genre so that it could perform its allotted task. They were critical of current writing in this genre on several grounds: detective novels were clichéd in their plots, lacked authentic contemporary detail, drew negative characters schematically, had a low intellectual level, and so on. At the same time names were hardly ever mentioned, though the critics' intense polemical spirit might make one suspect that they were concerned by more than just the low *quality* of detective/adventure literature. If it had only been a matter of isolated lapses, there would hardly have been anything to talk about. The critics were obviously concerned by the *quantity* of poor-quality works. The problem was not that Soviet literature of the Stalin and post-Stalin eras had no detective fiction, but rather that the fiction that did exist did not meet ideological requirements and was therefore pushed to the margins. The opinions of literary critics of that time are worthy of study in their own right, but they are not a particularly useful source of information. If they give information on readers' preferences, they do so only indirectly, as in an article that complained of the limited horizons of young readers who insisted on requesting books 'about spies' in the libraries – which only goes to show that these readers knew what they wanted.[21]

In the absence of full bibliographical information on the genres of so-called mass literature in Soviet Russia, I can only make the supposition, based on indirect indicators and on my own experience as a reader, that there were no breaks in the history of the Soviet detective genre: it continued to exist, adapting to the conditions of the time, sometimes camouflaging itself, sometimes declaring itself openly, largely independent of the recommendations that came from above. If we also recall that the whole of Soviet history was a constant struggle with and hunt for the enemy (internal or external), then it becomes clear that a genre like the *detektiv* was condemned to a long life as the literary form best adapted to this historical reality. All that changed over time was the material used and the ideological approach. For the first few years after the Revolution the needs of the

---

eraturnaia gazeta, 14 November 1953, p. 3; readers' responses appeared a month later in the issue of 12 December; G. Tushkan, 'O literature smeloi mechty i geroicheskikh prikliuchenii', *Znamia*, 8, 1955, pp. 182-187; 'Materialy III Plenuma pravleniia Soiuza pisatelei SSSR. Problemy prikliuchencheskoi literatury', *Literaturnaia gazeta*, 11 June 1957, p. 3; Ia. Polishchuk, 'Siamskie bliznetsy', *Literaturnaia gazeta*, 5 April 1958, p. 2; M. Cherkasskii, 'Chitatel' zhdet geroia', *Iunost'*, 11, 1958, pp. 77-80; L. Kovaleva, '"Daite luchshe pro shpionov..."', *Literaturnaia gazeta*, 2 June 1959, p. 2; A. Bortsagovskii, 'Chtoby vse prochli', *Literaturnaia gazeta*, 10 December 1960, pp. 4, 6.

[21] Koveleva, '"Daite luchshe pro shpionov..."'.

book market were met (more or less) by re-issues of prerevolutionary books (including the stories of Conan Doyle, stories about Nat Pinkerton, and those about the Russian detective Ivan Putilin). Next came the era of 'Red Pinkertons', which in due course would be deemed a complete failure (in the terms of the aesthetics and ideology of the 1930s).[22] At the same time literature started to include plots involving struggles against the 'bourgeoisie' ('former people'). These took the form both of 'search' novels (the search for bourgeois treasure, for hidden stashes on abandoned estates and so on) and of 'crime' novels, which in turn were represented by two types: the first was focused on the tracking down of an 'enemy', on pursuit and punishment, the second on the exposure of his criminal actions, which were otherwise known as 'wrecking'. In the 1930s the plot repertoire expanded thanks to the new theme of the struggle against kulaks. This kind of 'village detective' formed the counterpart of urban detective novels whose plots were taken from the lives of juvenile vagabonds (*besprizorniki*) along the lines of the 'slum novels' of the nineteenth century and from the 'bandit tales' of the NEP era. The general feature of texts in this period was the shift of emphasis from solving a crime or a mystery to exposing the 'criminal', who was deemed to be such only because he represented another, hostile, class. The opposition between one's own people and outsiders, implicit in all detective texts in the early stages of the genre's development, became absolutely fundamental to the genre, since the mere fact of belonging to the category of 'outsiders' constituted a 'crime' and served as sufficient justification for a 'counter-action' even if the adversary had not performed any 'action' as such.

In terms of the development of the genre, the 1920s and 1930s brought little novelty except new themes and a redistribution of priorities: preference was now accorded to 'crime novels' (in a broad sense) rather than to 'detective' fictions. In terms of theoretical reflection, however, these decades were extremely fertile. The Serapion Brothers developed a theory of narrative forms and provoked a noisy polemic with RAPP, and the Formalists adopted techniques of detective fiction in their own literary practice; all this contributed to the overall climate of literary discussion and exerted a significant influence on the development of a general theory of literature. But theoretical debates had no impact on the bulk of 'low' literature, which led its own existence beyond the cultural domain inhabited by party decrees and public declarations of artistic principle. The Party

---

[22] The literary 'failures' of this time were the subject of a special article on *pinkertonovshchina* in the *Literary Encyclopedia*, ed. A. Lunacharskii, M, 1934, vol. 8, p. 645.

demanded of literature a new hero, the builder of a new life, and attacked the 'heroes' of bourgeois literature (who were deemed to be the dregs of society, thieves, robbers, prostitutes and detectives protecting the interests of private property). At the same time, however, detective literature produced the first 'hero' of Soviet mass culture: Major Pronin, who from the 1940s onwards became a real idol of the mass reader.

The creator of Major Pronin was Lev Ovalov (L.S. Shapovalov), a Soviet writer with an almost 'traditional' Soviet biography: a nobleman by social origin, he was born in Moscow, and his father died in the First World War, when the future writer was nine; at the time of the Revolution the family was in the village of Uspenskoe in Orel province, where the fourteen-year-old Ovalov organised a Komsomol cell; a year later, in 1920, he entered the Party. After moving to Moscow, he combined his party work with a literary career. He became a prominent figure in RAPP, published widely and produced a number of novels that received serious attention from the critics (*Chatter* (*Boltovnia*, 1928), *Hunters of Doubts* (*Lovtsy somnenii*, 1931)). He worked at the newspapers *Rabochaia Moskva* and *Komsomol'skaia pravda*, and then became the main editor of the journal *Vokrug sveta*, where he published 'The Blue Swords', the first story of a cycle about Major Pronin. In 1940 the writer finished work on a book about the feats of the Cheka and offered it to the journal *Znamia*, where it was held up by the editorial process and appeared (in the fourth issue for 1941) only after a personal intervention by Molotov. Simultaneously the magazine *Ogonek* published the next instalment, and as early as May the story was published in a separate book edition. A month later, shortly before the outbreak of war, Ovalov was arrested and he had a fifteen-year 'career break' until 1956, when he was rehabilitated and allowed to return to writing. Soon after this the whole Pronin cycle was reissued, and a little later appeared the stories 'A Bouquet of Scarlet Roses' (Buket alykh roz, 1957), 'The Brass Button' (Mednaia pugovitsa, 1958) and 'The Secret Weapon' (Sekretnoe oruzhie, 1962), which together with the earlier stories represent an interesting document of the era.

Example 3: Lev Ovalov, *The Blue Swords (Sinie mechi)*
'The Blue Swords',[23] the story that opens the cycle, tells of a young chekist who manages to uncover an international counterrevolutionary conspiracy. The hero, Ivan Pronin, is a twenty-seven-year-old Red Army veteran who fought in 'the

---
[23] Lev S. Ovalov, 'Sinie mechi', in idem, *Sobranie sochinenii v trekh tomakh*, M, 1988, vol. 2, pp. 5-31.

German war' and volunteered for the Bolshevik side in the Civil War. Seriously wounded, he is brought to Moscow, where he is assigned to work in the Cheka. His first task is 'surveillance' over a lady from the 'former people', a certain Boretskaia, on whom Pronin is imposed as a flatmate by administrative fiat. To begin with the lady gives her young neighbour a favourable reception, but he becomes a hindrance when he grabs a note from one of her visitors who, it turns out, is engaging in counterrevolutionary activity under the cover of an antiques business. After a complicated plot involving also Pronin's younger assistant Viktor Zheleznov and his secret police mentor Kovrov, Pronin manages to save himself and, with his colleagues' help, to arrest all the member of the secret White Guard organisation 'The Blue Swords'.

Ovalov's stories offer a model of a new type of Soviet detective fiction, which, on the one hand, developed the traditions of the classic detective novel and, on the other, took on board the accumulated literary experience of the previous decades. The 'classical' detective, whether Sherlock Holmes or Ivan Putilin, whether he acts as a private individual (as in the case of Holmes) or an official (as with Putilin), protects the rights of ordinary people, but Major Pronin is a representative of the state, whose interests he defends and in whose name he acts. This gives the hero a specific moral code: just like his adversaries, he schemes, deceives, tracks down, constructs traps and even steals and kills, but all these actions turn out to be justified, because he is a chekist and serves not the Law but rather Order. This dual morality is reflected in a 'dictionary of synonyms' that we might compile for the Stalin era: intelligence officer – spy (if someone is 'one of ours', then he is an intelligence officer, if not, then he's a spy), traitor – assistant, operation - diversion, taking out - kidnapping, destruction/liquidation - murder, and so on.

A new aspect of characterisation in the Pronin stories was the revelation of the inner workings of the hero's personality (as well as his typicality). Major Pronin is in some sense a 'typical representative' of the revolutionary proletariat, but he is also shown in the process of development, which makes him different from his literary predecessors. In the first story Pronin is a poorly educated soldier who is motivated only by a romantic sense of struggle and looks on his work in the Cheka as something trivial and 'earthbound', but in later stories he toughens up, starts to understand the seriousness of the mission with which he has been entrusted, and is transformed from a 'man of the people' type to a representative of the elite. As early as the story 'The Chickens of Dusia Tsareva' ('Kury Dusi Tsarevoi'), Pronin is a staid major in the GPU who lives on his own with a housekeeper named Agasha and a meaningful set of domestic objects (a guitar that is a gift from a gypsy singer saved by Pronin; a bent dagger that is a souvenir of a case long in the past that almost cost the major his life; an expensive central Asian carpet adorned with swords and pistols; and so on). As further stories appeared, the hero became ever more refined, as is indicated by the professional credo he formulates in 'A Glass of Water' ('Stakan vody'): 'An agent should know how to write poetry, calculate logarithms, play cards, walk dogs and respect his elders, although some of us don't have anywhere near all the attributes I have listed'. Here there were clear echoes of Sherlock Holmes, who in the Soviet version was turned into an 'agent', although he only ever acted on his own territory. The transformation of detective into secret agent did not change his basic function or the general strategy for constructing a plot (which did not depend on the specific material in question, whether that be the mass murder of chickens in a state farm or sabotage in mines in the Urals), but it did change the pattern of events in the genre: the action invariably started before the 'event' occurred, the motivation for the hero's activities became his sense of an impending event (he takes measures without yet understanding what exactly he is looking for), and his inner driving force was 'vigilance' (a concept that entered common parlance before the war and later became established in the cultural consciousness of the postwar era). A fundamentally new feature was the emergence of 'morality' in the main character. Viktor Shklovskii, who wrote extensively on the detective genre in the 1920s, drew attention to this in a whole article he devoted to the Pronin stories: 'It took a long time for Soviet detective fiction to work because the people who wanted to establish it followed in the footsteps of Conan Doyle. Like him, they went for gripping plots. But instead you can follow the path of Voltaire or, even more so, that of Pushkin. These works needed a moral element ... Ovalov has managed to create a new character: the patient, brave, resourceful major of state security Ivan Nikolaevich Pronin ... A genre is being created before our very eyes'.[24] In actual fact it was not so much that the genre was being created as that its constituent elements were being rethought: the character of the criminal and the investigator, the context of the crime and its evaluation, the method of solving the crime and the nature of the punishment. Ovalov established a new kind of literary model which would later guide his many imitators and which quickly gave rise to various apocryphal

---

[24] Viktor Shlovskii, 'Rasskazy Maiora Pronina', *Ogonek*, 18 June 1941, p. 15.

legends from the life of Major Pronin. This oral folklore indicated that the model had become a commonplace.

The general features of texts of the Pronin type include the following:

- an evaluative framework that is based on the opposition 'one of us – outsider' (*svoe - chuzhoe*), where outsider status is determined above all on ideological grounds;
- the basic reason for the crime is the fact of the criminal belonging to another camp (as opposed to social or moral causes, as was the case in the crime and detective novels of the second half of the nineteenth century and the start of the twentieth);
- the absence of mystery: the main character either anticipates the crime or knows from the beginning who has committed it; his task is to expose, pursue, apprehend and neutralise;
- the repertoire of crimes is expanded: the traditional categories such as murder, theft and arson are joined by crimes against public property (cattle, factories and their equipment, and so on) and against groups of citizens (though the poisoning of wells, the adulteration of foodstuffs, gun-running, the distribution of seditious literature, illegal border crossings, the organising of secret anti-state societies and unions);
- the explicit evaluation of characters' behaviour; the presence of an ideal image of a representative of state power;
- the identification between the state and the executor of its will; the latter receives unlimited executive power and is guided not by the law but by his own or the state's notion of the seriousness of the crime;
- the plot contains many separate events which amount to not one but several crimes that are all interconnected and stem from a 'fundamental' crime. This not only conveys the scale of the occurrences and their exceptional nature but also creates a strange sense of everydayness, as these criminal events are tied in with daily life (an impression strengthened by the Soviet mass media); what results from this is the illusion that literature can be extrapolated to real lived experience if the reader conforms to the parameters set by the hero (vigilance, bravery, cleverness, skilfulness, and so on);
- a basic positive thrust: the traditional 'happy' outcome signifies not only the individual triumph of the stronger side (whether the victor overcomes his ad-

versary through brains, astuteness, or physical or moral strength), but also the triumph of society. Both life and literature inculcated in Soviet society the notion that it was engaged in an unceasing struggle from which somehow or other it was bound to emerge victorious, having overcome one obstacle after another; the new detective fiction served up a compelling illustration of how evil, as an external phenomenon, could be not only exposed and punished but exterminated, which corresponded perfectly to the general ambition to build a new society and form a new man.

At the end of the fifties literary critics became concerned with the overwhelming popularity of 'spy literature' and declared a kind of war on the Pronin model. Adventure literature (and detective fiction as before remained in this category) was expected to deliver the romanticism of heroic deeds, social consciousness, stark psychological conflict, demonstrations of endurance and courage, and edification. 'Human heroism – that is the content of adventure literature', wrote a certain A. Bortsagovskii in a discussion published in *Literaturnaia gazeta*. 'Not crime (or espionage) on its own, not the techniques of crime, but ... heroism underpinned by the total artistic authenticity of the character, the heroism of a historically concrete human being'.[25] Critics saw the proper hero of adventure literature as a knight in shining armour who 'is searching most of all not for a spy, or a thief, or a treasure ... he is searching for and affirming the truth'.[26] As argued above, such declarations of principle and abstract demands hardly had any direct influence on literary developments, which emerged more in response to shifts in the sociocultural situation than in response to literary criticism, which was itself registering these shifts.

Soon after Khrushchev came to power the population was informed that the construction of socialism in the USSR had been completed and that it was now time to start building communism. Official party documents drew up the moral code of a builder of communism, which differed little from the Ten Commandments. The announcement of the triumph of socialism in a single country signified the completion of a stage in the total struggle of all against all. The party leadership had established some sort of order in socialist reality. Only isolated failings remained, but these could be worked on. The hostile international environment also remained, but the consolidated and unified Soviet people could cope

---

[25] A. Bortsagovskii, 'Chtoby vse prochli', fn. 20.
[26] A. Elkin, 'Podvig sil'nykh ili "madril'skie strasti"?', *Literaturnaia gazeta*, 14 April 1964, p. 3 (à propos of Iu. Dol'd-Mikhailik's 'I odin vpolne voin', published in the same year in the journal *Ural'skii sledopyt*).

with this. These optimistic beliefs gave rise to a sense of what Soviet detective fiction should be. On the one had, it should show that crimes were rare, constituted no more than 'isolated failings', and could potentially be overcome or fully eradicated in the not too distant future. On the other hand, it needed to demonstrate the indestructibility of an existing social system that was not in thrall to any external enemies and was capable, moreover, of doing that enemy substantial harm from within, by acting on its territory. This basic belief system did not mean that the authors of detective fiction took it as a direct guide to action. It meant a change of overall psychological orientation, inspired from above and cultivated at all levels of society independently of what was happening in reality. On the ground, of course, the same old crimes (murders and thefts) were being committed, though these were supplemented by specifically 'Soviet' crimes that infringed socialist legal culture (individual private commercial activity with the aim of personal gain, today called business, but in those days considered a punishable activity). The general tone of everyday life changed. Limitless rapture and bottomless terror both departed the scene; an illusion of equilibrium took hold and gave rise to the era subsequently known as that of 'stagnation'. Newspapers no longer published stories about large-scale conspiracies, diversions and provocations; there was no longer any such thing as day-by-day crime reports; information on law-breaking mostly shifted to specialist journals. Social and political horror stories now came in strict doses.

In this light the development of detective fiction in the 1960s-70s seems quite predictable. The chekist novel broke down into two subgenres. First, the police novel, which in its structure and emphases approached the production novel. Second, the spy novel, which concentrated on the struggle with Western secret services and governments, using mostly subjects from recent history (above all the Second World War, less often the Civil War and the NEP);[27] on occasion it might use contemporary material, often including elements of the 'border novel', which became in the middle of the fifties a subtype of its own, or of the police novel.[28]

In each of these subgenres the main characters became increasingly professionalised. In the police novel the main role was taken by the investigator, who, as a rule, had higher education. In the spy novel the leading role was taken by a mil-

---

[27] See for example Iurii Klarov/Anatolii Bezuglov, *Konets Khitrova rynka. Povesti,* M/ Kaluga, 1994.
[28] See for example the very popular novels by A.O. Avdeenko: *Nad Tissoi, Gornaia vesna, Dunaiskie nochi.*

itary cadre. Romantic ideals gradually gave way to everyday realism: the ordinary activities or the Soviet police or of the Soviet secret service were the basic theme of detective fiction in the sixties. The focus was less heroism than professional activity. As a result the subject matter became more trivial, as did the character of the crimes under investigation. Authors placed great emphasis on the plausibility of the events they described. In the police detective novel this entailed a deeper psychological portrait of the main character, who now acquired a personalised biography (wife or girlfriend, free time, personal interests and likes, moods). In the spy novel, it meant using documentary material.[29] We should also note that documentalism, or at least stylised documentalism, became a genre characteristic in police fiction too. Here the plot was focused mainly on the process of investigation, which consisted both of 'brain work' and of interaction with innumerable administrative structures that could help to solve the crime.

---

[29] The phenomenon of novels based on documentary material was partly connected to the fact that many veteran chekists became writers in the 1960s. They included Dmitrii N. Medvedev, a colonel in the state security apparatus and commander of the special NKVD detachments 'Mitia' and 'The Victors', author of the documentary stories 'It Happened Near Rovno', 'The Detachment Heads for the West', 'On the Banks of the Southern Bug' (*Na beregakh iuzhnogo Buga*, M, 1963); Aleksandr A. Lukin, lieutenant-colonel, fought in World War Two, head of intelligence in the special NKVD detachment 'The Victors', author of the books *Sotrudnik ChK*, *Operatsiia Dar*, *Tikhaia Odessa*, M, 1963, *Obmanchivaia tishina*, *Razvedchiki*, *Devushka iz Rzheva* and others; Mikhail S. Prudnikov, major-general, commander of the detachment 'The Untouchables', author of the books *Soveshchanie sobiraetsia ekstrenno ...*, *Dal'nii billet*, M, 1983, *Operatsiia Feniks*, *Neulovimye*, M, 1961, *Neulovimye deistvuiut*, M, 1965, and others; Oleg M. Shmelev, lieutenant-general, whose books include *Oshibka rezidenta*, M, 1967, and *Vozvrashchenie rezidenta*, M, 1975/1997, which were subsequently adapted for the screen; Aleksei N. Zubov, Vladimir V. Vostokov, Ovidii A. Gorchakov and others. At the same time a few writers who had no direct professional connection to the intelligence services gained access to archive material. Their works include Lev Nikulin's *Mertvaia zyb'*, A. Ardamatskii's *Vozmezdie*, Vartkes Tevekelian's *Reklamnoe biuro pospodina Kocheka*, Vadim Kozhevnikov's *Shchit i mech*, and the novels of Iurii Semenov. The same process can be observed among the authors of police novels: more and more writers had some professional connection. Nikolai Leonov, author of a cycle of novels and stories about the criminal investigator Lev Ivanovich Gurov worked in the police for ten years. Leonid Slovin, who wrote about the activities of the transport police, knew about these activities from first-hand experience (*Sled chernoi ryby*, M, 1995, together with Georgii Vainer). Vasilii Vedeneev, who wrote a legal dissertation, was also a lieutenant-colonel who published the novels *Chelovek s chuzhim proshlym*, M, 1994, *Prem'era bez repetitsii*, *Volos 'Angela'*. Daniil Koretskii, whose novels are published to this very day, headed a department in the Rostov Higher Police School and was well-known as the author of academic studies on the distribution of firearms. This list could easily be extended.

This is what happens in the Vainer brothers' novel *I, the Investigator* (*Ia, sledovatel'...*, 1968).

Example 4: Arkadii i Georgii Vainer, *I, the Investigator*
The hero, a police detective, is investigating the murder of an unidentified citizen whose body has been discovered in a Black Sea town. The task is to determine the identity of the dead man, to reconstruct the event and to find the murderer. A scrap from a recipe and the brand of a comb found next to the corpse enable the detective to establish the name of the victim: he turns out to be Evgenii Koretskii, the first navigator of a Tallinn fishing boat. His killer was a conman who wanted to steal his car and money. Thanks to the first person narration, the reader is drawn into the process of investigation. We not only 'hear' the thoughts of the main character as he reflects on the nature of professionalism in his line of work,[30] but also help him to compose numerous requests and telegrams to various institutions (their text is provided directly in the novel) and to conduct an interrogation.[31] In other words, we become a participant in the process of communication between different state structures, which gives a sense of the coordinated activity of the enormous state mechanism standing behind the hero, who is seen to be acting both on his own and yet not alone.

Another characteristic of this period is a new attitude to the criminal: he is no longer perceived as an 'outsider', and as a result a new opposition takes shape between 'one of us' and simply 'other'. Contact between the two sides is now conceivable; not only that, the criminal may even be morally improved – that is to say, re-educated. When this happens, the investigator becomes not only a figure who surpasses the criminal in intellectual terms, not only a representative of the law and the state, but also the criminal's moral superior who therefore tries not only to bring the criminal to light but also to understand the reasons that have led him to follow the wrong path. The prominence attached to moral issues corresponds closely to the general orientation of literature in this period. Whereas

---

[30] Reflections on professionalism deserve special mention, because they help to formulate a new professional credo which only in part corresponds to the traditional investigator's code of the classical detective novel. 'My whole work', says the main character, 'is a struggle to solve mysteries ... You can only triumph over mystery by using logic and through *people's kind help*' (p. 66). An important point is the opposition regularly drawn between 'feeling' and 'professionalism': 'It may well be that the dead man was a great guy, and he may have been a real bastard ... But that didn't interest me at all back then. There's nothing to write – the profession stifles feeling' (p. 10). Vainer, *'Ia, isledovatel''*.
[31] The stylised documentalism of the text is heightened by the format of a few of the chapters, which are presented as 'pages from a case file'.

in the nineteenth century the motto of Russian literature was 'man is good, his environment is bad', which gave rise to the conviction that it was essential to change external circumstances, official literature of the twentieth century, after waging for many years a struggle to change circumstances, put forward another thesis: 'the circumstances of Soviet life are good, but man can be bad'. However, responsibility for the failings identified was placed not only on the individual himself but also on his immediate environment, the collective that was jointly responsible for the personal development of its members. This is what brought the general educational impulse of the era and a corresponding ethic of behaviour that was reflected at all levels of society. The dogged attempts in Soviet detective fiction of this period to understand the causes of crime often contain a note of sincere astonishment: all Soviet citizens are placed in identical conditions, all minimal existential requirements are met by the state, which also offers every citizen all the essential social guarantees (housing, work, guaranteed wages, medical care, education, pension and so on), but crimes are still committed, even if they are 'isolated occurrences'. The reason was found in moral imperfection, in the lack of spiritual values, lofty interests and aspirations, and sometimes even in the very type of personality that tended to oppose itself to the collective. 'All versus one' became in the 1960s-70s a cultural formula for interpersonal conflict, which was fixed in the language by the well-worn phrase 'All people are regular people, it's just him ....' (and variations on the same). These words could be heard in schools, shops, at home and at work.[32] Plots reflect this opposition in the sense that crimes in detective fiction are directed against 'others'. There are no family dramas with their resulting conflicts, nor are there 'family' emotions such as jealousy, envy, hatred, and so on; these motifs can be found in subplots, as minor sidelines, and even there not too often. The criminal's actions are seen as being directed against the norms of Soviet collective life in the interests of satisfying selfish personal interests of a purely material nature. The antagonism between 'spirit' and 'matter' becomes a central theme of conflict that takes over from the cultural myths of the previous decades.

---

[32] Phrases of this kind were favourite ways of speaking to one another in secondary schools: 'Why are you so special?', 'Do you need a special invitation?', 'All children are normal, it's just you ...' (vse deti kak deti, odin ty) – this was the standard repertoire of phrases of the average teacher, who worked from the general assumption that a universal ideal person must exist. To 'Be a person' (byt' chelovekom) meant both to be good and to be like everyone else. Note also the title of a popular children's book of that period, 'Barankin, Be a Person!', whose main character is constantly standing out from the general 'order' of schoolchildren.

Soviet detective fiction in its two main types (police and spy stories) was joined in the 1960s by foreign detective fiction, mainly the books of Conan Doyle, Agatha Christie, Georges Simenon, and Gilbert Keith Chesterton. In the 1970s the range of authors was expanded, and publishers began to release series such as *Masters of Foreign Detective Fiction*, *Contemporary Detective Fiction*, *Contemporary French Detective Fiction*, and so on. These included both stories and novels by contemporary Western authors. Naturally, the choice of these works and authors had an ideological underpinning, as they were designed to demonstrate the evils of capitalism and provide oblique evidence of the 'rotting West'. But we should all the same note the fundamental differences between this material and its Soviet equivalent. For all the variety of their themes, plots and narrative structures, all these texts were united by one thing: their orientation towards the private life of the private individual, in other words, towards a sphere practically absent in Soviet works. In this time and place Western detective fiction performed the function of a 'window onto Europe', because it gave information on everyday life and habits that were unknown or little known to Soviet readers of that era. Its function resembled that of travel novels with their heavy dose of ethnography. Translated detective fiction continued to be astounding and engrossing, even though its officially stated function was merely to edify.

The end of the 1970s saw a peculiar equilibrium between Western and Soviet detective fiction. Both occupied the niche of middlebrow psychological prose in which a gripping plot is combined with humanist moral baggage. At the end of the 1970s and beginning of the 1980s, psychological detective novels were taking a leading position in Soviet literary culture thanks to the works of Stanislav Rodionov, Daniil Koretskii, Vasilii Vedneev, and others.[33]

Detective fiction did, however, labour under certain constraints. Most publishing houses were so-called 'self-financing enterprises' (a change in policy of the Khrushchev era), which meant they kept themselves going mainly through publishing the classics and works of adventure literature. The quantity of the latter was capped by the State Committee on Publishing; it was not to exceed eighty titles per year. As a result publishers were forced to manoeuvre, to find not so much sales strategies as camouflage strategies. They devised new series of pub-

---

[33] It is also striking that even prestigious Soviet prose writers turn to the detective genre at precisely this time (note Iurii German's *Moi drug Ivan Lapshin* and Viktor Astaf'ev's *Derevenskii detektiv*). This phenomenon reflects the general sense of the time that the status of detective fiction was going up (note also the lengthy discussion that took place on the pages of *Literaturnaia gazeta* at the end of the 1970s).

lications such as *The Library of War Adventures* or *The Library of Detective and War Adventures*, some of them as supplements to journals like *Ogonek* or *Krasnaia zvezda*; they also published, along similar lines, almanacs with titles such as 'Heroism' or 'The Investigator'.[34] They produced collections of stories to mark the day of the Soviet police or the day of the Red Army. A few stories could be published under the category of children's literature, a few more in journals such as *Ural'skii sledopyt*, *Sel'skaia molodezh'*, *Volga*, series such as *Roman-gazeta*, or even periodicals apparently remote from literature such as *Nauka i zhizn'*, *Znanie – sila* or *Khimiia i zhizn'*. Especially important in this latter category was the journal *Grazhdanin i zakon*, which had a circulation of more than a million and published not only Soviet authors (Iulian Semenov, Vil' Lipatov) but also Western 'classics' such as Simenon. This set of publishing strategies placed the readers themselves in the position of a detective: in order to find the desired text, it was necessary not only to expend energy (this went without saying in an era of a total book shortage that was paradoxically combined with enormous print-runs), but also to work out where to start looking for it. Although detective fiction was among the most popular and potentially profitable branches of Soviet publishing, it was heavily reined in.[35] The relationship between readers and publishers in this era was very curious. Literary critics were not providing detailed guidance on reading matter and little information was available on new books. The result was that readers became extremely 'genre-orientated' in a way that was not affected by the tortuous manoeuvres of publishing policy.[36]

---

[34] These libraries often offered a home to authors who could not be published more openly. Thus, for example, Gaito Gazdanov's novel *Vecher u Kler* was published at the very start of perestroika in the *Library of Heroism and Adventure*, which was a supplement to the journal *Sel'skaia molodezh'*.

[35] At the end of the 1980s, at one of the annual meetings of the All-Union Bureau for the Propaganda of Literature, it was related that the book trade was the third greatest income generator in the budget after vodka and cinema; not only that, cinema revenues were falling, while book sales were rising. We can surmise that the profitable part of book publishing was not classic fiction or political literature, which sold at a much lower price than detective novels. For example, books in the series 'School Library' cost 1 rouble 40-50 kopecks at the end of the 1970s, whereas books in the series 'Contemporary Italian Detective Fiction' cost 3 roubles 50. For more detail, see Viktor Miasnikov, 'Bul'varnyi epos', *Novyi mir*, 11, 2001, pp. 150-158; in English, 'The Street Epic', *Russian Social Science Review: A Journal of Translations*, 44, 2003, 2, (March-April), pp. 67-81.

[36] Some detective lovers learned foreign languages specially so as to be able to read foreign novels in the original and get round Soviet publishing. The Ekaterinburg writer Viktor Miasnikov recalled that at the end of the seventies he worked at a factory with its own Polish

In the middle of the eighties book production started to turn towards the market, which at this stage was little more than a free-for-all. On the one hand, old strategies were maintained through inertia: old-style 'Libraries' continued to appear until the middle of the nineties, along with old-style collected volumes[37] and 'old' authors (Arkadii Adamov, the Vainer brothers, Iurii Klarov, Nikolai Leonov, Ivan Makarov, Vasilii Ardamatskii), several of these in the form of collected or selected works.[38] On the other hand, publishers began to look for new niches: they put together collections of prerevolutionary detective stories,[39] they published new Western detective novels (whose novelty was, however, only relative, as these were mainly authors whose works had appeared before 1972 and so did not fall under the copyright convention joined by the USSR in that year). They included familiar names such as James Hadley Chase, Earle Stanley Gardner, Rex Stout, Frederick Forsyth, and less familiar ones such as Joanna Chmielewska. The arrival of this kind of product on the book market had significant consequences. It was not that Russian readers gained access to books they had previously only heard about at second hand, or that the new texts offered new genre patterns or ethnographic material, but rather that the book market began actively to expand the social basis of readership, presenting ever more varied choices to as yet uncommitted consumers. Now, in order to read a detective novel, you did not have to go searching for it – the market forced it on you: bright cover designs, stalls in highly visible public places (by the metro, at bus stops and stations, on central streets, next to shops), a handy format (pocket size and paperback) with a correspondingly lower price – all these things drew readers in and made them accustomed to the idea of literature for rapid reading that

---

language society. The workers were learning Polish purely to be able to read the detective novels that were available in the 'bookshops of socialist literature'. Especially popular were the pocket editions of the Polish series '*Labyrinth*' and '*The Silver Key*', which included not only Polish but also American, French and English detective novels. See ibid.

[37] See for example: *Iskatel'. Sbornik*, M, 1994 (the final issue); *Podvig. Sbornik*, M, 1990 (and so on until 1995); *Ofitserskaia ruletka. Sbornik*, M, 1992; *Imenem zakona. Sovremennyi sovetskii detektiv. Sbornik*, M, 1989; *Militsiia v SSSR. Prestupnik i bor'ba s nim.* Sbornik, M, 1991; *Detektivnye romany i povesti*, M, 1996 (final issue), and others.

[38] See for example: Arkadii A. Vainer/Georgii A. Vainer, *Izbrannye sochineniia v 3-kh tomakh*, M, 1991; Nikolai I. Leonov, *Sobranie sochinenii v 4-kh tomakh*, Samara, 1993; Iurii Klarov, *Izbrannye sochineniia v 2-kh tomakh*, M, 1994, and others.

[39] *Russkii syshchik. Sobranie neveroiatnykh prikliuchenii*, M, 1992; *Nasledniki Van'ki Kaina. Sbornik detektivov*, M, 1994; *Russkie detektivnye istorii ne pokhozhie ni na chto*, comp. B.A. Leonaev, Pushkino, 1993; *Prestupnyi mir Moskvy* (reprint), M, 1991, 1994, 1996, and others.

had its own distinctive style of self-presentation. Detective fiction was, for example, packaged quite differently from fantasy books, which were published in hardback and promoted in other ways (through adverts in public places, in the mass media, and by using a number of other positioning strategies). This expansion resulted fairly quickly in the saturation of the market with Western detective fiction that on closer inspection turned out to consist of products from 'the day before yesterday': James Bond and Perry Mason seemed hopelessly old-fashioned against the background of the dynamic processes taking place in the new Russia. Publishers did the rounds, reprinting the same old works due to economic considerations. To buy up the rights to new authors required a substantial capital investment at a time when readers were becoming ever more immersed in the ready-made detective stories provided by news reporting on the mass media. The criminalisation of everyday life not only lowered the threshold of Russian society's sensitivity to crime, it also transformed the consciousness of people in a society where fear became the basic emotion. At precisely this moment new Russian detective novels arrived in droves and filled the empty space left after the selection of Western authors became exhausted and the old themes of Soviet detective fiction ceased to correspond to reality. As the main type of detective novel had long been the police novel, it became the first victim of a new social situation where the organs of security had lost their authority and were no longer considered to guarantee observance of the law, all the more so since the laws themselves had not only stopped working in reality but were perceived as being ineffective.

Contemporary Russian Detective Fiction

Russia detective writing in its current form is still very young: it is not even ten years old. It was not until 1996-97 that publishers began to follow a general policy with this genre. Separate 'series' started to appear, each having a single, recognisable design (Russian Bestsellers, The Black Cat, Russian Thrillers, Hard-Boiled Detective, Cure for Boredom, Home Detective, and so on). The visual presentation of the books was eye-catching, even aggressive. Publishers also developed a new attitude to their authors. Whereas in the Soviet era authors remained behind the scenes, now they became fully-fledged people. Certain basic but highly significant information was provided about them: their education, their occupation, a short list of their works. These short biographies indicate that all authors had higher education, and some of them had some experience of working in the security services, in the armed forces (for the men) or in journalism. Women detective writers, besides those (like Aleksandra Marinina) who also worked in the 'organs', included those with a background in literary studies, journalism or film studies.[40] This kind of professional history increased the fictional credibility of a story, or at least (in the case of people with a literary background) promised a certain literary competence. By establishing the 'series' format so firmly in readers' minds, publishers guarantee the commercial success of any text that fits the set model. It is worth noting that authors were first published in paperback and only then, after they had achieved obvious commercial and popular success, did they make it to hardback. The principle of 'seriality' served as orientation for readers who did without the services of literary critics.

Gender is a fundamental structuring divide in contemporary detective fiction: books can be split into 'men's' and 'women's', an opposition that does not, however, mean that the basic patterns of the genre are treated differently in the two categories. These designations are bestowed on the basis of simple criteria: the sex of the author and of the main character.

Women's Detective Writing

The emergence of women's detective fiction is a major innovation, though not because there have never previously been women detective authors.[41] The dif-

---

[40] The question of the reliability of the information presented by the publishers will not be discussed here, although it deserves attention. It is well known that many authors, especially at the dawn of the new Russian detective fiction, wrote under a pseudonym – some of them to avoid embarrassment (as in the case of graduates of the Literary Institute), others to avoid confusing their main profession with this 'sideline', still others under pressure from the publishers. One result of this has been situations where an author for one reason or another breaks a contract with a publishing house, but his name – like a brand name – remains in the possession of the publishers. So as not to lose the name they have worked to establish, publishers hire another, usually completely unknown writer, who continues to produce novels under the name of the already famous author. If the 'real' writer continues to publish books under the same pseudonym and the publishers dig their heels in, then literary twins begin to operate on the book market (as was the case, for example, with Anna Malysheva and Viktoriia Platova, both of whom existed in two manifestations). For more detail on this, see 'U avtora "Okhoty na Zolushku" otniali imia', *Komsomol'skaia pravda*, 19 July 2003. The existence of authorial 'teams' is sometimes discussed in the newspapers; there are rumours that authors such as Fridrikh Neznanskii, Aleksandra Marinina and others do not exist but are made up of various people who are dubbed 'negroes' in the professional slang.

[41] In the perestroika period, for example, women authors included Daliia Truskinovskaia (*Shaitan-zvezda*, M, 1998), Ol'ga A. Lavrova (*Umri v polnochi*, SPb, 1995), Vera P. Mal't-

ference is that now the main character can be a *woman* investigator. Her social position varies. Often she is a private detective or an ordinary citizen. Much less often she is an employee of the organs of state security.[42] The authors who take the latter option are headed by Aleksandra Marinina, who initiated the upsurge in women's detective writing.

This 'queen of Russian detective writing' has surpassed all her peers in terms both of print-run and of quantity of editions: her twenty-two novels have a combined print-run of 26 million in 217 separate editions.[43] All her books have the same heroine: Anastasiia Kamenskaia, who works in the analytical department of the criminal investigation service of the Russian Federation. She is a middle-aged woman of unremarkable appearance with an 'anti-heroic' set of attributes: she is negligent of her appearance, asexual, emphatically unsporty, sloppy around the home, not very competent in her everyday affairs (and inadequate in various other ways commonly associated with the 'weaker' sex), well-educated (she knows classical music and foreign languages, and does literary translations), immersed in her intellectual activity. All her thinking is bound up with her work, and this takes up all the time she might otherwise devote to family life, to which she appears entirely indifferent.

Marinina uses the traditional pattern of the detective or police novel, proceeding from a mystery to its logical resolution. In doing so, she focuses the reader's attention on the process of the investigation, the accumulation of information from various sources through analytical reasoning, and the working of this information into a general picture. As a result, the climax of the book comes not when the criminal is caught but at the moment when the crime is worked out. The plot is non-linear, because the actual pursuit of the criminal is not a major element. It is more like a spiral, as the heroine takes in more and more fields of investigation and gradually works towards a solution. This structure is bound up with the material the author chooses. The centre of each book is not a crime per se but

---

seva and Ol'ga Volkova.

[42] See for example the novels of Nina Vasina, who in 1999 published a series of four books under the general title *Zhenshchina-apel'sin*. The main character is a senior investigator named Elena Kurganova, whose motto is 'The criminal should go either to prison or to the grave'. The heroine follows this principle in her work: she is not only a extraordinary beauty but also an extraordinary sniper, agent and investigator. Although she uses the external attributes of police detective fiction, the author adopts the structure of the thriller: the heroine, who has lost her faith in Law and Justice, makes her goal the pursuit and destruction of the criminal.

[43] Figures from Marinina's official site http:// www.marinina.ru

rather a particular social problem that is manifested in a particular crime. Marinina's novels all have their own themes: the publishing business, pornography, show business, psychological experimentation and zombification, illegal trade, corruption, and so on. The subjects enable the author not only to show society's sore points but also to give a composite portrait of this society. She depicts representatives of varied social groups and strata (rich and poor, educated and uneducated, workers and unemployed, and so on). Her characters fit neatly into this system of social classification: they have not so much individual as group characteristics.[44] Additional suspense is created by the fact that the reader, immersed in this recognisable fictional reality, has to follow the heroine in solving a number of mini-mysteries along the way. These arise because the system of social stereotypes essential for people to make judgments about their environment is breaking down. Previously, for example, a certain professional affiliation (doctor, policeman, writer, actor, scholar) served in literature as a guarantee of high moral values, but now time has broken down into a number of separate 'pasts'. Every citizen has several different biographies, and society has witnessed the emergence of categories of 'former' people (yesterday a researcher, today a down-and-out; yesterday a school underachiever, today a showbiz star, yesterday an Afghan hero, today a contract killer; and so on). In fictional terms, this means that every character has a second, concealed face and every event exists in at least a second dimension. Duality – of biography, actions, personality, moral judgments and ethical criteria – becomes an essential feature of reality. The author follows the laws of the genre by taking every investigation through to its conclusion, but leaves the reader feeling that the underlying problem is still unresolved. As a consequence, the state and effective power are seen not to coincide. The state, in the person of Kamenskaia, makes efforts to eradicate crime and even hands over criminals to representatives of the Law, but ultimately it is devoid of real power that would enable it to bring under its control the chaos of events and circumstances and the conflict of individual interests or to make these correspond to a single social order with clear legal and moral boundaries. Marinina can be considered part a group of contemporary detective writers who engage with social issues and thus continue the traditions of the classical detective or police novel.

---

[44] This method of constructing social types is evident most of all in the depiction of the victim, who may be a model (*Igra na chuzhom pole*), a woman lawyer (*Stechenie obstoiatel'stv*), male teenagers (*Stilist*), Jewish youths (*Ne meshaite palachu*), and so on.

The alternative to the state investigator in contemporary women's crime fiction is the private citizen, who takes it upon herself for various reasons to defend the interests of the individual. This kind of character has many variants that boil down to two basic types: the private detective, who takes on a case on professional terms, i.e. for money, and the private citizen, who is an amateur.

Marina Serova was one of the first writers to make a woman private detective her hero.[45] Her main novels are contained in two series. The first features the private detective Tat'iana Ivanova, while the other showcases the professional bodyguard Elena Okhotnikova. Both these women have stable characteristics: they are young, beautiful, well-read, sporty, physically fit, expert in self-defence and the use of firearms. In other words, they have all the qualities that today's 'ideal woman' ought to possess (it is worth noting that the heroine is constructed precisely as an ideal woman) in order not only to play an equal part in a man's world but to take the lead and subject men to her will. The narration is entirely in the first person, which gives the author the opportunity not only to show her private detective in a private environment but also to bring the reader as close as possible to the heroine's inner world, which itself has ethnographic interest as an unusual reflection of today's values, above all personal freedom. This freedom is associated with a certain level of prosperity (money, flat, expensive clothes), with social independence (work outside state structures and private business), with personal independence (as expressed notably in an active sex life and a rejection of family life), with the absence of moral restrictions, and so on. The first-person narration allows the author to give full details of how the heroine conducts her morning toilette (she spends a long time in the shower, looks at herself in the mirror, applies her makeup, and so on), what she wears (all articles of clothing, right down to underwear, are painstakingly described), how she drinks her coffee (an essential ingredient in everyday life), what she reads (she often reads detective fiction, for example Marinina), how she has sex, and so on. In other words, the reader receives a mass of information that has no direct relationship to plot development but creates an image of the heroine that partly explains the behaviour of the men she encounters when the plot swings into action.

---

[45] According to the publisher's information, Serova is a 'graduate of the Law Faculty, an official in the General Prosecutor's Office, and at the present moment an official in one of the security services' (which seems unlikely to be accurate given the strange vagueness of the description). On Serova see H. Trepper, 'Philip Marlowe in Seidenstrümpfen oder Misogynie im russischen Frauenkrimi? Zur Figur der Privatdetektivin bei Marina Serova', E. Cheauré (ed.), *Kunstmarkt und Kanonbildung: Tendenzen in der russischen Kultur heute*, Berlin, 2000, pp. 243-260.

Whatever the underlying reasons for this style of characterisation (narcissism, the war of the sexes, sheer bad taste), the presence of a woman at the centre of the narrative has certain advantages for plot development. When the heroine takes on the male role in the narrative, she trumps the men because she brings an element of the unexpected, which gives the narrative additional dynamism and tension. In addition, the heroine, for all her perfection, is not only vulnerable in the same ways as her male counterparts (she may fall victim to her adversaries' strength or numbers) but is more vulnerable because of her pronounced femininity, which opens up a range of new plot manoeuvres. The choice of a private detective as the main character predetermines much of the plot structure. The story has to begin with a request from a client, who formulates a task: from the outset, the detective is confronted by the need to take vigorous action. Women detectives, however, have their own ways of getting information. Their feminine wiles often enable them to find a private route of access to state organisations. Serova's heroines, for example, always have a former husband, schoolmate, ex-lover or secret admirer who happens to be an employee of the state security organs. Serova adds to this traditional repertoire of tricks one novelty: fortune-telling. One of her heroines throws dice before taking any important decision and interprets the result by consulting the fortune-telling manual *The Oracle*. Thus, an activity with deep roots in female popular belief brings to women's detective fiction the theme of fate, which is so alien to the detective genre as hitherto conceived. The heroine not only listens out for the 'voice of fate' but even regards herself as the embodiment of fate. For this reason she bears with pride the nickname of 'witch'. In formal terms the kind of text represented by Serova's novels differs little from its 'male' counterpart, but it does stand out for the extreme intensity of the action, which in places is so great that the text becomes a kind of women's thriller. This tendency is most in evidence in the series devoted to the bodyguard Elena Okhotnikova.

Example 5: Marina Serova, *Taking a Long Aim*; *Laughable Money*
Taking a Long Aim (*S dal'nim pritselom*). Elena Okhotnikova is hired by the owner of a private restaurant to guard his premises, which have been targeted by racketeers. Elena not only finds out who is behind this but also carries out a successful operation to get rid of the racketeers and to liquidate the debt that the owner has incurred to one of the bandits.
Laughable Money (*Smeshnye den'gi*). Elena Okhotnikova is hired as a personal bodyguard by a rich American lady who has arrived in Russia to audit a charity

fund set up with her money. As she performs her duties Elena realises that the real reason for Miss Friedlander's visit is not the charity but her plan to recover treasure that once belonged to her Russian ancestors. The treasure hunt is joined by American competitors and by Russian bandits, who are defeated comprehensively by Elena Okhotnikova.

Texts of this kind consist of a string of minor plots that are held together by the basic thrust of the activities of criminal and investigator, and where unknowns are kept to a minimum. For every action by the criminal there follows a reaction, and so on until the successful resolution of the conflict. The roles of many of the characters are not fixed. Yesterday's victim can become today's criminal, a criminal can in turn become a victim, the investigator may become a pursuer, a victim or a criminal, and all this in an environment where the boundaries of right and wrong are all but erased. Characters move easily from the world of 'normal people' to that of bandits and back again, without experiencing any special emotions as they do so. The only point that is emphasised is the status of the characters: all of them (both the criminals and their victims) belong to the world of the rich, and as such they exist beyond the limits of ordinary moral and ethical norms in a criminalised social environment. All collisions between them, even if they have the appearance of a family drama born of greed or jealousy or an economic conflict arising from competing interests, eventually boil down to a struggle within the criminal world, which is presented as consisting of two interconnected parts: the legal and visible, and the illegal and concealed. The outcome of this struggle is not the triumph of justice or good or law or order but the meting out of local and, as a rule, temporary justice. This kind of crime fiction echoes the fairy-tale mythological world-view that was discussed earlier in connection with tales such as 'The Bear and the Peasant'.

The woman detective or bodyguard has as her counterpart the amateur detective, who figures prominently in the works of many authors. This role is often played by a reporter, as in men's detective fiction.[46] The association between private investigator and journalist became common in Western detective fiction of the 1960s-70s and it still functions successfully as a plot device for setting up non-state investigations. The adoption of this model has brought nothing radically new to the prototype except perhaps a few specifically Russian details (the

---

[46] See for example Anna Malysheva, *Pri popytke vyiti zamuzh,* M, 2000; Elena Arsen'eva, *Sud'ba streliaet bez promakha*; some novels by Tat'iana Poliakova (f.i. *Karaoke dlia damoi s sobachkoi*, M, 2004), and others.

heroine's exaggerated attention to her appearance matches the narcissism of her professional detective sisters, and she also shows a certain degree of cynicism and boastfulness, for example when she shows how successfully she can get in to elite social events).

A more original type is the 'pure' amateur, who is present in Russian women's detective fiction in several types: the pensioner,[47] the rich woman who does not need to work,[48] the ordinary citizen (a pianist,[49] twin sisters,[50] a self-effacing schoolteacher[51], and so on).[52] All these characters in one way or another echo Agatha Christie's Miss Marple and share with her the natural curiosity that makes them different from professionals and draws them to cases in the first place. Unlike the English lady, however, they all have at least some taste for adventure. Miss Marple's concern is to solve the mystery, and so each investigation reads like an exercise for her intellect and attention to detail; solving the crime is almost a chance by-product. The Russian heroines, by contrast, are motivated not only by curiosity but also by an explicit desire to help others; they do not only take an active involvement in the investigation, they start searching energetically for the criminal, acting often impulsively, unpredictably, unreflectively and incautiously. In the process, they may provoke a series of further unplanned crimes, which are sometimes only obliquely connected to the main crime. The heroines often cross ethical boundaries as they help out minor characters who, when they hear of the good cause, are glad to offer essential information or documents, or to break into someone else's flat, only to fall victim to a crime themselves. Compositionally speaking, these detective novels are very close to the adventure novel, as the action develops from one occurrence to the next and

---

[47] Note the cycle of fifteen novels by Natal'ia Aleksandrova about the pensioner Natal'ia Lebedeva that include *Shag v bezdnu* (M, 2003), *Svideteli zhivut ne dolgo*, *Tango vtroem* (M, 2003), *Dve damy s popugaem* (SPb/M, 2002), *Porvannaia struna* (SPb, 2004), and others.

[48] See the cycle of about twenty novels by Dar'ia Dontsova on the private detective Dasha Vasil'eva.

[49] See the cycle of novels by Ol'ga Volkova on the clairvoyant pianist Natal'ia Orekhova (*Tarantella*, *Kofeinyi serviz* and others).

[50] See the novels by Natal'ia Nikol'skaia about Polia and Olia, twin sisters who keep getting involved in detective stories: *Lapsha na ushi*, *Dushnym vecherom vdvoem...*, and others.

[51] See Tat'iana Poliakova, *Baryshnia i khuligan*.

[52] The 'ordinary' people who get involved in private investigations include some men. In general, this is the partner, husband or lover, who helps the heroine to hunt the criminal or untangles complex circumstances. See for example Tat'iana Ustinova, *Khronika gnusnykh vremen* and Elena Bogatyreva, *Naslednitsa*.

does not centre on a single event. The main crime becomes just a pretext for the heroine's adventures. The many plot lines achieve resolution only when the criminal is caught or exposed and all the events in the text have been explained. This kind of hybridisation of adventure novel and detective novel has given birth to a new type of detective narrative with a multiplicity of unknowns that are not quite the traditional 'mysteries' of detective fiction. Here the basic question is not who the victim and the criminal are but how to catch and punish the criminal; not why the crime was committed but how all these crimes, plot lines and characters are interconnected. This kind of text usually has a dual suspense mechanism, the first part of which comprises the immediate sequence of events while the second is the 'extratextual' story, which turns into a complex drama and constitutes the real plot. This technique has been frequently used, for example, by Dar'ia Dontsova, who works in the genre of ironical detective fiction.

Example 6: Dar'ia Dontsova, *An Inspector's Kiss* (*Kontrol'nyi potselui*)
An Inspector's Kiss (*Kontrol'nyi potselui*). A friend of the heroine (who is a rich middle-aged lady named Dasha Vasil'eva) has her children kidnapped. Dasha begins to look into the case. After a while she encounters a girl who looks like one of the kidnapped children begging in the metro. Dasha tries to establish the girl's identity and calls her mother to the metro, but the latter falls under a train in suspicious circumstances. After many adventures Dasha penetrates the world of professional begging and meets an image consultant who gives acting lessons to beggars: this turns out to be the grandmother of the kidnapped children, who once taught at the Theatre Institute. When Dasha pins her to the wall, Valeriia Petrovna (the grandmother) tells her story. Left helpless by the era of reforms, she was unable to cope with her poverty and inactivity. Her situation improved when she was approached by a successful businessman who offered her work coaching professional beggars. After discovering that her daughter-in-law was about to receive an enormous inheritance from France, the grandmother decided to make it hers. She plans to make a fake will for her son, to get rid of her daughter-in-law and so take the money. While she is working on this plan she discovers by chance that both her granddaughters were born not to her son but to another man. Deciding that the girls are not worthy of the inheritance, she stages a kidnap and 'places' them with her boss in the begging business. She is helped in organising the kidnap by a loyal pupil who shortly before that kills her own friend just to make it into Valeriia Petrovna's acting class. Dasha's intervention foils all the grandmother's plans. Not only that, she is blackmailed by her pupil, who demands her share for helping with the kidnap. Valeriia Petrovna turns to her boss for help, and the pupil is soon killed. Dasha is on the trail of the girls.

On hearing about this, Valeriia Petrovna asks her boss to take out her daughter-in-law, who nonetheless miraculously survives. Dasha manages to find one of the girls, who has been sold by the boss to a firm that trades children. The woman heading the firm becomes the next victim of the boss, who is getting rid of all witnesses. Dasha gets into the 'begging academy' and exposes the main culprit, but lets her go after her confession and promises not to tell the police.

The basic characteristic of this kind of detection fiction, which may be called the adventure variant of the detective novel, is the fact that all the crimes take place in the private sphere and concern personal relationships that have an emotional basis. The central figure is a private individual in private circumstances, a private investigation or pursuit which ends with a private 'sentence'. Although state structures nominally exist in the form of an acquaintance in the police or prosecutor's office, they take no direct part in the action and only appear from time to time at the decisive moment, if it is necessary either to save the life of the private investigator or to arrest the criminal. The private focus and the adventure style of narration (which implies numerous plot collisions) mean that the crime itself is nothing exceptional and becomes ordinary. This impression is confirmed by the ironic style of narration, which tends to downplay the social significance both of the crime and of the criminal. These are treated as ordinary parts of everyday life. This ironic type of detective novel, introduced to Russian literature by the Polish writer Joanna Chmielewska, is produced by a number of women writers.[53] Their books differ from equivalents in the West partly in the way they insist on treating even extraordinary events as everyday, but also in their relationship to social reality. The Russian novels contain elements of the 'slum novels' of the late nineteenth century: the characters find themselves entering the murky lower depths of urban society. They also act in an asocial space, a state within a state, with its own hierarchies.

Another distinct category of detective fiction is the crime novel, which allots roughly equal time to describing how the crime is committed and to how it is solved.[54] Texts of this kind have two vectors. On the one hand, they develop a criminal plot, showing the criminal making a number of mistakes. On the other

---

[53] See the books of Alena Smirnova, El'vira Bariakina, Anna Mikhaleva, Irina Asba, Marina Vorontsova and others.

[54] Writers active in this subgenre include Viktoriia Platova, Alena Kravtsova, Ol'ga Arnol'd, Tat'iana. Kravchenko, Svetlana Aleshina, Anna Danilova, Polina Dashkova (Dashkova's works are psychologically deeper and stylistically more accomplished than those of her colleagues).

hand, they tell the story of an investigation. Eventually, of course, the two plots meet. This kind of fiction does not have regular characters (who reappear in one novel after another of a big series), nor are they crammed full of subsidiary events. These texts are so various in their themes and narrative models that it is hard to systematise them. One important variant is the so-called 'economic detective fiction' created largely by the journalist and economic commentator Iuliia Latynina.[55]

Men's Detective Fiction

The types of detective narrative that I have identified (police/detective novels, detective novels with elements of the thriller, detective novels with elements of adventure, crime novels) are not the exclusive preserve of women writers. They all have analogues in so-called men's detective fiction, which deserves to be treated separately because it tends to favour different themes, place different emphases, and advance a different set of values.

'Male' themes include above all politics, which can be divided into domestic and foreign politics. The latter is concerned mainly with international political conspiracies, a theme that has not been particularly popular in Russia recently.[56] Much more popular has been the theme of corruption in the upper echelons of government. In the scale of the events they describe and in their formal principles, these novels resemble the classical Italian mafia stories of the 1970s. Fridrikh Neznanskii, for example, follows this pattern in his novels, which he has brought together as the series *Turetskii's March* (*Marsh Turetskogo*). The main figure of this cycle is a special agent of the general prosecutor's office, Aleksandr Turetskii, whose status is such that he only gets involved in especially complex

---

[55] See Iuliia Latynina's *Okhota na iziubra*, *Sarancha*, *Stal'noi korol'*, *Nich'ia* and others. Latynina is also succeeding in the fantasy genre. See chapter 6, fn. 60.

[56] The only author who consistently uses international material in his detective novels is Lev Gurskii, but his novels (*Ubit' prezidenta*, *Peremena mest*, *Postav'te na chernoe*, *Igra na gestapo*, and others) stand in a category of their own. They are a variant of the spy novel but have markedly fantastic elements, which leads their author to categorise them as alternative history or political fantasy, although in formal terms they could easily be classified as political detective fiction. The spy novel is itself near the bottom of the current hierarchy of genres, as indicated, for example, by the book *U samogo sinego moria* (M: Olma-Press, 2002), which is a collection of parodies of spy stories and jokes and anecdotes on the same theme. The emergence of anecdotes, very popular in Russia, is a sure indication that the culture has been oversaturated with a particular phenomenon, which is starting to become the butt of laughter.

cases. All of the plots are closely bound up with present-day events in Russia that are fully recognisable: the disaster on the Kursk, the ever more frequent plane crashes involving senior civil servants, the privatisation of major industrial firms, and so on. Unlike his 'colleague' Anastasiia Kamenskaia, Turetskii is not office-bound: he combines analytical intelligence with 'fighting qualities', which are further supplemented by personal charm and a clearly formulated 'code of honour', one of whose key points is loyalty to male friends (whereas faithfulness is absent in Turetskii's dealings with the female sex, and with his own wife in particular). Male friendship, along with this code of honour, enables Turetskii to investigate corruption cases while remaining within the corrupt environment. Following the traditions of the Soviet police novel, Neznanskii makes each investigation a collective affair – with only one qualification. Whereas the Soviet detective was fighting a battle on one front (the boundary between state or society and the criminal world was clearly drawn), these days the investigation is a struggle on several fronts: now even someone who appears to be 'one of us' can turn out to be an outsider and a renegade, and vice-versa. In their structure Neznanskii's books are similar to those of Marinina. The action follows a spiral, the resolution of the conflict generated by the plot does not imply a solution to the general problem, which in Neznanskii always has a political colouring. A peculiarity of Neznanskii's texts is that the 'real' criminal – the person who set in motion the whole chain of events – goes unpunished. As a result, the extra-textual implications are the same as in Marinina: the state (in the person of Turetskii) is separated from effective power, and society is separated from both. Because the state in Neznanskii's works is personified but power is not (the true criminals remain nameless), the representatives of state power are romanticised. This is more or less standard for contemporary Russian police novels, even if their main characters are acting in less romantic or extreme conditions than Turetskii; note for example the novels of Andrei Kivinov, which are devoted to the everyday life of the police and formed the basis for the popular series *Cops* (*Menty*) and *The Strength to Kill* (*Uboinaia sila*).

Another area where male authors these days are productive is retro-detective fiction. Its main representative is Boris Akunin, who overshadows all the other men and women who work in this genre.[57] Alongside fictional works, publishers

---

[57] Among the men, note Sergei Karpushchenko, who published with the Petersburg firm Amfora a small cycle of novels about the detective Vyzhigin. For women authors, see: Elena Basmanova, *Taina drevnego sarkofaga* (SPb/M, 2001) and *Serebrianaia vaza*; Natal'ia Aleksandrova, *Batumskii sviaznoi*, *Zakat na Bosfore*, *Volch'ia sotnia*, and other novels that

have started to issue historical works on the Russian police and penitential system. In 2002, for example, Eksmo, one of the major Moscow publishers for detective literature, put out the series *Archive of Russian Police Detectives,* which included stories about the above mentioned detective Ivan Putilin and a documentary volume by the prerevolutionary journalist Vlas Doroshevich, who made a journey to Sakhalin and described in his reports many different types of convict (from the legendary Sonka the Golden Hand to a false-pretender Van'ka Kain). The retro-detective style has experienced a major renaissance, and Akunin's success has been phenomenal, but it should be noted that Akunin has not done anything radically new with the detective form. On the contrary, the author consistently uses an old formula without attempting to fill it with the extratextual connotations of the present day (although the texts themselves offer plenty of clues to the author's chronological location in the way that he – whether consciously or not – applies to the past the values and experience of the present). Most contemporary detective fiction is saturated with negative emotions such as wounded honour and despair, but Akunin cultivates the 'optimism of memory', which makes the reader's encounters with his heroes Erast Fandorin and Sister Pelageia all the more pleasurable and comfortable. The author definitely gains from working with historical material: he can permit himself a slower tempo of narration, he can see to it that the culprit is caught and know that that will be good enough for readers who want to receive a nostalgic positive impression of the state: back then, in the past, good did have a fighting chance of triumphing over evil. Any attempt to transfer all this to the contemporary scene (the same type of hero and narration, the same happy endings) would undoubtedly result in fiasco, as the optimism would seem completely unconvincing to a society psychologically orientated towards a constant state of emergency. The only refuge for contemporary readers is to be found in Akunin's retro-fantasies or in the issue-free women's detective novels that appear to be edging aside male hard-boiled thrillers on the book market.[58]

The contemporary men's detective novel is not, however, exhausted by the types indicated above. It is supplemented by the various types that exist in women's detective fiction too: the investigative novel (where the investigator is a private

---

form part of a cycle about lieutenant Ordyntsev.

[58] According to A. Solntseva's figures, the sales of male thrillers fell by a factory of thirty just in 2001. See A. Solntseva, 'Russkii macho gor'ko plachet. Boevik otstupaet pod naporom damskogo detektiva', *Sankt-Peterburgskie vedomosti*, 14 February 2002, p. 3.

detective or a journalist, less often an ordinary citizen)[59] and the crime novel. While books of this kind follow common narrative models, they give them a masculine flavour in their details (the theme of male friendship, the masculine feelings of the main character, the male sense of humour, and so on) and in their general disdain for family life, which remains the territory of women's detective writing. The business of men's fiction is public, not private, life in all its forms from business (legal or illegal) to politics (above-board or secret).

Conclusion

The most natural, not particularly scholarly, conclusion to be drawn from all the above examples would run as follows. There are a lot of detective novels out there, they are all different, but in a funny way they all seem to differ from Western detective fiction, both quantitatively (in the size of the readership they have acquired) and in terms of their content. This otherness, however, does not mean that the Russians have invented new kinds of crime. The transgressions are the same as elsewhere – murder, violence, robbery, kidnap, blackmail, racketeering, deception of various kinds – even if some of these crimes became commonplace in Russia very recently, in the perestroika period and afterwards. Nor have the Russians come up with anything new in terms of narrative models: all authors in one way or another use the same basic patterns, which can easily be identified and analysed. But formal schemes do not help us to understand the significance of their constituent parts in a specific cultural context. In order to understand the symbolic roles taken by the various actors in Russian detective fiction, the first thing we need to do is abandon the clichés commonly used. In particular, we must give up the notions of 'criminal' and 'victim', because these are the great unknowns of contemporary Russian detective writing: who, in actual fact, can be considered a criminal or a victim when all characters, for various and fully understandable reasons, to one extent or another are breaking the law as well as transgressing social norms and general human notions of social order?

In the picture of the world drawn by Russian detective fiction, the state is at best something separate from society; at worst, it is a form of violence against society. It was not so long ago that collective consciousness held the view that 'the state

---

[59] Note for example Mikhail Petrov's novels about the private detective Goncharov, Andrei Konstantinov's about the journalist Obnorskii (*Travlia lisy*, M, 2002; *Zhurnalist*, M, 2002), Fridrikh Neznanskii's about the lawyer Gordeev, and others. The figure of lawyer as protagonist is a feature of men's fiction; one of the first to use this model was Konstantinov.

is us', but now the state is firmly considered to be 'them'. Note the recent election slogan put forward by one of Russia's leading political parties: 'We will force the state to be just!' Detective fiction demonstrates this negative attitude to the state in general, but heavily romanticises a few of its representatives, who are capable of acting not in their corporate interests but from a sense of professional duty or in line with universal ethical standards. Similar romanticised treatment can be accorded to the criminal, who is presented either as an evil genius or as a victim of circumstances. Against a backdrop of general legal nihilism,[60] the criminal world looks like an ordered system that operates according to its own iron laws and is governed by its own 'code of honour', which – at least in fiction – paradoxically corresponds to the code of honour held by romanticised members of the security services. The result is an erosion of the boundary between the ethical standards of 'normal' social conduct and those of the criminal world.[61] When the state, which is a precondition for and guarantee of a civilised justice system, is rejected so totally, its place is taken by natural law, and the concept of 'guilt' is completely excluded from the range of value categories, because it is always perceived as an external phenomenon (guilt is borne not by individuals, but by the system, by circumstances, by the family, by social conditions, and so on).

The supremacy of natural law partly explains the basic patterns of the Russian detective genre, which in certain key areas come close to the mythological patterns of Russian folk tales. An unreflective consciousness reacts to every action committed against it without giving a moment's thought to the problem of good and evil. Although it is traditionally believed that Russian folk tales always show the triumph of good over evil, in fact they offer many examples of an alternative 'social ethic': one that can justify all imaginable crimes as long as they are committed by a 'good' hero and condemns the same crimes if they are carried out by a 'bad' person. This implies commonly held informal notions of what constitutes a 'good' or 'bad' person in an androgynous world that does not yet know the difference between 'women's' and 'men's' worlds, and so places both

---

[60] On this theme in Russian legal consciousness, see A. Poliakov, *Obshchaia teoriia prava*, SPb, 2001, pp. 254-327.

[61] A curious illustration of this point of connection can be found in a word game found in a special crossword newspaper that has become exceptionally popular in Russia recently. One of the exercises requires readers to come up with the umbrella concept for a list of near-synonyms. In one issue (*777*, 23 July 2002), readers were presented with the following list of terms: 'Chivalrous, civilian, labour, bandit...'. What single term would be equally applicable to all of these?

sexes in the same conditions. For both men and women, the winner is the one who is stronger, cleverer, craftier, and that person feels he or she has the right to impose on others his or her notion of justice, which is the only relevant ethical criterion. Contemporary Russian detective fiction presents what is essentially an ancient mythological narrative pattern that has accumulated narrative layers from other, later, forms (the adventure novel, the crime novel, and others). It reflects the formation of an unspoken social contract which people have come to find essential given the complete transformation of the value system in contemporary Russia.

In the current social climate, detective fiction is produced through a kind of collective authorship. Everyone takes part: the media that make readers accustomed to the idea of an 'emergency' situation; TV, which reserves prime time for serialisations of the most popular recent detective stories (from Marinina to Kivinov); publishers; their grateful readers; and, finally, life itself. The result of this collective authorship is a special product whose social function and inner structure are analogous, strangely enough, to those of advertising. Adverts emphasise the features of a product that are considered positive by the community, but stress not only positive ideals and values but also their inverse: if health is being advertised, then fear of illness may be lurking in the background, youthfulness may thinly conceal ageing, leisure may be a direct response to fatigue. If we were to pull together all adverts, we would end up not only with a catalogue of national values and ideals but also the same kind of catalogue of fears. A precondition for successful advertising is the existence of a collective understanding both of the positive component of the product and of the negative. Russian detective fiction, as a form of collective production, a collective Russian folk tale, is exactly this kind of catalogue, with the single important difference that it, unlike advertising, makes explicit the negative side of reality while at the same time heightening consciousness of the positive, however amorphous that may be in the current conditions of ethical flux.

(Translated by Stephen Lovell)

Boris Dubin

The Action Thriller (*Boevik*) in Contemporary Russia

In this chapter I will offer a sociological analysis of one of the distinctive popular genres of post-Soviet Russia: the action thriller based on 'hot' contemporary material. Russian publishers, advertisers and readers call it the *superboevik* or simply the *boevik*. The closest equivalent in English is the 'hard-boiled' detective, but even this term does not fit the Russian genre precisely; to avoid confusion, I will use the Russian term throughout.
The *boevik* is popular above all among urban middle-aged men (from 25 to 49) whose status and earnings are average or below.[1] It is a kind of novel that features a confrontation between Russian and Western (almost always American) secret services. The hero is a top-secret super-agent who acts at his own risk and competes with powerful mafia structures, both in Russia and internationally, which threaten to destroy him. As he does so, he is not simply carrying out his duty; nor does he wish to earn money. Rather, his goal is to restore justice, to reaffirm a moral order that has been violated. There were several high-profile popular authors in this genre during the 1990s. Viktor Dotsenko, a pioneer in developing the potential of the *boevik*, is the author of a series of novels featuring as hero Savelii Beshenyi (the surname is a nickname that might be translated as 'Rabid' or 'Mad Dog': Beshenyi has been described as 'the Russian Rambo').[2] Like other *boevik* authors, Dotsenko has seen several of his novels adapted for the screen. Other significant figures include Daniil Koretskii, whose novels include *The Code-Name* (*Operativnyi psevdonim*) *Antikiller* and *Antikiller-2* (and have been made into films by Egor Konchalovskii); Chingiz Abdulaev,

---

[1] See M. Levina, 'Chitateli massovoi literatury v 1994-2000 gg.', *Monitoring obshchestvennogo mneniia*, 4, 2001, pp. 32-35.
[2] For the Rambo analogy, and for more information on Dotsenko, see H. Goscilo, 'Big-Buck Books: Pulp Fiction in Post-Soviet Russia', *The Harriman Review*, 12, 1999-2000, 2-3, pp. 11-12.

author of a series of novels entitled *Discovering Hell* ('Obretenie ada'); Aleksandr Bushkov, whose books include *The Pack of Wolves* (*Volch'ia staia*), *Return of the Piranha* (*Vozvrashchenie piran'i*) and *The Piranha Hook* (*Kriuchok dlia piran'i*); Evgenii Sukhov, whose series of novels is called *I am a Thief-in-Law* (*Ia – vor v zakone*);[3] and Andrei Dyshev, author of *Hour of the Wolf* (*Chas volka*), *Heart of the Wolf* (*Serdtse volka*) and their sequels.[4]

This genre is in several ways reminiscent of the hard-boiled detective fiction of Raymond Chandler or Mickey Spillane, or of the *film noir* in France or the USA, but in Soviet literature and cinema it had two main analogues. The first was the spy story, whose main landmarks included Vadim Kozhevnikov's *Shield and Sword* (*Shchit i mech*, made into a film by Vladimir Basov), Iulian Semenov's *Seventeen Moments of Spring* (*Semnadtsat' mgnovenii vesny*, screen version by Tat'iana Lioznova), and Veniamin Dorfman's film *The Resident's Mistake* (*Oshibka rezidenta*, based on a story by V. Vostokov and O. Shmelev). The second was the political detective story, which had among its main exemplars Semenov's *TASS Is Authorised to Announce* (*TASS upolnomochen zaiavit'*, made into a film by Vladimir Fokin) and Aleksandr Alov and Vladimir Naumov's film *Teheran '43* (*Tegeran-43*). The distinction between these Soviet precursors and the recent Russian *boevik* lies in the identity of the hero. Previously the main protagonist was accompanied on all his foreign assignments by his 'motherland' and its associated system of secret services, but now he is a loner who usually trusts no one in his own country. His own state's secret services are themselves often afflicted by corruption and betrayal. The hero used to embody the USSR, work selflessly for it, and turn to it for support. Now, however, his assessment of this social and political entity is radically changed. Incidentally, this former symbiotic relationship with the Soviet system was characteristic not only of the heroes of spy stories but of their authors, who saw their works subjected not only to the usual ideological censorship but also to the close scrutiny of secret services with a professional interest in this kind of writing.

---

[3] The 'thieves-in-law' were a criminal brotherhood formed in Soviet prison camps.
[4] In my more detailed analysis I will refer to the following books, which have all appeared with the Moscow publisher Vagrius: Viktor Dotsenko's *Vozvrashchenie Beshenogo* (1995, abbreviated as *VB*), *Komanda Beshenogo* (1996, *KB*) and *Zoloto Beshenogo* (1996, *ZB*); Vasilii Krutin's *Terror-95: Krasnaia ploshchad'* (1995, KP); and Sergei Taranov's *Vybor Mechenogo* (1996, *VM*), *Vyzov Mechenogo* (1996, *VyzM*) and *Vystrel Mechenogo* (1996, *VysM*).

The lonely and vulnerable existence of the *boevik* hero, and the often brutal conditions in which he finds himself, will here form the subject of a primarily sociological analysis. They will be treated as social actions and values encoded in narrative form. Above all, these stories assert, and put to the test, the male identity of the hero in a situation where social order is ill-defined – where the values and norms of Russian society are eroding and falling apart.

The Hero as Loner

The fundamental element in the narrative formula of the *boevik* is the hero. His name – or, more precisely, his testosterone-fuelled nickname – often figures in the book's title and recurs throughout a series of novels with the same protagonist. His visual image – often an aggressive pose from a film or TV adaptation of the given novel – is featured on the bright and glossy cover of each volume.
The hero is also, for the most part, alone. This is not the usual folkloric pair or threesome, not a bunch of seven associates as in a Western, not a crack team, not a family and not a clan. Here we have a fact of fundamental importance. The main protagonist is usually an orphan and has no children of his own. The women he loves, not to mention those with whom he has fleeting liaisons, will sooner or later perish. Afghan veteran heroes – such as Dotsenko's protagonist Savelii Govorkov (aka Beshenyi) – have more often than not emerged from orphanages. This background is emphasised insistently in the text and is shared by characters in all 'camps', independently of their proximity to the hero and of the other characteristics, positive or negative, that they possess. Thus, in the novel *Beshenyi's Team* (*Komanda Beshenogo*), Govorkov's compatriot Kolomeitsev-Bondar' has grown up without a father – but so have the Americans Michael James and Chester Walker (nicknamed 'Crazy Shark') and the latter's friend, the Iranian Ali. If parents are ever recalled, they belong to the distant past. And it is usually the mother who is mentioned: she conforms to the type of the homely, prematurely greying mother, and her image is usually constructed in the expressive manner of late Esenin ('Are you still alive, my old woman?')[5] or of the famous finale of Gogol's 'Notes of a Madman' ('Is that my house looking blue in the distance? Is my mother sitting under the window?...'). Govorkov is brought up not by a father, but by a Teacher. This does not work against the

---

[5] 'Ty zhiva eshche, moia starushka?', the first line of Esenin's poem 'Pis'mo materi' (1924).

hero's autonomy but rather serves as a source of his special independence and strength.

The hero is a being quite out of the ordinary. He is the Initiate, the pupil who has become a teacher and received from the hands of his own Teacher the sign of belonging to a special breed. This superhero is not just profoundly different from, and superior to, ordinary people and ordinary life: he is also separated from the wider world by an insurmountable barrier. What this means is that the given essential and awesome task (to restore order and justice) can be carried out by *no one* other than the protagonist, and that he can expect help from no quarter. *He must act and decide how to act, and he must do so instantaneously and on the spot.* He is the centre of the action, he sets the pace and sequence of events, their rhythm. Not only that, he has the sense of being at the cutting edge of world history. As one protagonist declares, in order to explain his destructive mission: 'I am at the cutting edge of humanism [sic], I am its sharp point'. He goes on to affirm his own existence in the defiant formula 'I kill, therefore I am' (*VyzM*, 33).

The main features of the hero – invulnerability, invisibility, orphanhood – are all, it seems to me, analogous. They are all connected to one of his principal and most strongly emphasised characteristics: his complete and wilful separation from the world, his total autonomy. This central element of the hero's self-definition, which constantly carries with it the themes of danger and self-defence, is found on several symbolic levels.

On the one hand, the hero exists at the crossroads of all the other human connections in the novel and constantly makes new connections. This extreme openness to contact works as a role and a strategy and is linked, paradoxically enough, to the hero's 'secret mission'. He brings to a focus the interests and motivations of all the various parties in the novel (rivalry in love, friendship ties, the agendas of criminal groupings and of the secret services). On the other hand, he is a man entirely free of attachments and devoid of weaknesses. He does not drink or smoke, he is not susceptible to women, he is incorruptible and has no family. It is crucial for him to be free of relationships that he cannot freely enter and leave – relationships (including sexual ones) that imply some kind of fixed social location.

The hero's separation from all that surrounds him is represented in the *boevik* as self-isolation. The corollary of the hero's paradoxical combination of freedom with security and invulnerability is his lifelong confinement to hermetically sealed spaces inaccessible to the outside world. These spaces range from the Kremlin to the prison camp, from exclusive hospitals to secret dachas, and they serve as the venues for crucial turning points in the plots of the *boevik* (whose principal theme is, after all, *security*). The defence of person and property against external threats – the guarding of flats and houses – betrays the same preoccupation with safety and autonomy: 'The country has just gone crazy ... Everyone is buying safes, super-secure locks, reinforced doors, CCTV cameras, alarm systems, gas canisters, pistols. It's a complete transition from the ideology of collectivism to the ideology of individualism' (*KP*, 165-166).

Of course, the theme of self-protection also has a state dimension and a geopolitical context: borders have to be sealed just like apartments. Here the novels regularly make use of erotic metaphors. 'It's as if a girl had decided to preserve her virginity to the end of her days': this is the malicious reflection on America's defence planning delivered by an infernal hero nicknamed Player-Manager (Igraiushchii Trener), who is both a political intriguer and a sexual predator (*KP*, 37). The greatest extent of defensive readiness comes when the hero is himself invisible but can penetrate totally the 'other'. For this reason he makes regular use of paid informers, phone taps, spy planes, and so on.

The hero is exceptionally open to contact but at the same time wholly 'untransparent'. He sees everything while remaining invisible and unreachable. All semantic boundaries in the *superboevik* can be penetrated by money and violent death, but the hero remains uncorrupted and invulnerable. Consequently, there are no limits to his capacities. His credo is 'I can do anything' (*VysM*, 274, 346). He interacts with his earthbound partners and antagonists, he carries out the specific task with which he has been entrusted, but at the same time he pursues much more ambitious plans. He has a special kind of hubris: he wants to find the source of world evil and destroy the main culprits.

The stereotypical opposition between the 'brightness' of the extraordinary and the 'anonymity' of the everyday is constantly challenged by the hero of a *superboevik*, who can choose, if he requires, to transform any normative or prescribed marks of identity: his appearance, his name, his biography. As a girlfriend asks the Mechenyi (Marked Man): 'It seems that you want to drop out of this life ... it's important to be an individual, a brilliant individual. But you'd prefer that you almost didn't exist?' 'Exactly', he replies. 'You can be a brilliant individual and at the same time try to make sure ... that nobody knows you. So as to lose yourself, to vanish completely' (*VysM*, 126-27). The hero is the personification of duty. As the same character reflects on his older assistant, who is almost a friend: 'We're in it together. But all the same ... I'm a loner ... I'm the judge, I carry out the sentence, I make my escape or die on my own. I'm a flash of lightning, a hammer blow. An avenger. And ... a lone wolf. I find it hard even to be with people who are on my side, I'm so much of an individualist' (ibid., 279).

In other words, the hero is purely a function of the action in which he participates. There is a clear symmetry between the protagonist and his various enemies in the way they understand the exceptionality of their role: they are the mirror images of each other, forming a peculiar twinned pair. Dotsenko sums up their relationship as follows: 'Savelii and Michael James were each doing their duty for their respective Motherland' (*KB*, 511). And the passage quoted above on the special psychology of the hero – as avenger and saviour – finds a neat counterpart in the following: 'Bandits have their own special kind of energy ... An evil energy ... The energy of evil ... Russia was now in no state to counter this source of energy ... Mechenyi sometimes thought that he was the product of this rootless time of troubles, not a man but the realisation of the feverish dreams of the weak and oppressed, of those who had suffered defeat in life - their dreams of wielding a powerful fist, of delivering a death-blow' (*VyzM*, 203). What follows is the kind of manichaean outburst that is quite characteristic of novels of this type: 'He bears not good but evil ... He considers that the world rests on evil - but evil put to good ends' (the justification offered by Goethe's Mephistopheles).

From the perspective of the historical sociology of culture we can see that the hero of the *boevik*, within his general profile of death-delivering saviour, combines several ethical and behavioural models that took shape in the feudal era and gained a literary lease of life in popular novels of the nineteenth and twentieth centuries. First of all, he is a monk in the ascetic tradition. Second, he is a warrior, a representative of a warrior caste, even of a holy order. Third - this is a later semantic layer deposited in the period when traditional social ties and feudal norms were declining - he is an adventurer, a risk taker and fortune seeker, even a rogue, but of a special kind: he does not have any self-interest and seeks no personal advantage, either in monetary or status terms. As one protagonist characterises himself: 'I love life, I like it when each day serves up to me something a bit new ... I need struggle and variety' (*VysM*, 271). But this self-perception coincides almost exactly with that of one of his opponents: 'I want excitement and risk. I'm an adventurer by nature' (ibid., 319). For both the hero and his counterpart, life is an ongoing bout of exceptionally dangerous combat, a potentially fatal sport, a game of risk where they are the main stakes: 'My stake is my life' (*VysM*, 319).

The Philosophy of the *Boevik*

The basic impetus for all action in the *boevik* comes from the realisation that everything is disintegrating into chaos: 'God, what is happening to this country?' (*KB*, 115). Both the disruption of stable normality and the restoration of violated norms are held to be the responsibility of the upper echelons of power. Thus, on the one hand, the hero can ask 'What on earth have our leaders brought us to?' (*KB*, 493, concerning the unravelling of the first Chechen war) and, on the other hand, as one conspiring KGB general observes, 'you can't blacken the name of our system of security' (*BysM*, 191). In spite of everything, the hero still keeps the 'system' on his side. This system may at the moment be falling apart in a shameful fashion, but it can be restored in the near future. Its enemies are driven by their private interests, their greed for unlimited power and wealth. The hero is motivated by a thirst for moral vengeance, his enemies by the quest for revenge against society.

The overall world-view of the *boevik* can be described as pantheistic. It may appear that its basic coordinates, like those of the Soviet epics of the 1970s, are provided by a well-known and traditional myth that recurs in popular fiction: the myth of fate, of a superindividual pattern of life and death – a convenient normative matrix for kin-based collective existence.[6] But the semantic thrust of the 1990s *boevik* is rather different. Here we learn of the protagonist's personal predestination: 'That was our hero's fate. It was hard, dangerous, laid deadly traps for him at every turn, and subjected him to constant ordeals' (*VB*, 79). This is not a version of the Fates of ancient drama. The *boevik* hero is not oblivious to the path he follows in life. 'Fate' is a structure of situations in which the hero reveals and confirms himself precisely as hero. It serves as a metaphorical construction of the heroic character. The hero is the active agent of his own fate, while fate is the hero's reward.

Another distinctive feature of the *boevik* is that the higher purpose of the hero's personal mission comes not from social allegiances (kin, class, nation or country) but from a more transcendental source: 'Who can anticipate his own fate? Only

---

[6] On the 1970s epics, see L. Gudkov/B. Dubin, *Literatura kak sotsial'nyi institut*, M, 1994, pp. 136-137, and S. Shvedov, 'Knigi, kotorye my vybirali', in *Pogruzhenie v triasinu (Anatomiia zastoia)*, M, 1991, pp. 389-408.

God and the Magi: it is beyond man's strength' (*KB*, 365). The building blocks of this world view are well-worn elements of naturalistic spiritualism, popular doctrines of 'spiritual salvation' and other metaphysical speculations that have become the common currency of Russian readers in recent times (theo- and anthroposophy, Western and Eastern mysticism, dianetics, and so on). The hero seeks and finds higher legitimation for his actions in a contemporary Russia where the old social hierarchies and authorities have collapsed and have not been replaced by universal legal and moral mechanisms. Here, I think, we find an explanation for the enormous interest the younger, more active sections of Russian society are currently showing in astrology, chiromancy, and various types of non-traditional belief.[7]

The appeal to an otherworldly dimension points to a different level of meaning held by events in the *boevik*: the persona and the actions of the hero serve as a metaphor for the higher significance of the example he sets. The primordial state of the world has been violated, the purpose of existence is problematic, existence itself is unpredictable, while events are unavoidable. 'The planet has come to a halt, time has lost its meaning – time is no more. Where then are we heading? And where have we come from?...' (*VyzM*, 182).

Temporal and Spatial Structures

The calibration of time as a means of explaining and analysing the characters' actions and motives is a general feature of the detective genre. But in the *boevik* physical time – the kind of time that depends on the physical interactions and movements of the characters – is complemented by two other types of chronology.

One of them is 'documentary' time that finds its points of reference in major political events and current affairs. In the mid-1990s the key markers were the war in Afghanistan and the coups of 1991 and 1993 (as pre-history) and, in the day-by-day present, the Chechen war of 1994-1996, with all its political accompaniments. 'Chechnia put his head on the block, just as Afghanistan had put his parents' heads on the block' (*VysM*, 6). As the time in which the novel's events unfold comes maximally close to the time in which it is read, the impression of 'reality' is heightened, as is the sense of the spontaneity of the hero's actions, which seem to be occurring for the first time here and now. In the first half of the

---

[7] For more detail, see Iu. Liderman, 'Sinteticheskie nebesa: Predskazatel'naia literatura v sovremennoi Rossii', *Novoe literaturnoe obozrenie*, 55, 2002, pp. 379-384.

1990s hard-edged contemporary reality provided rich material for popular literature, while it was largely ignored by 'serious' realist literature, which was experiencing an acute crisis in these years.

As the framework of events in the novel comes to coincide more closely with the picture of the world the reader sees on his television screen, he is drawn ever further into the plot: he is able to transfer meanings between the real and fictional domains and finds numerous points of emotional identification in the novel. Another way in which the *boevik* engages with commonly held notions of contemporary reality is through quotations from recent mass culture. This might include Soviet cinema (Vladimir Motyl''s *White Sun of the Desert* [*Beloe solntse pustyni*, 1969], or the comedies of Leonid Gaidai); films that were inaccessible until recently (such as *The Godfather* or *Emmanuelle*); the mass-cultural dimension of Bulgakov (the nickname Woland is used in *KB*), Nabokov or Borges; catalogues of fashionable brands of wine, furniture, clothing, watches and weaponry; Hemingway's daiquiri or the more recently fashionable tequila; the songs of Okudzhava and Vysotskii; or the cult rockers of recent years (Viktor Tsoi, Boris Grebenshchikov). We have here the mental universe of contemporary journalism, the communicative medium of newspaper headlines or the formulas of glossy magazines. In other words, this is the 'common culture' of the present day – by contrast with the common culture imposed on Russian society in its previous (Soviet) historical stage. This substantial reconfiguration is a result of the impact made by journalism on literature, a process typical of the dynamic socio-cultural changes of recent times.[8]

The other distinctive temporal framework of the *boevik* comes from within the fictional world of the novel itself. It is provided by references to episodes from the previous life of the hero – his fictional past from earlier volumes in the saga. The author may retell this 'pre-history' for the benefit of those readers who are making their first acquaintance with the series. Alternatively, he may present it as the protagonist's own reminiscences at moments when he is dreaming or raving or out of control. Memories may also come to the surface when the hero interacts with a consciousness of a higher order: such, for example, is the case with the mental dialogues the hero of Dotsenko's saga conducts with his Teacher. A more complex version of this device is self-citation or even a reference to a work by another author, which here features, for plot purposes, as reality. Thus, the

---

[8] See B. Dubin, *Slovo – pis'mo – literatura: Ocherki po sotsiologii sovremennoi kul'tury*, M, 2001, pp. 166-172, 178-181.

protagonist of *Beshenyi's Return* (*Vozvrashchenie Beshenogo*) watches the screen version of his author's first novel, *Destroy the Thirtieth* (*Tridtsatogo unichtozhit'*), which conveniently jogs his memory (*VB*, 186-187). Further on in the novel the sporting mafia (made up of experts in the Eastern martial arts that were formerly banned in Russia) comes on the scene, and among them we find 'the Marked Man from Belorussia', which refers us to the corresponding Belorussian episodes from the saga by Sergei Taranov.[9]

Although fictional time in the *boevik* has many dimensions, it is discrete and anti-determinist. It is punctuated by key episodes of combat where the hero shows his true 'nature', which remains practically unchanged through all the cataclysms that befall him in this novel and indeed the whole series of novels. In this sense the *boevik* stands in clear opposition to the most powerful – and, in Soviet literature, formative – novelistic tradition of the modern era: the Bildungsroman, in which the hero takes shape biographically, in numerous stages, from year to year, from one period of his life to another, and in the process acquires his own 'image' (*Bild*). The sense of time in the *boevik* is more reminiscent of genres like the saint's life, the courtly romance or the adventure novel (though, of course, it does not imitate these genres or act as their continuation but simply operates with the widely understood cultural codes that they have provided).

The other characters do not undergo any significant development either in the course of these novels. Only the hero, however, is endowed with his own, supplementary dimension of time: the dimension of memories and dreams. His inner clock, and his inner world more generally, are hidden from his enemies or his temporary allies, but they are revealed to us readers. The real identity of the protagonist is tactically concealed due to the demands of his role in the novel as spy and special agent. But this identity always exists already, there is no need to go looking for it.

The actions of the hero are justified in advance, because in the bipolar world of the novel he embodies the pole of justice. For this reason his final triumph is guaranteed and nothing disastrous can happen to him. The closest analogy here is with a cyborg, who may temporarily be disabled or thrown off track but who in general terms cannot be improved on. However, the result of any single episode

---

[9] The sporting mafia is by no means the only criminal grouping that figures in the boevik as an independent social force. Other mafias include those whose activities centre on drugs, antiques, holiday resorts, gun-running and prostitution: they reflect the full range of values, taboos and shortages in an until recently closed society.

of combat is not pre-programmed. The hero's triumph is due to his self-mastery, his absolute and rigorous pursuit of his identity and his destiny. By contrast, his enemies have a dual nature that is not hidden either from him or from the readers who see through his eyes.

Space, in all its symbolic dimensions, is also discrete in the *boevik*. First, it is structured by polarities that fit a clear hierarchy of values and also correspond to the relative social positions of the characters: from the 'height' of government to the lower 'depths' of society, from Red Square to the prison or camp, from the capital city to provincial obscurity, from charming old houses to faceless housing developments, from luxurious country villas to contemporary high-rises.[10] Second, as usually occurs in the adventure and detective genres, *closed* spaces with their own structure (from the Kremlin or the White House to a cell in the Butyrki jail or a labour camp barrack in the taiga) are opposed to *open* expanses that do not possess such a structure (no man's land, frontier zones such as wastelands on the edge of cities, the natural landscapes of Afghanistan, Siberia or Chechnia). The former are heavily populated spaces were power is concentrated, where the individual can be coerced, and where a person's power is defined by his position in the social hierarchy. The latter are spaces of potential danger, where the freedom of movement is greater than in any of the other arenas of the novel but restricted by possible interventions by the hero's antagonist, whose 'gaze' may be concealed somewhere in the vicinity.

In the symbolic geography of the novel, spaces without their own structure will sooner or later have structure forced upon them from outside. 'Stalin's men dealt with the back of beyond. They drove out the slaves and herded them into proletarian barracks. They built factories in Siberia and extracted ore from the harsh North. They built up the country's military-industrial potential and crushed Hitler' (*KP*, 7). All locations are equally penetrable for the hero, and for him alone. He exists as if beyond time and space, undergoing a kind of metempsychosis: 'The path of the exile lies across the deserts and the ages' (*VyzM*, 251).

Identity Creation in the *Boevik*

I now propose to examine the literary model of the *boevik* not for the image it provides of the hero but for the way its system of symbols and devices draws the

---

[10] The strict polarisation of social space is a characteristic of traditional and 'closed' societies: see Iu. Levada, *Stat'i po sotsiologii*, M, 1993, pp. 42-44.

reader into the action and provides him with an identity. This process determines the pace and the dynamics of the reading process, pulling the reader into a particular rhythm of response. He temporarily frees himself from external normative controls and sheds the social roles he normally plays. At the same time he follows with heightened attention the extreme states of consciousness presented in the novel, which are not just unusual but even taboo in real life.

The fundamental point here is the symmetry of this novelistic world: its categorical divide between 'self' and 'other'. Such bipolar structures have always underpinned thriller narratives. But in the contemporary world, which is polycentric and has a pluralist culture, bipolarity – along with the social stereotyping of the characters and the event-driven narrative style – is characteristic only of the 'mass' genres. In the *boevik* polarities and binaries drive on the plot in two main ways.

The first is that the hero and the generalised image of his enemy are mirror images of each other. The clearest example of their connection is the complete resemblance between the upholders of law and order and those conspiring against them, the mafia and the KGB. This model can be extended to the whole fictional world of the *boevik*, which is organised according to the famous Hobbesian 'war of every man against every man' (*VyzM*, 239). One person stands in opposition to another, men in opposition to women. 'For a person the main thing is to have another person. A friend, comrade and brother. A wolf. Someone terrifying yet needed. A man ready to strike with a lethal blow or with the illusion of immortal happiness' (*VysM*, 13). What results is the splitting of the imagined reader. On the one hand, the reader is programmed to identify with the hero, who has the initiative on his side, whose values he accepts and through whose eyes he assesses the situation. At the same time, socially unacceptable attitudes to these values, and forbidden methods of attaining them, are concentrated in the figure of the enemy, whom the reader also *understands* – because of his symmetrical relationship to the hero – but does not *accept*. Thus the rivalry between the hero and his antagonist has implications that go beyond the plot. It serves to organise the reader's response, it provides a model for the combat between 'author' and 'reader' – or, more precisely, between the author and those elements of the conceptual world of the reader that the latter needs to reassess and banish from his consciousness.

The second aspect of the *boevik* that conditions the reader's response is the play between the mysterious and the manifest, the closed and the open, and the transitions from one to the other. The motif of mystery was previously found in all kinds of genres from Greek tragedy to French melodrama, but it was pushed to the margins of European culture as the world became increasingly rationalised or 'disenchanted'. Now it is fully activated only in mass cultural suspense narratives: detective novels, thrillers, fantasy. In the *boevik*, mystery is generated by the metaphorical role of secret weapons and secret agents, hidden abilities, secret societies, conspiracies.[11] This motif of secrecy plays a large role for the text's implied reader. It is a way of making the reader focus on his own feelings and anxieties and then of introducing new symbols and meanings without casting doubt on the basic principles of reality. It does not perform the same function as mystery in the fantasy genre, which makes the reader unsure of the very nature of what is depicted. The split narrative of the *boevik* is even further removed from the 'communicative shock' of avant-garde art. There the subjective self-definition of the reader or viewer is provoked without providing any ready-made meanings to compensate.

The *boevik*, however, cannot be called a 'realist novel' as this term was understood in Russian and Soviet aesthetics and literary criticism. It draws its definitions of reality above all from the virtual worlds of mass communications. The models for the regular episodes of combat scattered through the text are probably drawn from American action films as viewed on pirated videocassettes. But the *boevik* also makes use of chronicles of daily events from the press and television, including crime reports. Authors attempt the stylised documentary manner of contemporary television. They only sketch in the background and the frame of events: the rest the reader can see for himself on TV any day of the week. The mimetic traditions of the classical Russian novel are alien to the *superboevik*. As Dotsenko has confessed to an interviewer: 'I don't like Russian literature. I don't like Tolstoi'.[12] For this reason, descriptions, portraits and conversations are reduced to a minimum. The author's task is, in Dotsenko's words, to 'plunge the hero into an extreme situation ... only then will life catch fire'. The author of a *boevik* is also indifferent to another requirement of classical mimesis: that the speech of the protagonists should be socially accurate and that the author's own language should be expressive.

---

[11] The conspirators include Masons, whom Dotsenko considers to be 'the descendants of an ancient line of Russian princes' (*KB*, 247) and the masterminds of the Russian coups of 1991 and 1993.
[12] I. Shevelev, 'Uspekh po prozvishchu Beshenogo', *Ogonek*, 11, 1996, p. 69.

In the *boevik* language sets the norms of reality, and consequently it is characterless, grey, 'nothing in particular'. Even the words of the supreme Teacher, spelled out in capitals in Dotsenko's novels, sound completely flat: he utters ungainly phrases such as 'an unusual situation' (*neordinarnaia situatsiia*), 'I don't have time to fix it' (*ne uspevaiu zafiksirovat'*). Against this colourless backdrop – which could only be illuminated by a sociological analysis of the text's abundant use of cliché – only two linguistic registers stand out. The first is aggression (obscenity) and the second is the language of uplift with its stereotypes of 'high', expressive speech (most often a stylised version of the romantic authorial digressions of Gogol' or Bulgakov).

The reader's sense of involvement and identification is also maintained by the emphasis placed on the body: its preservation and the threats to its wholeness. The hero's body is presented in counter-relief to the corporeality of his partner in a given scene. The protagonist is always viewed through the eyes of an 'other'. This generalised other can be for the hero a source of danger, in which case the hero's body is perceived as a target. But the 'other' can also be a source of pleasure. In erotic scenes the activity and passivity, the cold and heat, or the smoothness and roughness, of the hero's and the other's body are constantly mentioned and contrasted.

The minute-to-minute readiness of characters to engage in activities of either type – their improbable (from a 'realist' point of view) indefatigability in encounters violent or amatory – has, of course a symbolic function. One way or another, these are all scenes of ordeal, a kind of experimentum crucis. It is telling that the glossy covers of the Vagrius series contain advertising photos of the heroes in precisely these two key states: aggression and orgasm.

Conclusions: The *Boevik* in Contemporary Russia

An analysis of the social functions of the *boevik* is not the primary task of this chapter, which is rather devoted to the genre's poetics. I would, however, like to make a few general points towards such an analysis. It is worth emphasising the contrast between the formula described here and the motifs of self-realisation and self-betrayal that were so prominent in Soviet literature and cinema from the 1960s to the 1980s. The system of Soviet culture, fully formed by the late 1930s, kept under strict control the depiction of autonomous, independent action – not to mention the expression of desire and eroticism. Eventually these themes found their way into art that in some way or other set itself up in opposition to official values (even though it coexisted with these values and to some extent depended on them). This 'second culture' reacted against the myth of activism foisted on the population by Soviet ideology and against the eternal search for 'heroic characters' in the Soviet artistic mainstream. Instead, it tended increasingly to put action in the passive voice. It depicted the failure of the hero to find fulfilment, his predicament as a 'superfluous man', and finally his rejection of action and his apathy.[13] The anthropological implications of, and the social price paid for, this freeing of the subject from responsibility for the surrounding reality, lie at the centre of Iurii Trifonov's attention in his later works.

The depiction in a positive light of success and renown remained the prerogative of the official culture. The question of freedom of choice and action, and the possibility of independent existential and metaphysical engagement with the 'other', were kept tightly controlled. Thus, for example, official art increasingly excluded the theme of death. The issue of official controls over literature is usually raised in connection with 'real' art produced by famous authors with an established biography and a healthy reputation with the critics. But cultural products defined by those same critics as belonging to mass entertainment genres were censored just as closely by the state. Research into reading and public libraries in the Soviet period has shown that for several generations almost all genres of entertainment fiction – from detective novels to fantasy – were not allowed to reach the mass reader, had their print-runs severely curtailed, or were subject to other kinds of restriction. Yet precisely these works, like literature 'about love', were the object of huge pent-up demand from younger, more educated and urbanised library readers.

This shortage of appropriate cultural material had enormous consequences for the structure of the Soviet personality and for its life in society. In the 1990s mass culture set about filling the gap as best it could; one of the models it adopted was the *boevik*. However, this genre shows many signs of being transitional: it is caught between Soviet ideology, Soviet values and literary models, and new models, which are more universal, belong more to civilisation in general, and are often identified as 'Western'. The image of the West presented not only by the heroes of Bushkov, Dotsenko, Sukhov, Krutin and others, but also in the language of their authors, is double-edged and by no means free of the ideological stereotypes of earlier eras. Elements of nostalgia for the past and concern for the motherland are combined with envy and fear with regard to Germany,

---

[13] See Dubin, *Slovo – pis'mo – literatura*, pp. 262-272.

Japan and (especially) the USA; Western consumerism is one key focus of hostility. All this is only to be expected. Mass culture in contemporary Russia is taking upon itself the function of adapting to the changes that have occurred to society and in society. Most of the institutions of Soviet society have collapsed and lie inactive, formerly integrative cultural structures have fallen away, and old symbols and authorities have lost their meaning. Mass culture can slow down these destructive processes, which are occurring for the first time in fifty years for such a large proportion of the population.

In this light it is not surprising that as early as the mid-1990s the general interest in the hard-boiled *boevik* and its invulnerable, unbending heroes was gradually shifting in favour of the psychological family novel of everyday life with a plot centred on adventure and crime: the 'women's detective novels' of Aleksandra Marinina, Polina Dashkova, Tat'iana Poliakova and others, and the 'ironic' detective fiction of Dar'ia Dontsova, Irina Volkova, Dar'ia Kalinina and others.[14] Russians who read now crave most of all – at least in their imagination – inner peace and a stable, perhaps even boring, but at least predictable picture of the world. This explains the trend towards the themes of family, everyday life and a women's world where life is steadily reproduced in non-catastrophic fashion – all this at the expense of the life-and-death adventures of the former male heroes, who were lone and untamed beasts in a cruel and chaotic world.

(Translated by Stephen Lovell)

---

[14] On this, see B. Dubin, 'Ot krutykh boevikov – k prostym istoriiam?', *Knizhnoe obozrenie*, 38, 1994, p. 15, and Levina, 'Chitateli massovoi literatury', pp. 35-36.

Birgit Menzel

Russian Science Fiction and Fantasy Literature[1]

In dreams begin responsibilities
(Delmore Schwartz)

The dissolution of the Soviet empire had the effect of swallowing up visions of the future, which were a primary concern for seventy years of Communist rule. It is now fashionable to see the present as a state 'after the future'; conceptual artists and writers have been viewed as 'postutopian', while historians and philosophers discuss the reasons for the 'end of history'.[2] Instead of obsessing about the future, most people as well as public discourses have become preoccupied with the Here and Now, or with re-examining various pasts. Science fiction, the popular 'dreams our stuff is made of',[3] has been a literary genre defined by its speculations on the future and its fantasies of alternative worlds. Twentieth-century Russia developed its own variety of the genre, *nauchnaia fantastika* (hereafter NF), with specific ideological elements, literary traditions and philosophical roots. Despised and ignored by most highbrow scholars and critics, in the 1960-70s NF was nevertheless favourite or habitual reading matter for 70-80 per cent of the technical as well as the arts intelligentsia.[4] But it was

---
[1] I am gratefully indebted to Mikhail Bezrodnyi, Eliot Borenstein, Paul Hillery, Nikolaj Iutanov, Annett Jubara, Marina Koreneva, Andrei Rogachevskii and Sergei Pereslegin for material, information and most helpful critical comments for this chapter.
[2] Mikhail Epstein, *After the Future. The Paradoxes of Postmodernism and Contemporary Russian Culture*, Amherst, 1995; Vladimir Malakhov, 'Das Ende der Geschichte- the Ending of Stories', *Urania*, 2, 1999, 2, pp. 126-132.
[3] Thomas Disch, *The Dreams our Stuff is Made of. How Science Fiction Conquered the World*, New York, 1998.
[4] Patrick McGuire, *Red Stars. Political Aspects of Soviet Science Fiction*, Ann Arbor,

also a special genre different from all others. It was the only adult literature officially exempted from the demands of realism. It dealt with alternative, often utopian models of society, be they technological, social or moral, and for this reason alone it had the potential to compete with the party ideology. Yet at the same time it maintained close ties to the mainstream literature of socialist realism, officially approved as an instrument to popularise the achievements of Soviet scientific and technological progress. Therefore NF was always located on a problematic border between official and unofficial culture, presenting a controversial and speculative discourse. At the same time it was the only kind of literature that bridged science and the humanities and connected readers from different cultural spheres and social strata, from different generations and educational backgrounds.

Since the decline of communism, which was caused not least by the Soviet lag in technological development and brought to an end Russia's position as a superpower, since the abolition of censorship and the opening of Russian culture both to the West and to a new kind of readership, science fiction (hereafter SF) has undergone considerable changes. In the 1990s, NF almost vanished, while a new genre, fantasy, emerged and conquered the marketplace. By the end of the decade it had become, together with detective fiction, the leading genre of popular literature among Russian readers under the age of forty. The Strugatskii brothers, the enduring authorities in this genre, were all that was left to connect Soviet and post-Soviet SF. However, it is still widely ignored by academic criticism. Only a handful of young critics and writers publish articles in literary periodicals from time to time. Most of their communication by now takes place on the Internet. Thus, in spite of its popularity, Russian SF has always been and still is a literary ghetto.[5]

A few facts and figures will illustrate the popularity of post-Soviet fantasy: the first private publishing house was founded and the first special series issued in 1989, and by the end of the 1990s between 80 and 100 new titles of popular fantastic works were released per month in more than 40 different series by the three leading publishing houses, AST, Eksmo (both Moscow) and Terra (St. Petersburg). Annual print-run for fantasy books was several million out of a total

---

1977/1985, p. 87.

[5] Only few articles of literary criticism have been published in Russia on the Strugatskiis in the past decade or more. See Amusin, Filippov and Vasiuchenko in the bibliography. In a recently published history of Russian literature by the German slavist Heinrich Lauer they are not even mentioned (*Geschichte der russischen Literatur*, München, 2000).

publishers' output of 20-30 million. Average print-run for a single work of fantasy was 8,000-10,000 copies, while the most successful works reached as many as 150,000-500,000 copies.[6] In St. Petersburg in the years 2000-2002 14 per cent of all bestselling books belonged to fantastic fiction, which thus held fourth position behind detective novels (the front-runner, with 29 per cent), and professional and educational books.[7]

Now what exactly do NF and fantasy mean in Russia? Nauchnaia fantastika was based on the idea of science and progress, science in the Marxist interpretation including not only natural science, but equally the laws of social and historical progress. The genre was closely linked to the communist utopian project of wealth and happiness for the masses, and would help to overcome the traditional gap between high and low, or intelligentsia and mass culture. Especially after the end of the Thaw, the question of what had happened to Soviet utopia became more and more a preoccupation of NF, and this literary niche filled up with warnings, anti-utopian premonitions, and Aesopian ideological criticism. Yet, for all that, Soviet NF has always been known and valued for its orientation towards the future, its attention to social issues, its humanism and historiosophical optimism. Fantasy novels do not feature spaceships, scientists and engineers, extraterrestrial creatures and intergalactic journeys. Instead of technology and scenarios for the future we meet ancient worlds, medieval knights and nomadic tribes, magicians and dragons, swords and sorcery.

What is the meaning of this change of orientation from utopian or dystopian visions of the future to myth and fairy-tale? Does it cater to a new type of reader or to the new needs and interests of the old readers? Has it been brought about by a new cohort of authors? Is this a case of an imported foreign genre destroying an indigenous Russian/Soviet NF tradition? How are Russian cultural roots and socialist realist formulas related to Western science fiction formulas? Are all formula genres universal, and are we witnessing an enforced uniformity or even the colonisation of Russian popular literature along Western, mostly Anglo-American lines? Is there a new Russian popular fantastic literature, distinctive in its ideology and poetics, post-Soviet in more than just a chronological sense?

---

[6] Becker, *Verlagspolitik und Buchmarkt*, chapter 3, fn. 6, p. 193. Terra fantastika (SPb) and other publishers fell behind the increasing monopolisation (1997/1999 = 665/430 with 12.6/4.5 million copies). See *Delovoi Peterburg. Izdatel'stva Rossii. Spravochnik*, M, 1999.

[7] *Delovoi Peterburg*, 15 July 2002.

Why does it deserve investigation, and what role does it play in post-Soviet culture?

This chapter aims to show that there are signs of a new Russian fantastic literature with a variety of (sometimes conflicting) ideologies, authors and styles. I will approach this genre as popular literature, without attempting either to demonstrate its lack of artistic quality or to raise its status by claiming it as a form of literary-philosophical utopia. Rather, the fantastic will here be understood as a type of literature with its own conventions and functions. Three elements are considered here to be basic to the genre. First, its formulaic structure, which conforms to certain specific genre patterns including a clear narrative and moral message. Second, a certain scientific or psychological credibility. Third, a commercially driven orientation towards the collective desires and fantasies of the consumer.

Definitions and Historiography of the Genre

One of the greatest problems in the analysis of present-day popular fantastic literature is the lack of a reliable historiography of Russian NF. Writings on this subject are sparse and highly charged with ideology. Most of the Soviet Russian studies are of little analytical value. In Soviet criticism there was an abundance of scholastic discussion, but at the same time serious critics preferred to keep silent about NF in order to protect authors and works from uncomfortable revelations.[8] Both in Soviet and in post-Soviet times, popular fantastic literature, if it has been discussed in academic criticism at all, has been treated according to the norms of artistic literature, notably the utopian and fantastic novels of the canon. A few monographs have value for their rich material or their unconventional approach.[9] Most comprehensive are the studies by two long-term Russian investigators of the genre, Leonid Geller and Vsevolod Revich.[10] Geller's monograph covers the

---

[8] Interview with Natal'ia Ivanova in 1995.
[9] Vladimir Liapunov, *V mire fantastiki. Obzor nauchno-fantasticheskoi literatury*, 2nd revised ed., M, 1975; Aleksandr Britikov, 'Russkii sovetskii nauchno-fantasticheskii roman; Sovetskaia nauchnaia fantastika', in idem, *Zhanrovo-stilevye iskaniia sovremennoi prozy*, M, 1971; Tamara Chernysheva, *Priroda fantastiki*, Irkutsk, 1984; Evgenii Neelov, *Volshebno-skazochnye korni nauchnoi fantastiki*, L, 1986; Rafail Nudel'man, 'Fantastika', *Kratkaia literaturnaia entsiklopediia*, 7, 1972, pp. 878-895. For an overview of Soviet NF see Evgenii Brandis, 'Fantastika i novoe videnie mira', *Zvezda*, 8, 1981, pp. 41-49. For a bibliography of samizdat publications on NF in the seventies, see A. Chertkov, 'Fenziny, ili samizdat fantastiki', *Sovetskaia bibliografiia*, 1, 1990, pp. 114-122.
[10] L. Geller, *Vselennaia za predelom dogmy*, London, 1979/1985; V. Revich, *Perekrestok*

period from the 1920s to the 1960s, while Revich in his latest monograph goes as far as the 1990s. In Western scholarship, Russian science fiction has mostly been dismissed as both trivial and ideologically contaminated literature, and only a few valuable studies have appeared in the past decades: there are some informative studies, forewords and articles in encyclopedias and anthologies by Western experts like Suvin (1976) and McGuire (1987), and Yvonne Howell (1994) on the Strugatskiis. Oswald (1991) has taken a sociological perspective, Witt (1995) has covered the perestroika period, Greene (1987) has investigated the gender aspect, while Schwartz (2003) has analysed the NF of the Thaw period.[11] Western critics tend to set Western standards as norms, often generalise too fast, and almost all studies neglect the specific historical roots of the fantastic genre. Some critics, like Maia Kaganskaia, have claimed that there is no connection whatsoever between Russian classics, like Gogol', and Soviet NF. Others, like L. Geller, claim a continuous line between older Russian utopianism, including popular peasant utopian literature, and Soviet NF.[12] But the beginnings of Soviet science fiction in the journals of the early 1920s have not been adequately described; nor have its possible roots in popular literature and genre traditions such as the picaresque and adventure novel from Faddei Bulgarin to Mikhail Artsybashev, or from William Morris to Ray Bradbury.

Few Russian critics in the 1990s specialise in popular fantastic literature (Arbitman, Berezin, Pereslegin, Prashkevich).[13] Since 1995 the Internet has become a

utopii: Sud'by fantastiki na fone sudeb strany, M, 1998.

[11] Darko Suvin, *Russian Science Fiction 1956-1974*, Elizabethtown/New York, 1976; P. McGuire, *Red Stars*, N. Baron and B. Aldiss, *Anatomy of Wonder. A Critical Guide to Science Fiction*, New York, 1987, pp. 441-473; Y. Howell, *Apocalyptic Realism. The Science Fiction of Arkady and Boris Strugatskii*, New York/Bern, 1994; Ingrid Oswald, *Der Staat als Wissenschaftler. Das Gesellschaftsbild der sowjetischen wissenschaftlich-technischen Intelligenz in der wissenschaftlichen Phantastik der Sowjetunion*, Berlin, 1991; Uwe-Michael Witt, *Renaissance oder Neubeginn? Russische Science-Fiction-Literatur nach der Perestrojka*, Rostock (Diss.), 1995; Diana Greene, 'An Asteroid of One's Own: Women Soviet Science Fiction Writers', *Irish Slavonic Studies*, 8, 1987, pp. 127-139; Matthias Schwartz, *Die Erfindung des Kosmos. Zur sowjetischen Science Fiction und populärwissenschaftlichen Publizistik vom Sputnikflug bis zum Ende der Tauwetterzeit*, Berlin, 2003.

[12] On the neoslavophile NF of the 1970s, see Maia Kaganskaia, 'Mif dvadtsat' pervogo veka ili Rossiia vo mgle', *Strana i mir*, 11, 1986, pp. 78-84; 1, 1987, pp. 131-140; 2, 1987, pp. 131-136; L. Heller/M. Niqueux, *Histoire de l'Utopie en Russie*, Paris, 1985; in German: *Geschichte der Utopie in Russland*, Bietigheim-Bissingen, 2003.

[13] Vladimir Berezin and Roman Arbitman have published regularly in *Nezavisimaia gazeta*, *Oktiabr'* and *Literaturnaia gazeta*; Sergei Pereslegin, *Oko Taifuna. Poslednee desiatiletnie sovetskoi fantastiki*, SPb, 1994, and Gennadii Prashkevich, 'Malyi Bedeker po nauchnoi fantastike', *Esli*, 3-4, 2003. All are active critics in Internet publications.

dominant medium of communication in SF. Some journals (*Esli, Ta storona*, and a total of about 15 fanzines) and criticism are published only on the net. Thus an account of the history of this genre has to confront serious lacunae. Much more research needs to be done on subjects such as the influence on NF of the occultism and technological utopian fantasies of symbolism and the avant-garde, the relations between elite and popular utopian fiction, and between youth and adult NF, the role of journals in the early development of the genre and in the post-Stalin decades, reader reception, the influence of Western, especially American SF on Soviet NF, and the relations between Russian and Polish NF.

The term NF was introduced in Russia in the early 1920s for a new Soviet genre which was to combine fiction with the popularisation of scientific innovations and socialist propaganda. NF became a well-known term in Russia even before the term SF in the Anglo-American language.[14] But, although the genre of science fiction in Russia and the West has a basically common origin and function in bridging the 'two cultures" of science and the humanities through the medium of the fantastic, it has been treated and traced differently in Russian and Western criticism. A particular point of divergence has been the relationship of SF/NF to utopia and the literary fantastic.

Fantasy literature, both Russian *fentezi* and Western 'fantasy', first appeared in Russia only in the late 1980s. The general term *fantastika* for all popular fantastic genres – NF, SF and fantasy alike – seems to be preferred by now. How did fantasy come to Russia?[15] Young authors at the annual Strugatskii science fiction workshop in Leningrad tried their hand at this foreign genre by writing new Russian fantasy novels in 1985-86.[16] A veritable fantasy boom followed. An amazing Tolkien cult, propagated by the so-called *tolkinisty*, took hold of

---

[14] For the history of the term, see McGuire, *Red Stars*; E. Brandis, 'Gorizonty fantastiki, *Neva*, 10, 1979, pp. 171-181; Robert Stockwell, *The Poetics of Science Fiction*, Edinburgh, 2000.

[15] In academic criticism the origins of fantasy literature have been seen much earlier, mainly in romanticism, in the work of writers like Mary Shelley (Frankenstein), Samuel Coleridge, William Morris and Lord Dunsany. In Russia some fantasy novels had been translated and become popular before perestroika. Tolkien's *Lord of the Rings* was published fully only in 1990/92, *The Hobbit*, as children's literature, in 1982. In samizdat translations, however, Tolkien's works had been circulating since the mid-sixties. Hooker has listed 63 different translations by 10 translators of *Lord of the Rings* and 52 different translations by 14 translators of *Little Hobbit*; Mark T. Hooker, *Tolkien Through Russian Eyes. Tolkin Russkimi Glazami*, Zollikofen, 2003, pp. 90-98.

[16] See Sergei Plotnikov, 'Imperiia, magiia, pustota. Tri volny rossiiskoi fantastiki', *Nezavisimaia gazeta*, 4 December 1997.

readers' imaginations,[17] and a new subgenre, Slavic fantasy, emerged from the combination of certain Soviet NF traditions with Western patterns of fantasy writing.

Fantasy is one of the youngest genres in the history of literature, and its emergence is strongly connected to commercial strategies. A purely Western popular genre, it came about in the 1920s. There are two different traditions of fantasy: 'heroic' or 'sword-and-sorcery' fantasy, whose foundation stone was Robert Howard's series *Conan the Barbarian*, a commercial series of mostly teen fiction with links to the adventure novel and a pre-fascist cult of violence; and 'high fantasy', established by the Oxford professor J.R.R. Tolkien's *Lord of the Rings* in the late 1950s. The latter tradition is connected with – mostly Celtic and Nordic – myth and fairy-tale fantasy, and claims literary qualities. As a genre in its own right, not merely a subgenre of SF, fantasy has been acknowledged only since the 1960s, when British and American authors such as Michael Moorcock, Poul Anderson and Robert Zelasny were at the forefront of a New Wave in SF. In the following years the genre achieved commercial success and became widely popular as adult literature too.[18] Since the 1960s, another subgenre, 'urban fantasy' or 'dark fantasy', has become very popular. Its novels are based on the juxtaposition of fantasy world and contemporary reality, and often mix elements of fantasy, thriller, horror and science fiction. Vampires, werewolves, fairies and other fantasy characters are moving back and forth between their fantasy world and today's modern urban world. The most successful authors of this 'urban fantasy' include Neil Gaiman, Robert Zelasny, and in Russia recently Sergei Luk'ianenko, whose novel *Night Watch* (*Nochnoi dozor*) was made into a blockbuster film by Timor Bekmanbekov in 2004. Fantasy has gained unprecedented popularity and international commercial dominance since the 1980s. Today it has become the dominant literary genre source for films and computer games.

Now what is the key formula of each genre, and why is making a distinction between them more than just a matter of artificial academic classification? This question has become all the more pressing since NF and fantasy have started to merge and by now have become almost indistinguishable. Most authors write and combine both genres, and in the post-Soviet era commercial strategies no longer enable us to distinguish between NF and fantasy. SF/NF and fantasy can be

---

[17] For a detailed history of Tolkien's reception in Russia see Hooker, *Tolkien*.
[18] As a commercial category the genre-term 'fantasy' was first used in 1973 for Lin Carter's *Ballantines Adult Fantasy Series*. See Helmut Pesch, Fantasy. *Theorie und Geschichte einer literarischen Gattung*, Köln, 1982, p. 3.

considered as two different responses to modern, rational, industrial society. Their roots can be found equally in romanticism and in the fin-de-siècle, with its stirrings of mass culture and its powerful interest in metaphysics, evolution, eugenics and mysticism. Formally, NF and fantasy have several traits in common: both are based on the fantastic as a plot-shaping element, the worlds of both are populated by fantastic creatures, both are distributed as commercial, serial-based formula literature. Another common trait is that neither genre fits the concept of fantastic literature as it has been elaborated by Western scholars (Todorov (1975), Suvin (1979), Rabkin (1976), Cornwell (1990) and Lachmann (2002)).[19] While Western theory defines the literary fantastic as based on the unresolved suspense between the real and the fantastic worlds and therefore excludes SF and fantasy from the canon, East European theory tends to incorporate all fantastic literature into NF, tracing its roots back to the eighteenth and nineteenth centuries, to enlightenment investigation and romantic speculation, and placing it in a broad European context. Since all fantastic fiction was defined by its function of bringing rational insight to irrational or inexplicable phenomena,[20] it became closely tied in the twentieth century to the mainstream literature of socialist realism. Readers, public opinion and commercial strategies, however, conflate SF with fantastic literature in general (a category that would also include Kafka, Borges, Gogol' and Bulgakov). Some Russian scholars have traced Russian fantastic literature back to pre- and early Christian utopian writings of the Middle Ages.[21] Since NF and fantastic literature are different in

---

[19] Tsvetan Todorov, *The Fantastic. A Structural Approach to a Literary Genre*, Ithaca/New York, 1975; D. Suvin, *Metamorphoses of Science Fiction: On the Poetics and History of a Literary Genre*, New Haven/London, 1979; Eric Rabkin, *The Fantastic in Literature*, Princeton, 1976; Neil Cornwell, *The Literary Fantastic. From Gothic to Postmodernism*, Toronto/New York, 1990; Renate Lachmann, *Erzählte Phantastik. Zu Phantasiegeschichte und Semantik phantastischer Texte*, Frankfurt/Main, 2002.
For recent monographs on the SF-genre, see Damien Broderick, *Reading Postmodern Science Fiction by Starlight*, London, 1995, and Stockwell, *The Poetics of Science Fiction*.

[20] Nudel'man, *Fantastika*; Stanislaw Lem and Andrzej Zgorzelski, 'Understanding Fantasy', *Zagadnenia rodzajow literackich*, XIV, 2, 1971, 27, pp. 103-109; Witold Ostrowski, 'The Fantastic and the Realistic in Literature', *Zagadnenia rodzajow literackich* IX, 1, 1966, 16, pp. 54-71; Iu. Kagarlitskii, *Chto takoe fantastika?*, M, 1974.

[21] See the 20-volume series *Biblioteka russkoi fantastiki*, M, 1990-2001, ed. Iu. Medvedev, the ex-chief editor of the publishing house *Molodaia gvardiia*, one of the leaders of the 'Efremov school', where Lev Tolstoi's stories are introduced next to the theosophist writings of Elena Blavatskaia and Vladimir Nabokov next to the Stalinist science fiction writers Aleksandr Beliaev, Nikolai Fedorov and Konstantin Tsiolkovskii.

some aspects but interrelated in others, the broad definition of NF will be applied here in combination with the umbrella term 'popular fantastic literature'.
NF/SF and fantasy differ significantly from each other. NF/SF claims a rational, at least pseudo-scientific explanation for any fantastic incursion into the familiar empirical world, whereas fantasy – as a contemporary man-made myth and fairy-tale – presents a totally non-empirical world, all the fantastic elements of which have to be accepted and taken for granted by the reader to begin with. NF is oriented towards the future, fantasy often draws on the pre-modern or ancient past, preferring medieval or pre-historical settings. Its antirational, mythic approach to the world rejects scientific and technological progress and the achievements of modern civilisation. The laws of nature are suspended and give way to the rules of magic. Therefore fantasy makes no claims of scientific credibility. NF always relates to history – the future as prolonged history, or the development of present reality – while fantasy breaks with historical continuity.

Soviet notions rejected NF as a projection of utopia, because, according to Soviet Marxist theory, science had replaced former social utopias by connecting them with observed history and reality. Therefore NF, especially in Stalin's time, became not at all utopian: it presented the future as a near, almost realised, prolonged present. At the same time its formulaic structure brought it close to socialist realist mainstream literature. It fitted the prevailing master plot for novels and conformed to gender norms by focusing mostly on male adolescent heroes and readers.[22]

Popular fantastic and science fiction literature has one other quality that makes it different from all other artistic forms and even other genres of popular literature: its intense communicative power, the corporate spirit – maybe even corporate identity – that it fosters in the world of readers. NF has always created a parallel cultural universe, connecting and socially organising its readers, writers, publishers and critics, providing an environment in which heroes and stories continue to live and communicate in a collective mind. In spite of its official incorporation into the socialist realist canon, NF always existed in its own niche, and made a bid for legitimisation and approval as artistic literature. NF in Soviet times was almost never published in literary journals, but rather in popular-science journals like *Tekhnika-molodezhi*, *Smena*, *Nauka i zhizn'* and *Znanie-sila*. Even in the highly controlled public sphere of late Soviet society, but to an

---

[22] This refers to Katerina Clark, 'Polozhitel'nyi geroi kak verbal'naia ikona', in H. Günther/E. Dobrenko (eds), *Sotsrealisticheskii kanon*, SPb, 2000, pp. 269-284, and Dobrenko, *The Making of the State Reader*, chapter 3, fn. 22.

extraordinary extent since the late 1980s, popular fantastic literature has met an active response in fan clubs and magazines throughout the country: the most widely disseminated of these are *Polden'*, *XXI vek* (published since 2002, edited by Boris Strugatskii), *Esli* (since 1991), *Iskatel'* (since 1969 a supplement to the journal *Vokrug sveta*) and the almanac *Fantastika* (since 1962). Its impact has gone well beyond Moscow and Leningrad to reach provincial cities such as Krasnoiarsk, Kiev, and Khar'kov. NF is, moreover, distinguished not only by its culture of fandom but also by its intense intertextuality. Although (in Russia) mostly ignored by the arts intelligentsia and academic criticism, NF novels always communicate with each other, are extensively self-referential and have been substantially shaped by intertextual references ever since the 1960s. The whole literary field of NF has its own hierarchies, canons and criteria of value, which are negotiated by 'insiders', producers, distributors and consumers. Some of this negotiation takes place in an elaborate system of prizes and annual conventions spread over capitals and provincial centres. The first nationwide NF convention was held in 1982 and organised by the Sverdlovsk journal *Ural'skii sledopyt*. Since 1992 six national conventions have been held per year, each with 200-300 people attending and spread over several days. There are more than fourteen different national awards, the most respected in the 1990s being the 'ABS (Arkadii and Boris Strugatskii) Prize' (St. Petersburg), the 'Aelita Prize' (Sverdlovsk/ Ekaterinburg), the 'Ivan Efremov Prize' and 'Start' (both awarded by the journals *Ural'skii sledopyt* and *Esli*), 'Bronzovaia ulitka' (St. Petersburg), 'Strannik' and 'Mech Rumaty' (Interpresskom).[23] Academic and non-academic criticism and scholarship on NF is often written by insiders who are long-standing NF fans themselves.

A Brief Historical Outline of Russian Science Fiction

Since Russian scholars usually try to make NF respectable by integrating it into the canon of high artistic literature, it has not properly been investigated for its connections to popular literary forms. It is time to re-examine the history of the genre from a bottom-up rather than top-down perspective. We need, for instance, to explain how much influence was exerted on NF by popular utopian beliefs and

---

[23] In the 1990s there were six nationwide Annual Conventions of Fantastic Literature in Russia: 'Rosskon' (M), 'Interpresskon' and 'Strannik' (SPb), 'Silartkon' (Kazan'), 'Volgokon' (Volgograd) and 'Zvezdnyi most' (Khar'kov). For current information see the general Russian SF website http://www.rusf.ru.

traditions.[24] Through a cautious reinterpretation of the material it can be stated that popular fantastic literature has several roots in both Russian and translated foreign literature.

Early roots can be found as early as the eighteenth century, in Mikhail Chulkov's picaresque novel *The Joker, or Slavic Folk Tales* (*Peresmesnik ili slavianskie skazki*, 1766-68), but even more so in nineteenth-century utopian-fantastic and adventure literature, such as Vladimir Odoevskii's unfinished novel *The Year 4338* (*4338-i god*, 1835), a polemical response to popular mesmerism that alluded to Francis Bacon's *The New Atlantis* and to Halley's Comet, then expected to reappear in the year 4339. Also influential were stories by now neglected writers like Aleksandr Vel'tman, Mikhail Zagoskin and Faddei Bulgarin, who helped to shape early Russian short prose and catered to readers' interests through a combination of exoticism, suspense and entertainment. Bulgarin's story *Journeys across the World in the Twenty-Ninth Century* (*Stranstviia po svetu v dvadtsat' deviatomu veku*, 1829) describes a journey into the future to investigate the moral state of society. Besides time-travelling, readers could also find accounts of journeys to the moon and other planets and to unattainable places on earth and in the sea, all accompanied by fantastic-utopian technological devices and cosmic disasters. These works connected archaic dreams and fears with the utopian popular visions which followed the key inventions of modern natural science. Equally popular with Russian readers were Western European writers, like E.T.A. Hoffmann, Ludwig Tieck and especially Edgar Allan Poe.[25]

Another source for the fantastic genre is Slavic, Eastern and Western mythology, as well as popular utopian legends, which were mostly transmitted by the Old Believers and other sectarian groups. The Russian myths and folk legends of vampires (upyr') and werewolves (oboroten'), demon-magicians (Kitovraz), peasant paradise (Belovod'e), legendary kings (Svetozar) and sunken cities (Kitezh) were the equivalents of King Arthur, Merlin (Morol'f), Parsifal and the Holy Grail, Atlantis and Shambala, since all these myths referred to common apocryphal stories and migrated between various cultures.[26]

---

[24] Valuable material for studying this aspect of NF can be found in Geller (1979/1985) and Geller/Niqueux (1995/2003), who cite various influences of this kind.

[25] Grossman, *Edgar Allan Poe*, chapter 4, fn.4.

[26] On vampires, see Jan L. Perkowski, *The Darkling: A Treatise on Slavic Vampirism*, Columbus, Ohio,1989.
For popular utopias in Russia see Kirill V. Chistov, *Russkaia narodnaia utopia* (1967), 2nd revised ed.., SPb, 2003. For connections between the migrating mythologies, see Aleksandr Veselovskii, 'Solomon i Kitovraz i zapadnye legendy o Morol'fe i Merline', in *Sobranie*

In a narrow sense the fantastic genre was first introduced at the end of the nineteenth century by Jules Verne, who brought a socially oriented NF, and H.G. Wells, whose material was more technological. Both writers were very popular in Russia. They linked well with the preoccupations of symbolist poets and writers like Valerii Briusov and Nikolai Gumilev, who were intensely interested in occult traditions and introduced Western literature to the Russian public. The Russian translations of the novels of Verne, Wells and the French astrologist and popular writer Camille Flammarion caused a massive wave of Russian pulp fiction that was strongly influenced by foreign patterns.[27]

Although these roots and influences are mentioned here, all of them were filtered and processed by seventy years of Soviet history, so that they cannot be taken as a secure background of common knowledge. While a general acquaintance with the literature on the school syllabus can be taken for granted in the twentieth-century readership, the same does not apply to mythology, religion and other spiritual traditions. These topics were of course kept off the curriculum. Russian and Soviet classics were the main source of literary references for the mythmaking typical of NF. It is therefore not surprising that post-Soviet fantasy works, like detective novels, are full of literary allusions and often have writers as their main characters.[28] One of the novels most frequently referred to and used for popular mythmaking is Bulgakov's *The Master and Margarita*. Stalin and Woland serve as the prototypes for many evildoers in contemporary fantastic fiction.[29]

The origins of Soviet NF lie in the first novels connecting socialist with technological utopian concepts, such as *Plutoniia* (1915/1924) by Vladimir Afanas'evich Obruchev, a geographer and explorer of Siberia; *Red Star* (*Krasnaia zvezda*, 1908) by Aleksandr Bogdanov, a doctor who (self-) experimented in

---

sochinenii, 8, vyp. 1, Petrograd, 1921; Neelov, *Volshebno-skazochnye korni*, and A. Britikov, 'Nauchnaia fantastika, fol'klor i mifologiia', *Russkaia literatura*, 3, 1984, pp. 55-74. For the first publication on 'Shambala' in Soviet Russia see Lev Gumilev, 'Strana Shambala v legende i v istorii', in idem, *Sochineniia*, vol. 5 (Drevnii Tibet), M, 1994, pp. 298-317 (first published in *Aziia i Afrika segodnia*, 5, 1968).

[27] There were more than 140 different editions of Jules Verne's works in Russia after his first publication in 1872, and 24 editions of Flammarion's novels between 1874 and 1913. Henry G. Wells, whose 9-volume selected works were published in SPb in 1909, was a socialist and visited Russia three times between 1914 and 1934, even meeting Lenin; his works were especially promoted in the Soviet era.

[28] See for instance A. Lazarchuk/M. Uspenskii, *Posmotri v glaza chudovishch*, M, 1997.

[29] See V.E. Kaigorodova, 'Russkie fentezi i russkaia slovesnost'', *Slavianskie chteniia II*, Daugavpil's-Rezenke, 2002, p. 136.

psychotechnics, but above all *Aelita* (1922/23) and *Engineer Garin's Hyperboloid* (*Giperboloid inzhenera Garina*, 1925-26) by Aleksei Tolstoi. *Aelita* was turned into a film by Iakov Protazanov in 1924 (the spaceship equipment was designed by none other than Konstantin Tsiolkovskii). Tolstoi's *Aelita* not only carried a socialist utopian emphasis but also bore the marks of theosophical ideas. The hero, the engineer Gusev, plans to travel and liberate India before he develops a spaceship instead. The Martians and their king Tusklub appear as inheritors of the continent of Atlantis, while Tusklub's daughter Aelita alludes to the pagan Goddess Magr and tells a mythical tale of mankind. These works founded the Soviet type of NF. A major influence on NF came from Konstantin Tsiolkovskii, the 'father of Russian space-science', whose stories *On the Moon* (*Na lune*, 1893), *Outside Earth* (*Vne zemli*,1896) and *Dreams of Earth and Heaven* (*Grezy o zemle i nebe,*1896/1918) popularised early space-science and connected it with utopian ideas strongly influenced by the philosophical system of Nikolai Fedorov.

One aspect of the Russian cultural context has not been given enough attention hitherto in accounts of NF. The visions of the future and utopian concepts of NF were strongly influenced by the Nietzschean concept of 'new man' or 'superman',[30] but particularly by the philosophy of Cosmism, which became popular among Russian scientists and writers even before 1917, but especially in the 1920s. A number of religious philosophers and scientists associated with Cosmism at the turn of the century – above all, Nikolai Fedorov, Konstantin Tsiolkovskii and Vladimir Vernadskii – helped to provide early NF with its key postulates and preoccupations: the strongly anthropocentric connection between the creation of a 'new man' as a kind of (self-made) divinity and the idea of immortality; the quest for an end to all human diseases and weaknesses (including the planning of reproduction, eugenics and chastity); the idea of science and technology as devices to create perfect immortal human beings; the total faith in the moral legitimacy of all scientific methods, including collective social experiments; the dedication to science as a way of serving society by releasing cosmic

---

[30] Hans Günther, *Der sozialistische Übermensch. Maxim Gor'kij und der sowjetische Heldenmythos*, Stuttgart, 1993; Bernice Glatzer Rosenthal, *Nietzsche in Russia*, Princeton, 1986, and idem, *New Myth, New World: From Nietzsche to Stalinism*, University Park, PA, 2002. On Nietzsche's concept of 'superman'in Russian culture, see R.Iu. Danilevskii, 'Russkii obraz Fridrikha Nitsshe', in Iu.D. Levin (ed.), *Na rubezhe XIX i XX vekov. Iz istorii mezhdunarodnykh sviazei russkoi literatury*, L, 1991, pp. 5-43; and M. Koreneva, 'D.S. Merezhkovskii i nemetskaia kul'tura, Nitsshe i Gete. Pritiazhenie i ottalkivanie', *Na rubezhe XIX i XX vekov*, pp. 44-76.

energies. Although there was no coherent theory or philosophy, and the term Cosmism came into use only in the 1960s, recent studies by Western historians have begun to reveal the influence of these thinkers on political, scientific and literary concepts of utopia in postrevolutionary Russia.[31] This aspect has gone unnoticed for a long time. Tsiolkovskii has been mentioned as the leading authority for the science of the cosmos and therefore vaguely linked to NF. But Tsiolkovskii's legacy as a literary and philosophical essayist, as a writer of NF himself, and the impact of his philosophical cosmology on Soviet NF, have only recently been discussed. In Fedorov's and Tsiolkovskii's work, but even more so in the contemporary revival of their thought, Cosmism comes across as a powerful ideology drawing on the occult, esoteric and theosophical traditions of the early twentieth century; it forms an important part of the intellectual background of the history of Soviet NF.

From the 1930s to the 1950s, most of the utopian-technological fantasies of the avant-garde and the esoteric philosophical concepts of Cosmism were off-limits, and NF, shadowing the decline of science itself, was reduced to a marginal, insignificant genre of little literary quality. Whereas more than 100 NF novels were published between 1924 and 1929, between 1930 and 1956 they numbered altogether only 80.[32] The only periodicals which published NF were *Znanie-sila* and *Tekhnika-molodezhi*. Since the realm of utopia was occupied exclusively by Stalin himself, and since the distant future, according to the 'border theory' (*teoriia predela*), was declared to be near and almost present, the fantasy of the close-at-hand was now the only possible type of NF and became a mere function of propaganda. Besides Aleksandr Kazantsev, Vladimir Nemtsov and Grigorii Adamov, who wrote both detective and NF novels, the only author to achieve real popularity was Aleksandr Beliaev, whose novel *Amphibian Man* (*Chelovek-amfibiia*, 1938) became a classic and inspired a cult film as well. Many of Beliaev's novels are strongly influenced by Tsiolkovskii and cosmism, to mention only *The KETS Star (Zvezda KETS), Leap into Nothingness* (*Pryzhka v nichto*)

---
[31] Michael Hagemeister, *Nikolaj Fedorov. Studien zu Leben, Werk und Wirkung*, München, 1989, part II; idem, 'Russian Cosmism in the 1920s and Today', in B.G. Rosenthal (ed.), *The Occult in Russian and Soviet Culture*, Ithaca/London, 1997, pp. 185-2002; and idem, *Anti-Semitism, Occultism, and Theories of Conspiracies in Contemporary Russia: The Case of Ilya Glazunov*, in V. Papernyi/W. Moskovich (eds), *Anti-Semitism and Philo-Semitism in the Slavic World and Western Europe*, Haifa-Jerusalem, 2004, pp. 235-241.
[32] In 1927 alone there were 46 NF publications, while in the period 1931-1938 only 2-3 novels per year were published. Geller, *Vselennaia*, p. 71; Britikov, *Russkii sovetskii nauchno-fantasticheskii roman*, p. 268.

and *Ariel*. In this period, NF was closely tied to the 'master plot' of mainstream socialist realist novels, as Katerina Clark has characterised it, with its male adolescent hero growing from uncontrolled affective individual activism (*stikhiinost'*) to conscious and party-guided participation in the building of communism (*soznatel'nost'*). NF merged with adventure novels and later with production-based plots.[33] Outside the mainstream, Mikhail Bulgakov's novel *The Master and Margarita*, like Evgenii Zamiatin's *We* in the twenties, became an influential source for later popular fantastic literature.

The massive revival of NF in the 1950s and 1960s was above all linked to the Soviet conquest of the cosmos between 1957 and 1965, which raised Russia's status as a superpower and gave it a lead in the space race with the US. This officially declared 'Cosmic Era' brought such achievements as the first Sputnik in 1957, Gagarin's first space flight in 1961 and the first TV satellites in 1965. All this was accompanied by the revival of a boundless faith in an attainable socialist utopian society based on scientific and technological progress. The literary corollary was an unprecedented boom in NF from the late fifties until the late sixties, when both technological triumphs and liberalisation came to an end. The Thaw was also an era of giant, almost fantastic industrial-scientific schemes that ranged from melting the North and South poles to diverting the Gulf stream and transforming the globe's climate. Tsiolkovskii, the centenary of whose birth was massively celebrated in 1957, was duly canonised, his rocket inventions of the early decades proving profoundly prophetic. Conquering the cosmos and flying to the stars and the moon was considered to be the final stage of communism. In these years, as cybernetics, telepathy, artificial intelligence and life on other planets became topics of research committees in the Academy of Science, as astrophysics took inspiration from Verne's and Wells's NF, scientific discourse merged with the fantastic literary discourse.[34] Along with this, traditional popular beliefs and myths of stars and planets, even ideas of immortality, were revived and officially supported as a means of mass propaganda.

---

[33] Clark, 'Polozhitel'nyi geroi,' pp. 570-571.
[34] From the 1930s to the 1950s, Russian scientists as well as NF writers had been forced to fight and ignore new scientific theories such as the theory of relativity, cybernetics and Mendel's laws of inheritance. See Alexander Vucinich, *Einstein and Soviet Ideology*, Stanford, 2000.

Example 1: The optimistic-utopian model: Ivan Efremov, *Andromeda Nebula (Tumannost' Andromedy*, 1957) and *Starships* (*Zvezdnye korabli*, 1957)
The first of these loosely paired stories describes the adventures of the spaceship Tantra's mission to a remote planet, once populated but laid waste by a nuclear disaster; the second is a detailed account of a utopian society in the thirtieth century, when all nations on earth and in the cosmos are united in the 'Grand Ring' (Velikoe kol'tso). This future stateless society is ruled by a 'Council of Astronauts' and a 'Council of the Economy'. People have been transformed by advances in genetics and biotechnology, and most of the communist ideals, both social and technological, have been realised: nature has been conquered, 50 per cent of the population are scientists, the separation between physical and mental work has been eliminated, child-rearing has become collective, and women are fully emancipated.

The revival of NF in this era is connected above all with Ivan Efremov's novel *The Andromeda Nebula*. With its static, stereotyped characters, its tediously extensive digressions to explain and justify this utopia on a scientific basis, its contradictions on matters such as emotions, women, art and language, its pathos-laden style and total lack of humour, this novel is anything but convincing in a literary or ideological sense. However, by pulling off the straitjacket of the production novel plot and opening up fantastic visions of a distant future, it spoke to the reborn faith in collective communist utopia and had a powerful effect on Soviet readers. In spite of their low artistic quality, Efremov's novels were significant simply for reviving the elements of esoteric and occult mysticism that had long been an undercurrent in Soviet NF, as well as drawing attention to love and gender. These themes are raised more clearly his later novels *Hour of the Bull* (*Chas byka*) and *The Razor Blade* (*Lezvie britvy*). Other NF writers of this era influenced by Cosmism were Gennadii Gor, Eremei Parnov, Genrikh Al'tov and Vadim Nazarov.[35]

The Thaw period and the following decade is the main point of reference for the post-Soviet popular fantastic. Before 1957 only an average of ten NF books were published per year. In 1963 eighty new Russian and eighty foreign translated titles appeared. In 1965 the figure rose to 315. Between 1959 and 1965 1,266 new titles were published. From 1959 onwards anthologies and yearbooks were

---

[35] G. Gor, 'Ol'ga Nsu', *Glinianyi papuas. Nauchno-fantasticheskie povesti i rasskazy*, M 1966, pp. 159-177; 'Zamedlenie vremeni', in *Geometricheskii les,* L, 1975, pp. 384-423; V. Zhuravleva/G. Al'tov, 'Legenda o zvezdnykh kapitanakh', *Port kamennykh bur,* M, 1967; in English, *Ballad of the Stars*, New York, 1982.

established; in 1962 the *Fantastika* and *Biblioteka sovremennoi fantastiki* series opened; and *Molodaia gvardiia* became the leading journal and publishing house for NF. For the first time since the 1920s, a wave of translated fantastic literature entered the country, mostly Anglo-American writers such as Ray Bradbury, Isaac Asimov, H. Ryder Haggard, Rudyard Kipling and Mayne Reid. Polish writers, especially Stanislaw Lem, became very popular too – some writers called Lem's novel *Solaris* the bible of Russian NF.[36] A new generation of writers, the so-called 'third generation', appeared and became very popular: Kir Bulychev, Sever Gansovskii, Il'ia Varshavskii, Sergei Snegov. NF was now renamed 'the literature of dreams taken wing' (*literatura krylatoi mechty*). With its clearly stereotypical positive and negative heroes, its historiosophical concerns and revolutionary romanticism, with its clichéd language and style, NF still remained within the norms of socialist realism, but motifs and characters became less static and more complex.

Two authors more than anyone else best represent the Soviet Thaw yet at the same time transcend both the ideological and literary dimensions of NF. They were in a sense antipodes to Efremov, and their names made Russian NF world famous. Arkadii and Boris Strugatskii's novel *Hard to Be a God*, is one of the most popular and most quoted Russian NF novels of the twentieth century. It matches in significance Solzhenitsyn's 'One Day in the Life of Ivan Denisovich'. Even today the Strugatskiis remain leading authorities and models for a great variety of popular fantastic writers.

Example 2: The dystopian model – A./B. Strugatskii,
Hard to Be a God (*Trudno byt' bogom,* **1964**)
Don Rumata, the alias of the Russian communist Anton, is sent to the kingdom of Arkanar on a distant planet, where a feudal regime is repressing the population. His orders are to watch and closely monitor social conflicts and to prepare revolution, without taking part himself. After getting involved with a woman he arouses the suspicions of the Jacobin aristocratic leaders. Persecution causes his resolve to waver, and he finally decides to stay on the planet instead of returning to earth.

---

[36] Iurii Kagarlitskii, 'Wissenschaftlich-utopische Literatur aus dem Ausland und in russischer Übersetzung', *Sowjetliteratur*, 5, 1968, pp. 174-179; Mikhail Kovalchuk, 'English and American Science Fiction in Russian Translations', *Soviet Literature*, 1, 1982, 406, pp. 162-168.

This novel connects two main topics of Thaw NF: totalitarianism and the exploration of the cosmos. In this way, Stalinist and fascist totalitarianism were for the first time in the Soviet Union compared and interrelated. Here is a model for the master plot of Thaw NF. The encounter with an extraterrestrial unknown civilisation, conceived as a mission to export progress, the communist system, and the determinist theory of historical materialism, is now questioned from a dystopian perspective. One of the key questions which passed from the book into countless discussions at Russian kitchen tables was: Is history predetermined, thus evolving according to iron laws, so that backward societies or stages of development have to wait for their time, or is it open to spontaneous action and intervention? Has man a right to intervene violently in a stagnating foreign civilisation in order to accelerate historical development? The underlying socio-political theme introduced and questioned here was the Soviet colonisation of the Third World.

In the 1960s for the first time a few women writers, such as Ol'ga Larionova and Natal'ia Goncharova, made their debut in NF. Their contribution to the genre, however, only confirms the strong chauvinist and even misogynist general character of NF. This can be illustrated simply by the small quantity of female characters and, wherever they do occur, by their subordinate position or negative impact on space missions or male leaders.[37]

Four main socio-philosophical themes dominated in Soviet NF of the Thaw period: the conquest of the cosmos; the reconstruction of planet earth and nature, a topic which became dominant after the Soviets lost the space race, especially after the first US mission to the moon in the mid-60s; totalitarianism, both Stalinist/communist and fascist; and lastly, the immortality of man as a goal of human scientific effort.

Extraterrestrial aliens – the secretive, inexplicable and therefore most fascinating Other of the genre – were still presented as basically similar to humans, as in earlier Soviet NF. In Efremov they are represented as ideal organisms, in Strugatskii as communities representing backward stages of the present civilisation on earth. But from the late 1960s writers began to introduce into their work encounters with genuinely different other people and civilisations, in which extraterrestrial beings remained strange and inexplicable in their language or their character. Sometimes these creatures appeared as threatening, warning forces, sometimes they appeared as prehistoric or mythological Slavs. As to the theme of

---

[37] Greene, 'An Asteroid'; McGuire, *Red Stars*, pp. 45-53.

immortality, Cosmism, which makes this a part of its goal of the universal transformation of mankind, became an operative ideology from the late 1960s, when neo-slavophile intellectuals rediscovered the work and legacy of Fedorov, Tsiolkovskii, Vernadskii and others. The striving for immortality as a reflection of philosophical ideas derived from Cosmism can be found in the novels of Efremov, who influenced the Strugatskiis in their early novels, in Gennadii Gor, Georgii Gurevich, Georgii Al'tov and Natal'ia Goncharova. In the first post-Soviet decade Cosmism became one of the most powerful and influential NF ideologies.

There is a significant difference between Russian NF and contemporary American SF in the presentation of extraterrestrial beings. Traditionally, in SF, extraterrestrial beings, Martians or robots, were images of a conquered race or its conqueror and therefore metaphors in the popular colonial discourse and the discourse of Cold War both in Russia and in the US.[38] Since milestones like Philip K. Dick's *Do Androids Dream of Electric Sheep?* (1968), Stanley Kubrick's film *2001: A Space Odyssey* (1968, based on Arthur C. Clarke's novel) and especially William Gibson's first cyberspace novel *Neuromancer* (1984), the imagery of Anglo-American SF has moved away from robots in the nonfictional sense to aliens, who represent the suppressed unconscious fears, desires and dark sides of man, and to androids, cloned creatures with artificial intelligence who replace man and raise problems of identity and moral responsibility. In Russian NF, however, robots figure very rarely, often under the name of 'cybers' (*kibery*) and, according to the socialist philosophy of work, mostly serve the function of replacing human hard physical labour to ease the future life of the collective. Extraterrestrial creatures are mostly anthropomorphic, almost never equal or superior to men, and in Russian SF we find neither aliens (horrifying monsters with an ugly frightening appearance) nor androids (intelligent beings, either cloned or of cosmic origin, who challenge the human mind and human control).

From the early 1970s the Zeitgeist changed, in both official and unofficial Russian cultural spheres. The enthusiasm engendered by political reforms that had propelled writers and scientists in the 1960s towards social-utopian beliefs, fell away, to be replaced by another authoritarian state-controlled regime. Gerontocratic leadership and stagnation cancelled out the ferment of de-Stalinisation, and resignation and scepticism took over from the pathos of youth. From politics and

---

[38] Disch, *The Dreams our Stuff is Made of*, p. 188.

natural science the intelligentsia turned to philosophy and religion. Socialist internationalism changed into neo-slavophile Russian nationalism; instead of the early Soviet avant-garde, writers and artists turned to symbolist fin-de-siècle culture for guidance. Research on and reference to Russian and Slavic folklore became permissible again and took its place in the NF genre.

The publication of translations of foreign SF literature was stopped just at the time when the British and American 'New Wave' revival of SF began, which led to a new period of Soviet isolation. In 1973 – following a resolution of the Central Committee ordering more severe ideological criticism and control – the chief editor of the journal *Molodaia gvardiia* was dismissed and replaced by Iurii Medvedev, a Russian nationalist and strongly antisemitic author of NF, who exerted much influence on publishing policy until perestroika. He was followed by Vladimir Shcherbakov in 1976. During the following decade, the Strugatskii brothers and other reformist NF writers like Sergei Snegov, Vladimir Mikhailov and Kir Bulychev were marginalised and criticised. Consequently, a gap opened up between official and unofficial NF, and divisions appeared between writers, readers, ideologies and cultural spheres.

The officially approved writers of the so-called 'Efremov school', Iurii Medvedev, Iurii Nikitin, Viacheslav Nazarov and Vladimir Shcherbakov, shaped a new type of popular fantastic literature, which under the name of NF moved away from the future to the prehistoric Slavic past, and which can be seen as an early Soviet type of Heroic or Slavic Fantasy. Medvedev, Nazarov and Shcherbakov wrote radical Russian nationalist novels, in which their anti-Semitism was barely disguised. Elements of occultism and theosophy, and allusions to the faked 'Protocols of the Elders of Zion', were eclectically mixed with pseudoscientific theories on UFOs and on Slavic ethnogenesis.[39] A number of motifs and fantasy elements entered Soviet NF at this time, though they came to popular prominence only in the 1990s.

The Perestroika Period

Perestroika was the 'endquote' period of Soviet NF. The gradual abolition of censorship had several consequences. Formerly censored works like *The Ugly Swans* (*Gadkie lebedi*) and *The Snail on the Slope* (*Ulitka na sklone*) by the Strugatskiis finally appeared as well as several novels written long before but

---

[39] Iu. Medvedev, 'Kuda speshish', muravei?' in: *Fantastika -80*, M, 1981; V. Nazarov, 'Silaiskoe iabloko', *Biblioteka russkoi fantastiki*, vol. 18, M, 2000, pp. 272-372.

never offered for publication, such as Kir Bulychev's *On Fear* (*O strakhe*, 1992). NF authors launched politicised and polemical criticism of the dominant *Molodaia gvardiia* group. As in the 1960s, pro- and anti-reform writers took opposite poles, while conflict over ideology and access to publishing began to rage. Several writers fell silent or gave up writing NF altogether after it ceased to be a niche for nonconformist thinking. Others ceased to write fiction of any kind, and some critics even considered NF superfluous after the fall of censorship.

At the same time, however, the publication of NF continued with renewed energy. One of the first cooperative publishing projects in Soviet book production came in 1989 with the series *Novaia fantastika* by Slovo in Riga, its chief editor being the ardent fantasy fan Vladimir Mikhailov, who did a lot to establish a 'new wave' of fantasy. Translations of US New Wave authors – Robert Heinlein, Philip K. Dick and others – followed in the early nineties. Fan clubs mushroomed: in 1988 more than 200 were registered, even the Komsomol still served as an organisational cover. NF journals and fanzines sprang up from Saratov to Omsk, from Nikolaev to Khabarovsk. New prizes were awarded, and the Internet began to replace printed fanzines as a crucial factor in the production and reception of SF. Some awards were made by special juries, others relied on a 'democratic' vote by publishers, readers and writers. These activities strengthened the traditional Soviet NF community and ensured that a SF boom began even before the commercialisation of culture and the book market in 1991. In the NF novels of the perestroika period, scientific and technological experiments almost vanished. Once again, the work of the Strugatskiis is emblematic.

Example 3: A./B. Strugatskii, *The Doomed City* (*Grad Obrechennyi*, written 1969-72, published 1987/89)
People from all countries and eras of the twentieth century meet in a city on an unknown planet to participate in a grand experiment to find the ideal means of harmonious human coexistence. Each one, including the main hero, has his own concept of the ideal and adopts antihuman totalitarian methods to fight for it, even lending support to fascist and anti-Semitic enemies in order to reach his utopian goals. The experiment fails and will have to be repeated. The depiction of the 'doomed city' contains many symbols of hell, and the approach of dictatorship and chaos strongly implies the ultimate and eternal victory of Evil. The novel is a parable of the end of history.[40]

---

[40] Here I am indebted to Annett Jubara: 'Farewell to Progress. Motifs of Russian Popfantastic Literature in the Late 1980s and 1990s', unpublished lecture given at the Freie Universität Berlin, October, 2000.

This is clearly an apocalyptic vision. The novel has no positive heroes and no historical optimism. Humanism appears to be dismissed altogether, and there is more explicit violence than in all the Strugatskiis' previous works. It is apocalyptic not only in the biblical sense, but in the philosophically transformed sense of the Russian symbolist tradition: the imagery and motifs of the novel clearly refer back to texts such as Vladimir Solov'ev's *Short Tale of the Antichrist* (*Kratkaia povest' ob Antikhriste*, 1900) and Pavel Florenskii's *On the Goal and Meaning of Progress* (*O tseli i smysle progressa*,1905), and reveal a deeply pessimistic view which rejects not only socialist humanism but any belief in humanism. It has been stated before that the Strugatskiis, having brilliantly mastered the formula of the genre, transcended its limits and introduced philosophical and moral issues into their novels. But these philosophical aspects, their context and sources, have only recently been investigated. Yvonne Howell has shown the influence of Russian symbolist religious philosophy on the work of the Strugatskiis and offered new interpretations of their major novels by revealing their underlying sources. This sheds new light on their NF oeuvre and connects their popular literary genre to the renaissance of Russian religious philosophy in the 1970s intelligentsia.

This was, roughly speaking, the NF model of the Thaw generation that prevailed at the end of the Soviet era, which was renamed 'Katastroika' in apocalyptic style. More examples of this kind are Vyacheslav Rybakov's novel *Letters of a Dead Man (Pis'ma mertvogo cheloveka),* famous more for the film by Konstantin Lopushanskii, which was scripted by Rybakov and Boris Strugatskii (1986).

The Strugatskiis exert a dominant influence on post-Soviet fantastic literature both as a model and as a focus of satirical reference or parody: they symbolise NF of the Thaw and post-Thaw eras. Their popularity was boosted by film adaptations of their novels. For some of the adaptations they wrote the script themselves: Aleksandr Sokurov's *Days of the Eclipse* (*Dni zatmeniia*, 1988/ 1991, based on the Strugatskii novel *Definitely Maybe* (*Za million let do kontsa sveta*)), *Five Spoons of Elixir* (*Iskushenie B*, based on the novel *Khromaya sud'ba* (*The lame fate*, 1990) by Arkadii Sirenko), *Wizards (Charodei)*, directed by Konstantin Bromberg, based on the novel *Monday Starts on Saturday* (*Ponedel'nik nachinaetsia v subbotu,*1982), *Hotel 'At a Lost Climber'*, based on the novel *Otel' u pogibshegosia alpinista*, directed by Grigorii Kromanov (1980), and – most famous – Andrei Tarkovskii's *Stalker*, based on *Roadside Picnic*

(Piknik na obochine, 1978/79). In 1989 a German-Russian-French joint venture adaptation of *Hard to Be a God* (*Trudno byt' bogom*) was made by Peter Fleischmann, and in 2004 Aleksei German announced the release of a further version of this novel.

Popular Fantastic Literature in the First Post-Soviet Decade

After the downfall of communism and the end of perestroika fantastic realism has become the major paradigm for all post-Soviet literature.[41] Authors of mainstream literature, like Aleksandr Kabakov, Vladimir Makanin, Liudmila Petrushevskaia, Tat'iana Tolstaia and Andrei Kurkov, have written fantastic novels. Others, who are considered postmodern or neo-avantgarde, like Vladimir Sorokin and Viktor Pelevin, use NF/SF formulas to create virtual realities as devices and metaphors, because their major concern is to construct and deconstruct language. Mainstream NF, however, even if it sometimes transcends the formula, never breaks the basic rules of realistic narrative conventions. Its primary concern is telling stories: adventure, entertainment and suspense rather than metafiction. The Soviet type of NF is exhausted and seems to be on its last legs. Very few Russian writers now continue the Strugatskii SF tradition.[42]

At the same time, Russia has ceased to be a technological superpower, and the miserable decline of the MIR space program has put an end to the grand Soviet space myth. Yet, in the 1990s, *fantastika* is booming more than ever before.[43] In the first half of the decade the market was flooded with translations. In 1993, the peak of the foreign literature boom, almost every second popular fantastic book was a translation, mostly from Anglo-American SF (the leading authors were Robert Sheckley, Clifford Simark, Robert Asprin, Harry Harrison, Ursula K. Le Guin). Since the second half of the 1990s, however, Russian readers have clearly

---

[41] See Alexander Kabakov, *Nevozvrashchenets*, Vladimir Makanin, *Laz*, Liudmila Petrushevskaia's fairy tales, Tat'iana Tolstaia, *Kys'*, Andrei Kurkov, *Zakon ulitki*; Vladimir Sorokin, *Goluboe salo, Led, Put' Bro*, Viktor Pelevin, *Chapaev i pustota, Pokolenie P* , and others.

[42] See V. Kaplan, 'Zaglianem za stenku', *Novyi mir*, 9, 2001, pp. 156-170; in English: 'A Look Behind the Wall: A Topography of Contemporary Russian Science Fiction', *Russian Social Science Review: A Journal of Translations*, 44, 2003, 2 (March-April), pp. 82-104; and Revich, *Perekrestok utopii*.

[43] According to readership surveys by VTsIOM, in 1997 11 per cent replied that SF/fantasy was their preferred reading matter, and in 2000 the figure rose to 15 per cent; while 27 per cent in 1997, and in 2000 34 per cent, answered that they didn't read books at all. Levina, chapter 3, fn. 13, p. 30.

turned to homemade SF again, and the number of Russian titles has increased steadily. In 2001 forty of the 100 best-selling books were translations.[44] The majority of readers are male and range from fifteen to thirty in age. Of all foreign fantasy writers Tolkien has done the most to fuel the corporate identity of SF readers throughout the country. Long before the film version of *Lord of the Rings* was released, Russians had got used to the sight of numerous groups of *tolkinisty* heading out into suburban woods on Sundays and holidays, playing roles and fighting with swords in medieval or fairytale costumes.[45]

1994, however, was a year of crisis for the new market of popular fantastic literature. All previously founded smaller publishing houses and semi-private co-operatives (like the St. Petersburg Terra fantastika), had to close due to economic crisis, and hence a new stage of commercialisation and monopolisation of the market began. Only the above-mentioned leading publishing houses (AST, Eksmo, Olma-Press) and two minor ones (Terra, Tsentropoligraf) remained. In the late 1990s some efforts were made to counteract the uncontrolled flood of trash from within and outside Russia. Several smaller publishing houses, like Zakharov in Moscow, Azbuka and Terra in St. Petersburg, aimed to combine commercial appeal with quality by promoting certain authors, by launching series of historical and contemporary fantastic literature, and by devising new promotional strategies. The Soviet type of NF, presided over by the *shestidesiatniki* writers of the Thaw period, has been almost totally replaced by fantasy.[46] This apparently new genre on the Russian book market is, however, not altogether imported from the West. Its two main strands are post-Soviet fantasy and what might now be called ex-Soviet fantasy produced by the authors of the so-called 'Efremov school' of the 1970s.

Most NF and fantasy literature can hardly be distinguished from Western pulp fantasy: it consists of serial imitations and unoriginal adaptations of standard plots with poor language and style. There is, however, a so-called 'fourth genera-

---

[44] *Knizhnyi biznes*, 11, 2001, pp. 57-58; Becker, *Verlagspolitik*, p. 189. According to a survey in 1995, the ratio of foreign to Russian fantasy was 5:1; 50 per cent of the foreign fantasy came from the US; only 25 per cent of all titles mentioned were Russian. E.A. Voronina, 'Zarubezhnaia fantastika i ee chitateli', *Zvezda*, 5, 1997, pp. 232-235.

[45] Besides the *tolkinisty* there are other role-playing fan groups like the 'amberisty", named after the popular cycle *Chronicle of Amber* by Robert Zelasny, and the 'Liudeny', a Strugatskii fan club dedicated to the study and distribution of their works. See H. Pilkington et al. (eds), *Looking West? Cultural Globalisation and Russian Youth Cultures*, University Park, PA, 2002, pp. 108-109; and Hooker, *Tolkien*.

[46] Kaplan, *Zaglianem za stenku*; Revich, *Perekrestok utopii*.

tion'[47] of new writers who have moved on the ideology, poetics and style of the genre and thus shaped a Russian New Wave of the popular fantastic. These include Andrei Lazarchuk, Mikhail Uspenskii, Viacheslav Rybakov, Sviatoslav Loginov, Andrei Stoliarov, Sergei Luk'ianenko, Pavel Shumilov, and a few women authors: Mar'ia Semenova, Elena Khaetskaia, Mar'ia Diachenko, Dar'ia Truskinovskaia and Iuliia Latynina. Eclecticism, a typical element of the genre, in the 1990s rules more than ever before: NF and fantasy elements are mixed together, as well as historically and geographically incompatible, real and imagined times and spaces, (pseudo-) science and magic. Popular fantastic literature can be classified into four groups according to its ideology and poetics:

1) 'Final-stage' NF

2) Ex-Soviet fantasy (heroic fantasy)

3) New Russian Slavic fantasy (high fantasy)

4) Parodic fantasy

1):

This tendency is represented for instance by Viacheslav Rybakov, Eduard Gevorkian, Kir Bulychev, Sergei Luk'ianenko and Oleg Divov.[48] They all continue the dystopian tradition of the later work of the Strugatskiis, now extending it to a 'global catastrophic' stage. Although the typical genre attributes – spaceships, star wars, technological inventions and pseudoscientific explanations – still determine plot and action, Russian NF novels are now rarely preoccupied with advanced technology such as artificial intelligence, cloning, genetic engineering, androids or cyberspace, but mainly with an alternative national future, i.e. with sociological and political fantasies rather than the future of science, space and technology.

Example 4: Viacheslav Rybakov, *Spaceship 'Tsesarevich'* (*Gravilet 'Tsesarevich'*, 1993)
The story is set in a politically united world, the federal government of which is led by an Emperor and cooperates with confessions like communism. The hero,

---
[47] They are also called the 'Maleevka' generation after the small town near Leningrad where the Strugatskii workshops were held until 1991.
[48] See for example V. Rybakov, *Ne uspet'*, *Gravilet Tsesarevich*; Kir Bulychev, *Reka Khronos*; Eduard Gevorkian, *Vremena negodiaev*.

Count Trubetskoi, an honest communist and secret agent, investigates the assassination of the tsarevich and discovers that communist rebels were responsible. They were, however, mentally deranged as a result of a chemical program, the origins of which Trubetskoi discovers only in the historical archives of the Socialist International and by cooperating with the German secret service: in the 1870s a Russian revolutionary and a German chemist invented a procedure to create a cloned microplanet of the earth and thereby manipulate people's minds. The creation of an alternative world went out of control, however, when the two creators split over the direction they wanted to lead it: hell or paradise. Two alternative endings of the novel are offered in a epilogue.

This novel combines a setting in contemporary Russia, complete with real TV shows and brand names, with the fantastic attributes of SF – a future society, spaceships, scientific inventions. The intention is clearly to present an alternative social constellation after ideologies and political boundaries have collapsed. Although not convincingly depicted, the reinvention of humanity precipitates new gender relationships, as the hero struggles to establish a harmonious life with two women and two families.

2):
A major new subgenre Slavic fantasy mixes the nationalist anti-Semitic tradition of the *Molodaia gvardiia* writers with Western heroic fantasy, transforming the Celtic-Germanic mythological context of Western fantasy into a Slavic pseudo-myth. It tends to go under the name of 'Sword and sorcery'('Fantastika mecha i koldovstva'). Some authors of the old generation, such as Iurii Nikitin and Iurii Petukhov, have been prolific in this genre ever since the 1970s.[49] Nikitin's cycle *The Three Men from the Woods* (*Troe iz lesa*), 20 volumes of which had been published by 2003 in a Tsentropoligraf series called *Enigmatic Russia*, is one of the most popular fantasy series in Russia.

Example 5: Iurii Nikitin, *The Three Men from the Woods*
(Troe iz Lesa, **1993)**
Three archaic heroes representing typical Slavic qualities – Mrak, a combative beowulf, Oleg, an intelligent magician, and Targitai, a sensitive, naïve but lazy

---

[49] Iu. Nikitin (*1939) has published since 1972 in *Molodaia gvardiia*. Between 1991 and 2003 he published 54 novels. On Iu. Petukhov's *pentologiia Zvezdnaia mest'* (1997), see Abram Reitblat, "'Zvezdnaia mest'" Iuriia Petukhova', *Nezavisimaia gazeta*, 19 June 1997.

musician – have been expelled from the Nevry, their tribe in the woods and move out into the steppe, where they fight against various tribes. Their main adversaries are the Cimmerians, the nemesis of the Slavs, who are superior in technology and civilisation, but have the evil goal of conquering and killing the Slavs by black magic. The three heroes conquer their enemies' capital and succeed in murdering their chief, but they cannot prevent a takeover by the evil magician of the Cimmerians.

This type of fantasy typically contains an alchemist's brew of various historical periods that are made to coexist at the same time – from the Nevry of the sixth century BC and the much earlier Cimmerians to sixteenth-century Kiev, from Apollo and the centaurs, who appear as ancestors of the Slavs, to Baba Yaga and the pagan God Svarog and hero Sviatogor, from Pushkin's *Ruslan and Liudmila* to Samuil Marshak and non-Russian classics like Robert Howard's *Conan the Barbarian*, another Cimmerian hero whom the three heroes encounter on their way, and Mao Tse Dong ('Let a hundred flowers blossom'). All these sources are quoted and recycled at random, as the language equally mixes pseudoarchaic stylisations and post-Soviet vernacular. But beneath these narrative and stylistic devices there is also an ideological bedrock, which, revealed throughout the novel in scattered allusions and motifs, comes to a focus in Eurasianist theories of a neoslavophile, esoteric and racist bent. All the positive heroes in this prehistoric land are Slavic, as tall and blond as the Germanic ideal race, superior to all other peoples and committed to the communal life, while their stereotyped enemies are alien and hostile Semitic aggressors. Nikitin, along with other writers like Evgenii Kurdakov, Viacheslav Nazarov, D.V. Kandyba and Sergei Alekseev, popularises ethnogenetic theories held by many rightwing intellectuals in and outside of Russian academia since the seventies and especially since the mid-1990s. This school of thought is most powerfully represented by Lev N. Gumilev, who asserts the geo-biocultural ideologies of Atlantic-Semitic and Etruscan-Arian-Slavic races and cultures and advances the theory of the Vlesova Kniga, a forged document purporting to prove the common Slavic-Arian race as the true ancestors of all Indo-European civilisation.[50] In this literature politically

---

[50] On Lev Gumilev see Marlene Laruelle, *L'Ideologie Eurasiste Russe ou comment penser l'empire*, Paris, 2002; in Russian, *Ideologiia russkogo evraziistva ili mysli o velichii imperii*, M, 2004; Hildegard Kochanek, 'Die Ethnienlehre Lev Gumilevs. Zu den Anfängen neurechter Ideologie-Entwicklung im spätkommunistischen Russland', *Osteuropa*, 11-12, 1998, pp. 84-97. On Gumilev's impact on Russian SF, see Kaigorodova, *Russkie fentezi*, pp. 140-146. On the impact of the Vlesova Kniga myth on Soviet NF, see Kaganskaia,

instrumentalised occultism and Russian racist-nationalist fundamentalism merge with a legacy of Soviet imperialism and anti-Semitism.

3):
A new post-Soviet Slavic type of fantasy novel is connected with Mar'ia Semenova and Nik Perumov. Semenova, who lives in St. Petersburg, is the author of *Wolfhound*, the first Russian fantasy bestseller, which has outstripped its foreign competitors by selling 300,000 copies. Like many other successful fantasy novels, *Wolfhound* has since become a series 4 volumes came out in 2001, including a version with a female protagonist (*The Valkyrie* [*Val'kiriia*, 2002]) – and has been adapted for the screen (in 2001 and 2005).

Example 6: Mariia Semenova, *Wolfhound* (*Volkodav*, 1996)
Situated in a nomadic medieval world permeated with tribal violence, the story centres on the hero Wolfhound, the last surviving member of the clan of Grey Hounds (*Serye Psy*), who was sold as a slave, but frees himself and, after gaining all the skills necessary for wild and cruel warfare, goes around murdering and conquering enemies until he enters the gate to another world, where only the Good and the Just exist and conflict and violence are absent. Volkodav is presented as a true Slavic hero, who, like the *bogatyr'* Il'ia Muromets, conquers not only his personal archenemy, but all the omnipresent Evil forces threatening the Slavic world, and who, thanks to his noble heart and in spite of being uneducated and non-verbal, is tender and courteous to women. Wolfhound becomes civilised mainly through protecting and serving his Countess Helene.

This prototype novel of Slavic fantasy contains most elements of the new genre: few or no Tolkien-like fairytale figures, but many elements of Slavic myths and folklore are recycled. Old Slavonic names and grammatical forms (Velimor, Luchezar, Knezinka Elen) are used, and the archaic mythological setting is presented as Slavic history. There is something esoteric in the dark secrets of Wolfhound's origins, and there is even esoteric feminism, when in the end of the novel in front of the Gate to the Future women are promised privileged access to the Truth of the Gods and the energy of the cosmos. Semenova shows a clear intention to deliver a moral message in generalising statements: to establish a moral code of fighting based on chivalric traditions, to hail the civilising power of physical violence exerted with self-control. Many digressions describe ancient

---
Rossiia vo mgle, part 3.

Slavic habits, tools, customs, and everyday life. Without being didactic, her novels show an intention to disseminate formerly suppressed historical knowledge and to encourage the emergence of a national identity; they also display some sense of humour.[51] Semenova, like most writers of fantasy, uses a wide variety of narratives, heroes and themes from Slavic and Northern mythology: *kolduny* (sorcerers), *znakharki* (magic healers) and the Slavic gods Svarog and Veles all influence the fates of the heroes, who are named Count Vladigor, Sviatogor or Valkyrie.[52]

4):
The most interesting branch of new post-Soviet fantasy, represented by authors like Andrei Lazarchuk and Mikhail Uspenskii (who have co-authored several novels), Iuliia Latynina, Maks Frai and Pavel Shumilov,[53] is the ironic and parodistic type. Whether their works have been classified as 'turborealist', as 'economic detective fantasy' or as postmodernist, these writers have made a fresh contribution to the mixing of old and new traditions.

Example 7: A. Lazarchuk/M. Uspenskii,
Look into the Eyes of Monsters (*Posmotri v glaza chudovishch*, **1999**)
The symbolist poet Nikolai Gumilev, instead of being shot by the Cheka in 1921, was saved by an ancient Secret Order of White Magic, hidden in Siberia and educated in magic for decades. He returns to perestroika Moscow to organise and win the superhuman struggle fought by his Order, the 'Fifth Rome', against the Order of Black and 'Red' Magic, which consists of an alliance between Communists and Nazis organised under the name of 'Rabkrin'. The story of Gumilev's masked wanderings through the Soviet past is told in flashbacks and timetravelling episodes, and is juxtaposed by details from political and cultural history. The story features a funny parody of the first Congress of Soviet Writers

---

[51] See Evgenii Ponomarev, 'Knizhka na vse sluchai zhizni', *Novyi mir*, 11, 1997, pp. 217-212. Mariia Semenova has also written non-fiction of this kind: *My – Slaviane*, M, 1998, a popular book on Slavic culture, where the author stresses the academically reliable character of the content by mentioning research in many archives and libraries and expressing thanks to various scientific specialists. Revich, *Perekrestok*, pp. 340-343.

[52] For examples see M./S. D'iachenko, *Rubezh*, SPb, 1999; Sviatoslav Loginov, *Chernaia krov'*, M, 1996, Leonid Butiakov, *Vladigor*, SPb, 1995; Sergei Alekseev, *Sokrovishcha Val'kiriia*, M, 1999; Mariia Semenova, *Val'kiriia*, SPb, 2002. See Kaplan, *Zaglianem za stenku*.

[53] A. Lazarchuk, *Vavilonskie soldaty*, M. Uspenskii, *Tam, gde nas net, Kogo za smert'iu posylat*, Lazarchuk/Uspenskii, *Posmotri v glaza chudovishch*' and P. Shumilov, *Odinokii drakon*).

in 1934, where Gumilev appears disguised as a loyal Kirgiz poet and is greeted with enthusiasm. The novel also contains a supposedly previously unpublished collection of poems by Gumilev.

Besides the breathtaking action and adventure plot, which together comprise a forced march through the history of literary life under Stalin, readers find an almost encyclopedic abundance of topics, heroes and mythical themes from occult history and New Age popular culture. Gumilev corresponds with E.R. Howard and H.P. Lovecraft, members of the German Thule-society visit Himalayan Shambala monasteries, Gumilev visits the cabbalistic Rabbi Lev in sixteenth-century Prague, Siberian shamans meet American Quakers and Russian *skoptsy*, and GPU officer Iakov Agranov cooperates with Rudolf von Sebottendorf's occult Nazi laboratory for racial experiments, 'Ahnenerbe'. Andrei Lazarchuk introduced motifs of Nazi occult mysticism into Russian SF, using the device of a 'virtual history' in which the Nazis conquer and ally with Stalinist communism.[54] This is a technique widely popular in American SF ever since Philip K. Dick's novel *The Man in the High Castle* (1956), but publications about Nazi occult mysticism had also been officially available in Russia since the late 1960s.[55]

Another source of material in Russian fantasy novels is reflection on the magical power and ethnic significance of language. In Nikitin's, Petukhov's and other novels by nationalistic Slavic fantasy writers, regular references are made to the Japhetitic theory of N.Ia. Marr, which presumed to prove the common Aryan-Indian ethnogenesis of one population from the Etruscans to the Himalayas through the reconstruction of a common Japhetitic language. Marr's theory was widely held in the 1920s,[56] then dismissed as vulgar Marxism by Stalin and academic linguistics, but from the 1960s was promoted and even popularised by the writings of Lev Gumilev, one of Marr's disciples.[57]

There are some differences between parodic fantasy of this kind and the rest of NF/fantasy. The former contains humour, irony and self-irony that are absent

---

[54] More explicitly in: A. Lazarchuk, *Shturmvogel'*, M, 2000.
[55] See for instance the excerpts from and discussion of Louis Pauwels/Jacques Bergier's international bestseller *Matin des magiciens*, Paris, 1960 in *Nauka i zhizn'*, 9, 1966, pp. 63-69, 10, pp. 82-89. For the context of this discussion see also Iurii Stepanov, 'Dikii chelovek v zheleznom stolbe', *Literaturnoe obozrenie*, 3-4, 1994, pp. 63-68.
[56] Nikolai Ia. Marr, *Iazykovedenie i marksizm*, M/L, Nauchno-issledovatel' skii institut sravnitel'noi istorii i literatur Zapada i Vostoka, [1929?]; idem, *Jafetidologiia*, Zhukovskii, 2002.
[57] See L. Gumilev, *Drevniaia Rus' i velikaia step'*, L 1969/M, 1989; Kaigorodova, *Russkie Fentezi*, p. 141

elsewhere in the genre (except for a few Strugatskii novels, like *Monday Begins on Saturday*. Parodic fantasy plays with subjects, motifs and stereotypes from both Western fantasy and the Slavic folk tradition, it treats ironically the Soviet NF tradition, above all the Thaw and post-Thaw paradigms, and it is full of sometimes polemical allusions to Strugatskii novels and heroes; in other words, it challenges the NF canon. Like other fantasy fiction, it adopts the stock repertoire of occult and esoteric motifs (black and white magic, cabbalistic and masonic symbols, symbolist and Nazi occultism), but at the same time undermines them by hyperbolic overcrowding and metafictional commentary.

Mikhail Uspenskii was probably the first to use fantasy to satirical and parodic ends. As a writer from Krasnoiarsk, far away from the more established metropolitan network of samizdat fantasy, he made himself familiar both with Western fantasy literature and with Russian folk literature. His bestselling first novel *Dear Comrade King* (*Dorogoi tovarishch korol'*, 1994) tells the funny story of a provincial Party secretary who after his death is miraculously transferred into a magical other world and elected king there. In his subsequent novels *Where We Are Not* (*Tam gde nas net*, 1997)[58] and *Whom to Send for Death* (*Kogo za smert'iu posylat'*, 1999) we find all the inhabitants and supernatural attributes of a fantasy universe. But the story and action are so obviously absurd and the heroes' goals are so abstract that the novels cannot but be read as a parody of the genre. One hero has 'to re-establish the linearity of time which had once been stolen by an evil magician who brought the wheel to mankind and hence the curse of eternal rebirth', the other's mission is to seek death, which has got lost in modern society. Although Uspenskii is travelling well-trodden ground in Western SF,[59] his novels introduce something new to popular Russian culture by transferring the King Arthur legend to a Slavic context. The fairytale fantasy of the Tolkien type, which is based on Germanic mythology, is parodied along with the Anglo-Saxon Celtic myths that provided the source of New Age ideology. There are many puns on Russian proverbs, and in *Where We Are Not* the narrator himself explicitly discusses his fantastic story according to Vladimir Propp's structural analysis of the folk tale.

---

[58] The title refers to a Russian proverb and ironises the escapist character of fantasy novels. The novel was reprinted in 1999 and awarded both the 'Zolotoi ostap' and the 'Strannik' prizes and is part of a trilogy (*Vremia ono, Kogo za smert'iu posylat'*)

[59] For a witty parody of the Western genre see for instance Terry Pratchett's nearly thirty-volume series *Discworld*. Pratchett's books are widely known in Russia by translations and through the Internet.

Fantasy disguised as political satire has also been used successfully by the young writer Iuliia Latynina. As one of the most highly reputed young economists and journalists, she became well-known as a correspondent for the newspaper *Kommersant*. More and more of the corrupt practices which she revealed in the New Russian economy bordered on the fantastic and led her to the decision to write SF novels as a literary encryption and thus less dangerous revelation of the present. Three bestseller novels were published between 1996 and 2000 as the *Chronicle of Veia* (*Veiskaia khronika*), alluding to the Strugatskiis' cycle on a fictitious empire.[60] Most characters in Latynina's *Magicians and Ministers* (*Kolduny i ministry*), which was shortlisted for the Booker Prize, can and have been deciphered as real contemporary figures, although the novel is set in a timeless and spaceless world. Latynina uses the store-room of fantasy only as a convenient disguise for the revelation of criminal economic practices in Russia.

Pavel Shumilov can serve as an example both of the continued reference made to the Strugatskiis in Russian fantasy and of the playful treatment in ironic fantasy of the idea of the end of history.

Example 8: Pavel Shumilov, *The Lonely Dragon* (*Odinokii drakon*, 1996)[61]

This is an adventure story that relates a dragon's discovery of his identity. Expected to conquer a hostile medieval world, a dragon with human psychology seeks his unknown origins and finds out that he was produced as a genetically engineered tool by a race of masters who had once tried to colonise this planet. The dragon decides to complete his ancestors' mission, fight the barbarian priests, save this alien civilisation from its medieval darkness and lead it into a bright future. In language and style the novel clearly alludes to the New Russian vernacular.

The story obviously refers to the Strugatskiis' canonical novel *Hard to Be a God*. But in Shumilov's dragon novel, we do not find the pathos of the 'triumph of Evil' as conveyed in the Strugatskiis' later novels, nor do we find their historiosophical pessimism after the grand experiment has failed. The world is not depicted as the dead-end of history, as condemned to reach via apocalypse the

---

[60] Between 1991 and 2004 Iuliia Latynina published 24 novels. The *Chronicle of Veia* (*Veiskaia khronika*) comprised *Sto polei* (1996), *Kolduny i ministry* (1997), and *Insaider* (1999).
[61] The novel is part of a cycle *Tale of the Dragon* (*Slovo o Drakone*) and has meanwhile been serialised by Tsentropoligraf.

eternal state of hell. It is a post-apocalyptic world accepted by the hero, who nevertheless tries to act and make sense of it; sometimes he is successful, sometimes not. There is, however, no global vision or idea of progress. Dragon-man is ruled by chance and subject to blind evolution, but has plenty of fun in the process.

Some Conclusions

All contemporary Russian fantasy novels have switched their attention from utopian futures to alternative concepts of history, from the prehistoric past to recent history (with barely concealed references to the present day). The idea of connecting history to concepts of justice and truth still seems to stimulate the utopian vision of writers. All writers are more or less preoccupied with the topic of the vanished empire. No matter whether and to what extent new genres like romance and fantasy have been imported, all contemporary popular literature is framed by the Soviet cultural context. Allusions to Soviet novels and stereotypes are abundant, and often carry an ironic charge (*Wolfhound* as a rerun of Nikolai Ostrovskii's Pavel Korchagin, for example). Also palpable is the legacy of pre-revolutionary traditions and philosophical concepts like Cosmism, which were rediscovered and re-ideologised in the 1960s and 1970s. A special influence on post-Soviet fantasy was exercised by the Soviet Thaw, which turned towards a dystopian mode, manifested a growing disbelief in linear progress, and shifted its main points of reference from science and politics to religion and magic. In post-Soviet popular fantastic literature, man is no longer presented as a subject able to move, determine and change history. History is rather presented as being moved by fate, magic or blind evolution. As has been shown, occult ideas and philosophical elements of Cosmism generally have had a stronger impact on Russian SF than hitherto assumed. All this does not mean, however, that no further development of the genre is occurring, or that defeatism or resignation is ruling the genre. It is true that writers of the older Thaw generation do not conceal their frustration, but new fantasy literature offers a variety of new heroes and preoccupations.

One general element of Soviet NF has not changed so far, though: its all-encompassing misogyny, which even exceeds that found in Western SF. Also striking is the near total absence of sex, which has invaded all other genres of contemporary Russian fiction and non-fiction. Misogyny can be explained both by the traditional deeply rooted patriarchal system in Russia and by a desire, shared by writers and readers alike (the absolute majority of SF writers as well as the bulk of its readers were and are still males between 12 and 40), to find a fictional escape from the female who in reality absolutely dominates boys' education and everyday life.[62] While in American SF since the 1970s a whole variety of women writers have developed their own female utopian fiction and criticism,[63] Russian women writers, like Larionova, Goncharova, Gromova and Zhuravleva, have tended to confirm the male-dominated role patterns. At the same time, an element of romance and the idea of worshipping beauty as female have always been part of Russian NF, possibly more than in Western SF, and this has continued from Tolstoi and Efremov to new fantasy writers like Rybakov and Khaetskaia.

What are the possible functions of this literature now, given the fact that most readers of SF/F are male adolescents and young adults? First of all it meets a need for male individual action heroes and positive self-identification. It offers a temporary escape from a rough and often cruel reality which leaves young males especially helpless, and it can thus ease the confrontation with new responsibilities and challenges. In a society turning more and more back to traditional institutions for spiritual orientation, it offers popular visions of non-traditional beliefs, of alternative worlds, history and geography. Whether this stimulates mindless superstition or rather provides a source of spirituality outside the Orthodox tradition, is a moot point.

---

[62] Greene, 'An Asteroid of One's Own'.
[63] See Carol A. Whitehurst, 'Images of the Sexes in Science Fiction', *International Journal of Women's Studies*, vol. 3, 1980, 4, pp. 336-344, and T. Staicar (ed.), *The Feminine Eye, SF and the Women who Write it*, New York, 1982.

Mariia Cherniak

Russian Romantic Fiction

The subject of this chapter differs from the other genres of popular fiction covered in this book because it requires a less elaborate pre-history. Unlike detective novels or fantasy, romantic fiction was an entirely new arrival in post-Soviet Russia. It was received by critics and readers as a wholesale import from the West. For the first few years that this genre existed on Russian soil, its most popular practitioners were translated foreign authors. It was not until the second half of the decade that native Russian romances began to carve out a niche in the market.
This is not to say, however, that elements of the romance cannot be found in Russian culture before the post-Soviet era. As elsewhere in Europe, women gained a distinct authorial presence in Russia in the first half of the nineteenth century, and they did much to establish in Russian letters the tension between emotional fulfilment and social convention that gives romantic fiction much of its narrative impetus. In a more popular cultural domain, from the late eighteenth century onwards, Russia had a flourishing market in (largely translated) fortune-telling works that were targeted explicitly at a female audience and formed part of women's domestic recreations. This feminine character of the material was often recognised in titles such as *A Girlish Trinket, With Which Men Too May Be Diverted* (1791) or *A Lady's Album, or a Fortune-Telling Book for Entertainment and Pleasure* (1816 and 1820). Books of this kind regularly offered advice on how to assess people's character by their appearance – and, by extension, how to find a suitable husband.[1] The first literary journal explicitly for women, Nikolai Novikov's *The Fashionable Monthly, or Library for Ladies' Toilette*, had come on the scene in 1779. In the late eighteenth and early

---

[1] Faith Wigzell, *Reading Russian Fortunes: Print Culture, Gender and Divination in Russia from 1765*, Cambridge, 1998, esp. chapter 5.

nineteenth centuries, educated women were also heavily involved as the producers of their own entertainment literature. They produced elaborate domestic albums full of light verse, improvised *bouts rimés*, word games and all kinds of decorations (such as flowers and miniature paintings). There was, in other words, a flourishing female subculture that can be seen to have performed at least some of the functions of later romance fiction.[2]

But women's writing, and writing for women, have also been more than usually disparaged in Russia. For male commentators they have traditionally connoted 'sentimentality, banality, and lack of intellectual power'.[3] In the early twentieth century critics would happily sound off about the successful melodramas of Anastasiia Verbitskaia, viewing these works both as low-grade and as emblematic of women's reading matter. Their prejudices were shared by the masters of Soviet culture, who also had a whole set of reasons of their own to object to romance and melodrama. These genres symbolised a kind of meretricious femininity that, in the Soviet world-view, went hand-in-hand with bourgeois decadence. Quite apart from this, Soviet women were supposed to dedicate themselves to the cause of socialist construction, not to their own emotional and sexual drives. Women's primary loyalty was to the collective or to their family, not to themselves.

It was not quite the case that love had no place in publicly disseminated Soviet culture. In the socialist realist novel, girls met boys as well as tractors. Soviet cinema, especially in the 1970s and early 1980s, served up a few emotionally fulfilling love stories. But the kind of romantic women's culture that almost invariably accompanied modernity in Western Europe was absent – at least in the public domain. This is not to say that Soviet women did not feel the romantic urge. When Western-style romances finally hit the bookstalls in the early 1990s, they met a huge pent-up demand. In the absence of published romantic fiction, Soviet teenage girls from the late 1950s onwards had made do with home-made love stories. These were a little-known form of Soviet samizdat that circulated very widely in the subculture of young females. The handwritten stories of the 1960s and 1970s ranged from the romantic to the erotic, their endings might be tragic or happy, but they tended to fit a first-love narrative formula. They changed hands frequently and were taken down by their latest readers; at each new copying new details (ranging from the weather to names of characters)

---

[2] G. Hammarberg, 'Flirting with Words: Domestic Albums, 1770-1840', Helena Goscilo/ Beth Holmgren (eds), *Russia-Women-Culture*, Bloomington, 1996, pp. 297-320.
[3] Catriona Kelly, *A History of Russian Women's Writing, 1820-1992*, Oxford, 1994, p. 2.

might be added. These stories met cathartic and educational needs that were not catered for adequately in Soviet culture. Girls had no other authoritative way to learn how to fall in love and how to behave with the opposite sex.[4]

That said, there were a few signs by the 1970s that officially published Soviet literature was becoming more informative on problems of everyday life, personal psychology, and individual fulfilment.[5] A few of the most sought-after authors in the years of the Soviet 'book hunger' – Alexandre Dumas, Serge and Anne Golon – may also be considered to have partly assuaged the growing demand for romance in the female reading public. Even classics such as *Jane Eyre* and *The Woman in White* continued to rank among the preferred reading of women before the publishing boom of the 1990s. Just occasionally, 'new' works such as *Gone with the Wind* and *The Thorn Birds* were made available to the Soviet reading public; they quickly attained cult status, especially among women.[6]

However, full-blown romance of the Harlequin variety remained strictly out of bounds until very near the end of the Soviet Union. The first signs of the incursion of female-orientated romance into Soviet culture came with the arrival of imported soap operas (usually South American) from 1989 onwards. Romantic novels followed hard on the heels of the soaps, and quickly showed their appeal to women of all ages and social groups.

Since the beginning of the 1990s Russians of both sexes have been free to make their own choices of reading matter. Until then they were kept apart from literary developments abroad, were brought up on the opposition between unofficial cultures, between 'permitted' texts and works that circulated in samizdat, and were taught from school age onwards that detective novels and melodrama were the genres of the rotten West. All of a sudden these ex-Soviet readers found themselves in an unaccustomed position: they could select books according to their own taste, mood or situation.

Translated romantic fiction immediately became extremely popular with female readers.[7] In 1992 Harlequin launched a line of romances in partnership with the Russian publisher Raduga: in the first instance six translated titles (each with a

---

[4] Sergei Borisov, 'Prozaicheskie zhanry devich'ikh al'bomov', *Novoe literaturnoe obozrenie*, 22, 1996, pp. 362-366.

[5] See N. Natov, 'Daily Life and Individual Psychology in Soviet-Russian Prose of the 1970s', *Russian Review*, 33, 1974, 4, pp. 357-371.

[6] Ol'ga Borisova, '"Damskii roman" i ego chitateli', *Zvezda*, 12, 1993, pp. 198-200.

[7] In Russian there are several equivalents for the English terms 'romantic fiction' and 'romance': 'ladies' novel' (*damskii roman*), 'love novel' (*liubovnyi roman*), 'pink novel' (*rozovyi roman*), and (more neutrally) 'women's novel' (*zhenskii roman*).

print-run of 100,000 copies) were released, but by 1997 more than 160 titles had appeared. By this time translated romances had surged forward in the fiction charts to lay claim to second place after detective fiction, and they ranged from the virginal to the racy.[8] The novels of Barbara Cartland, Judith McNaught, Danielle Steel, Judith Krantz and others were published in enormous print runs. They provided material for many new series that varied little in their content and bore such titles as *Novels about Love* (published by Panorama), *Temptation* (Raduga), *Happy Love* (Eksmo), *Passion and Disappointment* (both by AST), and so on.[9] In the early stages of capitalist accumulation in the Russian publishing business, romantic fiction received the same unscrupulous treatment as other genres. Several books by well-known American authors were published under false titles to get round copyright issues; alternatively, Russian authors might publish under foreign names in order to cash in on the prestige of the West.[10]

Romantic fiction did not have appeal just for housewives or the less educated sections of the population. By 1997, according to sociological data, as many as 70 per cent of women readers had a fondness for this genre – though it was less popular in the capital cities than in the not so prosperous provinces.[11] By the middle of 1998, romance was established as a very strong second to detective fiction on the book market.[12]

How should we account for this rapid rise to prominence? Part of the reason lies in the format of publication. All of a sudden women readers were presented with a new mode of book consumption. These romances were explicitly serialised rather than individual products. They constructed a world that transcended individual works in the genre. A reader could step out of one fiction and enter another without feeling any sense of narrative or emotional rupture. Yet it was not clear how Western Harlequin romances would be received in post-Soviet Russia. After all, these novels were written to the specific requirements of a well-established and largely predictable market in prosperous and politically stable

---

[8] Helena Goscilo, 'Big-Buck Books: Pulp Fiction in Post-Soviet Russia', *The Harriman Review*, 12, Winter 1999-2000, 2-3 pp. 18-19.
[9] The 'series' (*seriia*) is a much favoured form of publishing in Soviet and post-Soviet Russia whereby books in a particular genre or by a particular author appear gradually over a number of years and are collected by readers.
[10] Piracy practices are briefly discussed in O. Borisova and A. Makarova, 'Damskii roman i ego chitateli: Prodolzhenie razgovora', *Zvezda*, 11, 1994, pp. 206-207.
[11] V. Musvik, A. Fen'ko, 'Zhizn': Prochitat' i zabyt'', *Kommersant-Vlast'*, 30 July 2002.
[12] Boris Dubin, 'Predpochteniia', *Itogi,* 10 June 1998.

parts of the world. Russia, by contrast, was a country in social and political turmoil, and it had acquired a book market in a huge hurry.

The success of romantic fiction was largely due to the opportunities it gave women to obtain the information they wanted about the world. Starved of popular publications on gender issues in Soviet times, women were now able to plunge into an unknown 'other' world with its own fashions, lifestyle, and habits, and to gain at least a passing acquaintance with extraordinary distant locations such as Paris and New York. As well as satisfying a deep curiosity, these novels also served their readers as a kind of textbook on the psychology, ethics and practice of relationships and family life. As a rule, in popular literature the focus of attention lies not on aesthetic matters but rather on the representation of human relationships, which are modelled by certain patterns of behaviour, situations and motifs. The reader of popular literature becomes an imaginer or dreamer, a consumer and observer, whose task is to experience the passions of other people.

One of the main functions of popular literature is escape: a flight from reality into another, more comforting world, where goodness, intelligence, beauty and strength are triumphant. When readers are asked why they like one genre or another, they most often reply that they want to switch off, relax, forget their troubles, plunge into an alternative reality, join the hero on a journey into another world. Escapism of this kind offers refuge in a simplified world where people do not struggle to realise their potential but rather enjoy a reassuringly reduced set of options.

For contemporary Russian women, romantic fiction performs the important function of making good an acute shortage of positive emotions. Readers of romances tend to suffer from what contemporary psychology calls 'frustration': a state that results from chronic disappointment and manifests itself in stress, anxiety, and a feeling of hopelessness. All of these emotions are characteristic of contemporary society, and romantic fiction offers an escapist solution to them. The mindset of a typical reader is encapsulated in a poem penned by the heroine of Liudmila Anisarova's novel *Blind Date* (*Znakomstvo po ob"iavleniiu*): in a tone of heightened emotion, she imagines a romantic retreat into a world of her own:

> In my violet dreams
> I am tall. And thin. And beautiful.
> And I'm garlanded for my goodness
> And I'm loved for my intelligence.

But in my black-and-white everydays
I'm so ordinary, untalented, small.
Petty thoughts and petty deeds
Are reflected in the mirror.
And when it hurts too hard,
When heart and reason are not in unison,
I say 'I don't want this. Enough'
And enter my violet dreams.[13]

Ol'ga Vainshtein has likened romantic fiction to a placebo for its predictable therapeutic effect.[14] No wonder that in the West books of this kind are often sold in drugstores or in big department stores in the toys and games sections. Romances usually have a theatrical quality, relying heavily on external signals. Albert Zuckerman, a well-known literary agent in the USA, notes that a successful novel should come across as a kind of tourist trip during which the reader becomes acquainted with the ways, rituals, fashions, etiquette, and social and political conditions of the country where the action takes place.[15] In the early 1990s, when the book market was inundated with translated novels, this informative function of melodrama was very important. Novels were a crucial source of knowledge about the Other, Western, world that beckoned from afar. One of the most popular types of publishing venture was the so-called 'tourist' series, where the hero and heroine would invariably meet at an exotic resort. In other words, romantic fiction became not only a textbook of practical psychology but also a special kind of reference work for travellers.

By 1995 the situation in publishing had come to resemble that of the 1920s, when the critic Boris Eikhenbaum famously complained that Russia had become 'a country of translations'.[16] The post-Soviet mass reading public had been oversupplied with translated Western fiction and with Russian fakes (whereby a Russian author took on the persona of a Western author to boost sales). At this point the market started to provide home-grown detective novels by the likes of Aleksandra Marinina, Fridrikh Neznanskii and Chingiz Abdulaev and fantasy by writers such as Nikolai Perumov, Andrei Stoliarov, Mikhail Uspenskii and

---

[13] L. Anisarova, *Znakomstvo po ob"iavleniiu*, M, 2000, p. 232.
[14] Ol'ga Vainshtein, 'Rozovyi roman kak mashina zhelanii', *Novoe literaturnoe obozrenie*, 22, 1996, pp. 303-330.
[15] Al'bert Tsukerman, *Kak napisat' bestseller: retsept prigotovleniia superromana, kotorym budut zachityvat'sia milliony*, M, 1997.
[16] See B. Eikhenbaum, 'V poiskakh zhanra', *Russkii sovremennik*, 3, 1924.

others. There was also some discussion of the status of Russian Romantic Fiction (hereafter RRF). Many critics were sceptical about the emergence of RRF, which began approximately in 1995. Tat'iana Morozova noted that the first novels in this genre tended to work with the traditional Cinderella image of the heroine. 'Whereas a Western heroine is desperate for independence, the most our worn-out former Soviet women can dream of is a man with a purse shaped like a suitcase. To give our girls credit, I should say that the hero's riches are only a pleasant supplement to her elevated love'.[17] Other commentators verged on the vitriolic. V. Dolinskii spoke of readers of RRF as 'invalids of the Great Fatherland Sexual Revolution', as children of 'Americano-Soviet pidgin' who were in thrall to a 'virtual reality'.[18] Tat'iana Sotnikova, who has herself made a fairly successful attempt to write romantic novels under the pseudonym Anna Berseneva, believes RRF has no future because, in her opinion, 'love novels' (as opposed to novels about love!) can only be American. This is just as much a distinctive national product as the Hollywood action thriller, and its rules are just as strict. 'To make a Russian romantic novel is the same as making Lego out of breadcrumbs. Lego is Lego'.[19] Even Western observers have made the point that romantic fiction, constructed in the West and transplanted to Russian soil, has a difficult relationship with traditional aesthetic ideals and with the image of positive heroes provided by the Russian classics.[20]

Discussion of the status of RRF was even carried on in other works of fiction. For example, in Marina L'vova's novel *The Teacher* (*Uchilka*), the heroine does not only find happiness with her beloved but also become a successful writer of romantic novels. In the process she shows herself to be a keen reader and observer of the book scene: 'You get sick of reading translated books. You might say that you feel offended on behalf of the motherland. Why is there such a genre in the West but not here? In what way are we inferior? What sort of distractions do our women have? Think what's happened: the first romances appeared here three years ago. People started buying them. First they read them on the quiet. It wasn't easy for women to admit that they were relaxing by reading sentimental

---

[17] Tat'iana Morozova, 'Posle dolgogo vozderzhaniia', *Druzhba narodov*, 9, 1997, p. 180.
[18] V. Dolinskii, '"...kogda potselui zakonchilsia" (O liubovnom romane bez liubvi)', *Znamia*, 1, 1996, pp. 235-238.
[19] T. Sotnikova, 'Funktsiia karaoke', *Znamia*, 12, 1998, p. 171.
[20] Nensi Kondi [Nancy Condee]/Vladimir Padunov, 'Proigrannyi rai. Ruletka sotsializma. Rynochnyi determinizm po obiazatel'noi programme', *Novaia volna: Russkaia kul'tura i subkul'tury na rubezhe 80-90 godov*, M, 1994, pp. 9-10.

books of this kind. But why can't we create this genre ourselves? It makes you angry.'[21]

Whatever the critics may have said about RRF, and although it still took second place behind translated and pseudo-translated fiction, from 1995 onwards it started to gain a presence on the Russian book market. The key novels authors included Marina Iudenich (*I Opened the Door for You, Offspring of Heaven, Sainte-Geneviève de Bois*, and others), Dar'ia Istomina (*The Lady Boss, The Lady Down-and-Out*, and so on), Natal'ia Kalinina (*The Loved and the Abandoned*), Marina Mareeva (*A Princess on Her Uppers*), Natal'ia Nevskaia (*Friends, Vasilisa the Beautiful, The Icy Steed*), Anna Kravtsova (*Games for Three*), Inna Ul'ianina (*All Girls Love Rich Men, All Girls Love Married Men*), Anna Alekseeva (*The Love of a Provincial Woman or Difficult Experiments with Love, The Married Life of Zinochka Penkina, Auntie Shura, Love and the Old House*), Anna Dubchak (*Visits to a Solitary Man*), Elena Bogatyreva (*Three Fates*), Ekaterina Vil'mont (*The Travels of an Optimistic Woman, or All Women are Fools*), and others.[22]

Novels of this kind were readily taken up by the post-Soviet publishing industry and slotted into a lengthening list of titles. Romantic fiction was strongly promoted through the usual publishing strategies. Many series made a clear pitch for the female audience in their very titles: *Women's stories, A Lucky Chance, Cosy Detective Stories*, or *Ironic Detective Stories* (a series put out by Eksmo which features a pistol cutely tied with a ribbon on the individual book covers). A visit to the Eksmo website (http://www.eksmo.ru)
reveals just how extensive and sophisticated the market for romantic fiction has become. By the early twenty-first century, romance fans were generously catered for by the Internet.[23]

Literary and cultural studies over the last few years have amply shown that culture and language are permeated with gender relations. This insight has a crucial

---

[21] M. L'vova, *Uchilka*, SPb, 1997, p. 65.

[22] The original titles of the works listed in this paragraph are: *Ia otvoril pered toboiu dver', Ischadie raia, Sen-Zhenev'ev de Bua, Ledi boss, Ledi-bomzh, Liubimye i pokinutye, Printsessa na bobakh, Podrugi, Vasilisa Prekrasnaia, Ledianoi kon', Igry dlia troikh, Vse devushki liubiat bogatykh, Vse devushki liubiat zhenatykh, Liubov' provintsialki ili nelegkie opyty liubvi, Zamuzhestvo Zinochki Penkinoi, Tetia Shura, liubov' i staryi dom, Vizity k odinokomu muzhchine, Tri sud'by*, and *Puteshestvie optimistki, ili vse baby dury*.

[23] Note for example the women's portal WWWomen.ru, which invites browsers to submit their own 'tales of passion', and Romance.narod.ru (a site which aims to classify and keep up to date with Western novelties in romantic fiction).

bearing on mass literature. The creation of a new female identity requires the rejection both of the stereotypes imposed in Soviet times and of common male notions of femininity. As Lev Gudkov and Boris Dubin have observed, 'formulas give the audience the opportunity to test the limits of the permissible in the controlled and secure environment of an artificial world'.[24] Ol'ga Bocharova has reached a similar conclusion. She identifies three key characteristics of formula literature (a high degree of standardisation, escapism, and entertainment), and observes that romantic fiction 'illustrates well the hypothesis that formula narratives reflect and repeat no real-life experience outside their own world and experience, which they have created and made familiar to the reader precisely because they have repeated (and reinforced) it from one book to the next, from novel to novel'.[25] The values of the fictional universe of romantic fiction are frequently reiterated to the reader in the text: 'Ira opened the window, breathed in the spring morning, and realised that Lenka was right. She needed not to hide away from life but to get herself together: buy plenty of expensive clothes, have her hair done by the hairdresser, go to the beautician every week and go swimming regularly. She needed to have a beautiful, intelligent little child and take it out in a pram near her home. The only hitch was that all this required money. Money and yet more money.'[26]

'Women gravitate towards order, but men force upon them chaos and sin'. These words from Viktoriia Tokareva's story *The Avalanche* demonstrate the simple stereotypes of male and female identity that are in common circulation. These are amply reflected in popular literature. At the start of the twentieth century, in an intellectualised rewrite of the romance novel, Nikolai Berdiaev observed that 'The sensation of existence, its intensity and colouring, is rooted in sex. People's sexuality manifests the metaphysical roots of their being. Sex is the point of intersection of two worlds in the human organism. The mystery of being is contained in sex.'[27] At the end of the century this idea received a new twist: RRF gained such mass status that it began actively to provide a model of reality that shaped the values, preferences and notions of status held by the reading public. Women were offered a fiction of their own: one that performed a compensatory

---

[24] Lev Gudkov/Boris Dubin, *Literatura kak sotsial'nyi institut*, M, 1994, p. 113.
[25] O. Bocharova, 'Formula zhenskogo schast'ia: Zametki o zhenskom liubovnom romane', *Novoe literaturnoe obozrenie*, 22, 1996, p. 294.
[26] L. Makarova, *Drugoe utro*, M, 1997, p. 78.
[27] Nikolai Berdiaev, *Smysl tvorchestva*, M, 1991, p. 98.

function, allowing them to transport themselves imaginatively into a domain where the conflicts and problems of their existence were overcome.[28]

It can be argued that 'women's reading' is different because 'women always read in the text an experiment with their own real life. The result of this kind of reading is a woman's own text – her own ego right there in the text'. Once this literary experiment has been conducted, it is 'written back' into the woman's everyday life.[29] RRF plays an important part in constructing a new woman's identity distinct both from Soviet stereotypes of women and from male notions of femininity. It serves Russian women with models of how to live their lives.

Yet there is no escaping the fact that romantic fiction takes up an essentially antifeminist position and reflects above all a male view of the norms of female behaviour. In the romantic universe, the conquest of a man is the main test of a woman's worth. As Ol'ga Vainshtein notes, 'the traditional meaning of gender roles is reinforced. The essence of the conflict which drives the novel's plot is that a woman declines her traditional role, and the function of the man is to show the heroine her true purpose, return her to her prescribed role and thus restore sociocultural order. All her adventures are a form of initiation, and the novel is a tale of female initiation'.[30]

Romance novels accordingly make frequent reference to stereotypically 'masculine' and 'feminine' characteristics, as in the following example, Tat'iana Ustinova's novel *Born of the Same Blood* (*Rodnia po krovi*):

> Andrei was angry with himself, because he was secretly dreaming of something quite different, which he wouldn't have been able to name, because the word 'love' wasn't in his vocabulary. He never admitted this to everyone, this thirty-six-year-old, divorced, cynical, cold-blooded, unforgiving, harsh and successful professional. He was a major in the police. He was a mass of strong and well-trained muscles, ninety kilos without an ounce of spare flesh, three bullet wounds, a broken nose, a CV as long as your arm – and he secretly dreamed of having a round puppy named Tiapa and a woman who would accept him the way he was.[31]

In his *The Psychology of Art*, Lev Vygotsky wrote that the emotional impression formed by the reader or viewer is 'extremely weak compared to the very strong

---

[28] See for example G. Ponomareva, 'Zhenshchina kak "granitsa" v proizvedeniiakh Aleksandry Marininoi', *Pol. Gender. Kul'tura (nemetskie i russkie issledovaniia)*, M, 1999, pp. 181-191.

[29] I. Zherebkina, *'Prochti moe zhelanie...':Postmodernizm, psikhoanaliz, feminizm,* Moscow, 2000, p. 69.

[30] Ol'ga Vainshtein, 'Rossiiskie damskie romany: Ot devich'ikh tetradei do kriminal'noi melodramy', *Novoe literaturnoe obozrenie*, 41, 2000, p. 310.

[31] T. Ustinova, *Rodnia po krovi*, M, 2002, p. 112.

affects that form part of the aesthetic response'.[32] In the romantic novel this thought could be neatly reversed: the emotional response of the reader becomes central, and the aesthetic qualities of the text lose their function.

Popular fiction of recent years has put forward new norms for women's behaviour and identity. The titles of some novels immediately signal this trend in their titles by making reference to women's work roles: *The Stewardess*, *The Actress*, *The Waitress*, *The [Woman] Banker* (*Bankirsha*), *The [Woman] Trader*, and so on. And professions such as banker and trader lose their conventional negative connotations in the course of these novels. Advertisements for these books claim that they offer everything the reader needs to know about 'women in the new Russia'. This promotional line implies a whole new set of socially prestigious forms of employment. As in the production novels of the Soviet era, professional success and the respect of colleagues can often be more important for heroines than personal happiness, but the criteria for that success are now very different. RRF presents a new women's identity that energetically distances itself from the role models of the Soviet period.

In the canonical Western romantic novel a 'happy end' has to entail union with the beloved, imminent marriage or simply the prospect of a long and happy life, but in RRF this does not have to be the case. Thus, in Natal'ia Levitina's novel *Intimate Services* (*Intimnye uslugi*) the heroine, the beautiful Katia Antonova, who arrives from the provinces to take Moscow by storm, becomes a cleaner, then marries a businessman, then works as a secretary and waitress when her marriage collapses and she faces complete destitution. What finally saves her from all her misfortunes and agonies is not love but a modelling career. We find here a line of social ascent (cleaner – businessman's wife – secretary – waitress – model) that reflects a change in the values of the mass audience. There are undeniable resemblances to the formulas of socialist realism, which tended to offer a simplified view of people as a function of some kind of impersonal process. Even the taste for laconic titles indicating a profession is shared with the 1940s, when novels bore names such as *Constructors*, *Drivers*, *Miners*, *Metalworkers*, *Sailors* and so on.[33] Evgenii Dobrenko has claimed that socialist realism 'sailed between the Scylla of "mass literature" and the Charybdis of "elite literature"'.[34]

---

[32] Lev Vygotskii, *Psikhologiia iskusstva*, M, 1987, p. 195.
[33] These novels were written, respectively, by Nikolai Pavlov, Anatolii Rybakov, Viktor Igishin, Aleksei Bylinov and Aleksandr Perventsev.
[34] Evgenii Dobrenko, *Formovka sovetskogo chitatelia: Sotsial'nye i esteticheskie predposylki retseptsii sovetskoi literatury,* SPb, 1997, p. 126.

As is well known, melodrama did not fit into the genre scheme of socialist realism and barely existed for several decades. All the more interesting then, that a kind of inversion seems to have occurred at the end of the twentieth century. To paraphrase Dobrenko, we might say that RRF is sailing between the Scylla of melodrama and the Charybdis of the socialist realist production novel. The 'moral teleology' of melodrama was noted in early Soviet times by Sergei Balukhatyi: 'Melodrama drives towards a moralising interpretation ... it offers instruction and consolation, it hands out punishments and rewards, it synthesises elements of "life" and of human behaviour, it reflects on specific instances of human actions and feelings'.[35]

One of the first attempts to apply the structure of 'ladies' fiction' to Russian material was Natal'ia Nevskaia's story *Vasilisa the Fair* (*Vasilisa Prekrasnaia*). Here the norms and motifs of folklore become an effective instrument for constructing a modern discourse of female identity. The text makes clear reference to the archetypes of Russian folk tales. Vasilisa, an ungainly, poorly dressed ugly duckling of a girl, attracts the loving attention of a handsome prince – a New Russian banker. The novel has all the elements of a fairy tale: both an obstructive friend (Marina) and an older friend, Nina, who acts as saviour and good fairy by turning the ugly duckling into Vasilisa the Fair.[36]

But RRF does not simply present a fairy-tale world thinly dressed up as post-Soviet reality. As Vainshtein notes, the so called 'pink novel' is often tinged black: it is not just romantic fiction but also a variant of 'criminal melodrama'.[37] The traditional Western Cinderella story tends to become a sad tale of the impossibility of living beautifully in contemporary Russian conditions. As the heroine of Marina Mareeva's novel *A Princess on Her Uppers* (*Printsessa na bobakh*) observes: 'There's nothing you can do. Dreaming of Hans Christian Andersen isn't going to keep the wolf from the door. Out in the big wide world other fairy tales are going on. Horrible, scary ones'.[38] The sequel to *A Princess*, entitled *The Sturdy Tin Soldatov* (*Stoikii oloviannyi Soldatov*), exemplifies how happy fairy tale scenarios are transformed when they come into contact with Russian reality. The 'New Russian' Dima takes to drink, his business collapses, the aristocratic Nina Sheremet'eva starts washing floors again and counting her

---

[35] S. Balukhatyi, 'K poetike melodramy', in idem, *Poetika (sbornik statei)*, L, 1927, p. 68.
[36] N. Nevskaia, *Podrugi*, M, 1999 (this includes the stories *Podrugi*, *Vasilisa Prekrasnaia*, and *Ledianoi kon'*).
[37] Vainshtein, 'Rossiiskie damskie romany, p. 114.
[38] M. Mareeva, *Printsessa na bobakh*, M, 1998, p. 56.

kopecks. The novel brings forth a new type of hero: not a prince from the camp of the New Russians but a 'real man' with unbending principles and a tough character. Through her heroine the author comments ironically on traditional models of behaviour for Russian women: 'This is the age-old way of Russian women: first to tie men hand and foot by your constant loving care and then to complain that he won't lift a finger for you.'[39]

The heroines of RRF are very often themselves writers: authors of romantic fiction or detective novels, translators of popular literature, or journalists. This choice of profession attests to the continuing prestige of literature in the Russian hierarchy of values, but also to a fundamental change in reading tastes. In interviews, contemporary authors regularly reveal some of their professional secrets, which usually include working to a strict formula. 'Who are they, these writers of women's fiction?', asks Elena Muliarova, who writes under the pseudonym Iuliia Snegova. 'They are young and middle-aged women, they have a literary education, they're journalists, former translators. Men can't survive in this genre, they can't stand the test of monotony. But women are successful in all the commercial genres: they write fantasy, science fiction, mystical thrillers, action thrillers (under male pseudonyms), detective novels, romantic fiction. Those who have no literary ambitions write with much greater ease than those who aspire to serious literary status ... You'd think there was nothing particularly complicated in producing this kind of novel. It all boils down to a few simple rules: simple language without unusual metaphors; everything, even reminiscences, should take place in real time; at least three detailed erotic scenes, and the inevitable *happy end*. I don't only guarantee my heroes success in their private life but also fix their everyday problems, their career and their health, if it has suffered in their quest for love.'[40]

Other authors view their writing as a form of self-affirmation, and thus reduce the gap between themselves, their heroines and their readers. Iuliia Shilova, author of women's detective novels, confesses that 'My husband didn't value me at all, he didn't read a single one of my books. That was his principle: a woman should just be a wife and not draw attention to herself. I would say to him: "Have a read of my book". But the answer I got was "That's all I need ... why should I

---

[39] Mareeva, *Printsessa na bobakh*, p. 198.
[40] E. Muliarova, 'Zhenskii roman kak shkola muzhestva dlia avtora', *Russkii zhurnal*, located at www.russ.ru.

read any old rubbish". My novels are a warning to women who marry for money.'[41]

Women's self-affirmation in RRF is often bolstered by phrases culled from popular articles on psychology and self-help manuals. For example: 'Women's independence is not about empty chatter. I'm not trying to turn you into a feminist. But you mustn't forget about yourself. It is possible to have a happy family life and to keep your own personality. To do your own thing and earn your own money. Because material dependence really chains you down'.[42] A prevalent model of behaviour is that of a strong, self-confident woman who often takes upon herself male responsibilities. This represents a rejection both of Soviet norms and of male stereotypes of femininity. Anna, the heroine of Liudmila Milevskaia's ironic detective novel *The Pocket Woman* (*Karmannaia zhenshchina*) is an independent woman, she supports her husband, but she is unable to go as far as divorce. She comes up with a clear formula for family relationships: 'Men are necessary for lots of things. For their salary, for love, for presents, for care and tenderness, to have someone to shout at without getting into trouble, to get on someone's nerves. All this can be put into a single phrase. Women need men so they can feel sure of themselves. I reckon men need women for the same reason.'[43] Similar reflections are offered by the heroine of Elena Iakovleva's *If You're Going to Bluff, Do It with a Flourish* (*Blefovat', tak s muzykoi*): 'At the same time the kettle was peacefully snuffling on the stove, which put me in the necessary mood – that is to say, emotional. I am only a woman, and for this reason I sometimes have an urgent need for a shoulder to cry on with some minimal degree of comfort.'[44]

Romantic fiction works at a high level of generality. As many critics have noted, novels in this genre can be read as part of an unending sequence of narratives that present a women's perspective on men, sex, love and gender roles. The authorial first person is absent, and reality is seen entirely through the eyes of the heroine. As Bocharova notes, 'you won't find a first-person narration here, which you can regard as an indication of the "objectivity" ... of the models presented in the novel. The novel reproduces the heroine's point of view, it is

---

[41] Interview with Iu. Shilova, *Ogonek*, 14, 2000, p. 14. On the same point see N. Pod"iablonskaia, 'Kak voznikaiut zhenskie romany', *Oktiabr'*, 12, 1998, pp. 168-175.
[42] M. Mareeva, *Stoikii oloviannyi Soldatov*, p. 190.
[43] L. Milevskaia, *Karmannaia zhenshchina*, M, 2000, p. 76.
[44] E. Iakovleva, *Blefovat', tak s muzykoi*, M, 2000, p. 98.

always on her side. Readers become intimately acquainted with her spiritual and sexual concerns, while they see the hero only through the heroine's eyes'.[45]
Kornei Chukovskii, a writer intrigued by the mass culture of his own day in the early twentieth century, once observed that 'The filmmaker has his own legends, ballads, comedies, dramas, idylls and farces. He composes stories and presents himself to the audience as a poet, playwright, chronicler and novelist'.[46] This observation has become even more resonant a century later. As Aleksandr Genis notes, 'these days books have become so dependent on films that they have become ready meals for cinematic consumption. In America the major writers – John Grisham, Stephen King, Tom Clancy – write novels that work both for the reader and for the producer. Even their heroes are designed for particular Hollywood stars. When it reaches the screen, this literature loses nothing but gains a lot. Most of all – economy and intensity'.[47]
Cinema, television, advertising and the Internet have given rise to new ways of seeing human beings. These can easily be taken up in popular literature, which is concerned not with aesthetic purity but with the problem of representing human relationships. In Russia over the last ten years, cinema has served up countless templates for depicting human beings. It has done nothing less than 'transform our means of taking in the world. Its frames have imprinted themselves on the consciousness of authors and readers and viewers'.[48] Accordingly, the representation of human relationships and gender roles that we find in RRF has much in common with the aesthetic of commercial cinema.
The characters that feature in cinema and TV have begun to multiply on the page. In mass literature, the written text no longer has to come first. Innumerable books have been published on the heels of successful TV series. The boundary between mass fiction and the audiovisual media has all but been eroded, as the North and South American soaps shown on Russian TV (*Simply Maria, The Rich Also Cry, Santa Barbara*, and so on) have given rise to Russian-authored books. As Lev Rubinshtein has suggested, for some readers cinema may serve as a way in to the written word. Rubinshtein tells an anecdote from the Soviet era to illustrate his point: when the celebrated TV adaptation of Il'f and Petrov's *The*

---

[45] Bocharova, 'Formula zhenskogo schast'ia', p. 296.
[46] K. Chukovskii, 'Nat Pinkerton', in idem, *Sobranie sochinenii v shesti tomakh*, M, 1965-69, vol. 6, p. 120.
[47] A. Genis, 'Fotografiia dushi: v okrestnostiakh filologicheskogo romana', *Zvezda*, 9, 2000, p. 134.
[48] I.A. Mart'ianova, *Kinovek russkogo teksta: Paradoks literaturnoi kinematograficnosti*, SPb, 2001, p. 216.

Twelve Chairs was showing on Soviet TV, he overheard a young woman say to her friend: 'You wouldn't believe it, Liuska, the series isn't over yet but there's already been a book written. I saw it myself: a bloke was reading it on the metro'.[49] Now this kind of situation is no longer the stuff of jokes. Contemporary literature has acquired a new genre: the cinemanovel. Anna Malysheva, a popular detective author, makes clear the connection between literature and film as she describes how she started writing: 'I just sat down at the keyboard and imagined that I was about to watch a film, and started writing the film down ... And now, when I'm writing my sixteenth novel, everything starts with that film'.[50]

Contemporary writers are so used to appealing to the cinematic experience of their readers that they can produce shorthand descriptions of their heroes: 'She was beautiful like Sharon Stone', or 'He was strong like Bruce Willis'. Alternatively, characters in books are assessed by the standards set by cinema idols: 'Katia couldn't help comparing her new acquaintance with Di Caprio. Amazingly enough, the real-life Leo wasn't at all inferior to his cinematic prototype. This was incredible, but true! Chavoisier had a pleasant voice and refined manners. Katia caught herself thinking that she had lost her grasp of reality. She had the feeling that she was caught up in some kind of exciting film and was playing a role that she didn't know properly'.[51] By denying their characters individual physical traits, by making them anonymous calques of film stars, the authors of RRF turn them into markers of particular human types. Heroes become simulacra, in Jean Baudrillard's phrase. Or, as Mark Kharitonov observes, 'the cinematic version of life can replace real life precisely because of its documentary, photographic verisimilitude'.[52] In a neat case of life imitating art, scenes from popular cinema serve as emblems of the good life in numerous works of RRF. To return to the example of *Titanic*: 'Ekaterina Shadrina could not get to sleep for ages, turning over in her mind for the hundredth time images of her voyage. Here she was standing on the prow of the ship, like Kate in the film *Titanic*, casting a glance into the unknown, and rushing fearlessly towards the waves of her fate... In fact, many lovers had tried to restage the famous scene on the prow of the ship. Several such attempts had come perilously close to tragedy'.[53]

---

[49] L. Rubinshtein, 'Dvenadtsat' s pliusom', *Itogi*, 20 January 1998.
[50] Interview with Anna Malysheva, *Ogonek*, 24, 2000, p. 10.
[51] O. and S. Tropinin, *Titanik-2*, M, 2000, p. 36.
[52] M. Kharitonov, *Sposob sushchestvovaniia: Esse*, M, 1998, p. 34.
[53] O. and S. Tropinin, *Titanik-2*, p. 70.

Although the plot is a source of enjoyment for readers of RRF, it is not sufficient on its own. It also serves as an opportunity for readers to immerse themselves in the world of their heroes, much as cinema-goers gaze lovingly at every last gesture and expression of their favourite stars. And the analogy with cinema is more than a casual allusion. Often authors of RRF are quite explicit in the way that they borrow plot elements and motifs from well-known films. And the characters constantly look back at their screen prototypes and reflect on their connection to them. Dilia Enikeeva's novel *Casanova* was promoted as 'a romantic history of love, a Russian version of the famous film *9 1/2 Weeks*'. The text of the novel took up this connection self-consciously: 'He remembered the final scene, when the inimitable Kim Basinger was leaving – she turned round briefly, as if still wondering what to do, with a tragic face, but then strode decisively forward. She was leaving her lover, who had given her an ocean of pleasure, because she didn't want him to break her as a personality.' But her Casanova is not reconciled to her departure: 'Wait a minute, darling. I think the analogy with this film is too transparent. I never tried to break you as a personality. Don't I know what you're like?! You're not like anyone else. That's why I love you.'[54] In Ol'ga and Sergei Tropinin's *Titanic*, the reference to a cinematic prototype is even more unambiguous: 'Suddenly there was a terrible crack. And then a howl of terror. The Titanic had split down the middle like a walnut. Hundreds of passengers were plunged into the water around the drowning ship and tried to grab hold of its fragments ... Katia realised that she had seen this nightmarish scene somewhere before: 'My God', she whispered, 'it's just like in the film'.[55]
Nor does the Tropinins' novel limit itself to allusions to Winslett and Di Caprio. It deals liberally in the cinematic myths that make film-star ideals the common currency of everyday life. As a dress designer explains à propos her new collection (entitled *Roman Holiday*): 'I must confess I'm in raptures over the film with the delightful Audrey Hepburn in the main role. I wanted to present women as light, airy but also sexy. I believe that dresses should not be too open. You need to leave space for men's fantasies. Women should remain a mystery for them, and before solving the mystery he should go through a bit of agony.'[56]
Still more elaborate references to films can be found in novels where heroines use cinematic prototypes to model their own experiences and aspirations. In her novel *I Want a Woman on Roller Skates* (*Khochu babu na rolikakh*), Ekaterina

---
[54] D. Enikeeva, *Kazanova*, M, 2001, p. 114.
[55] O. and S. Tropinin, *Titanik-2*, p. 32.
[56] O. and S. Tropinin, *Titanik-2*, p. 56.

Vil'mont has her heroine wander into an elite shopping centre, where she is pointedly ignored by the assistant in the first shop she enters. At this moment the first association that comes into her mind is Julia Roberts in *Pretty Woman*.[57] Liudmila Boiadzhieva's novel *The Masks of Love* is based totally on the patterns of Western thrillers. Here we find Hollywood, lost diamonds, expensive cosmetic clinics that can give you a new face, and an actress who goes to war with her husband over an inheritance.[58] Publishers also tend to play on visual symbols in their cover designs. Contemporary detective novels often bear collages of scenes from films made out of the book (the covers of Aleksandra Marinina's novels, for example, often feature the actress Elena Iakovleva, who plays Kamenskaia).

Like cinema, RRF offers its consumers the opportunity to move into a parallel world where other people's lives can be experienced as their own. Romantic novels are print versions of soap operas. Characters are treated in narrowly evaluative ways: either as objects of disparagement or as models for emulation. Cinematic heroes very often fall into the latter category. As one character remarks, old films 'show a different kind of life, one that I would perhaps like to live myself'.[59]

The treatment of everyday life marks out RRF as being different from its Western counterpart. In 1996 Ol'ga Bocharova carried out an analysis of translated romantic fiction that had appeared in the early 1990s in series such as *Novels about Love* (published by Panorama) and *Love Novels* (Raduga). She found that precise indications of time were almost absent, and that 'only by the frequent references to personal computers can you guess that the action is taking place in the early 1990s and not at the end of the 1960s'.[60] There was practically no mention of important events, of famous people, or even of specific details of everyday life (firms, shops, restaurants) that might help to date the narrative. By 1998, however, Natal'ia Pod"iablonskaia was observing that 'in ladies' fiction the effect of recognition is important...Reality creeps out from between the lines. And this is a kind of reality that does not wish to accommodate itself to the strict rituals of the genre'.[61]

---

[57] E. Vil'mont, *Khochu babu na rolikakh*, M, 2002.
[58] L. Boiadzhieva, *Maski liubvi*, M, 2000, p. 34.
[59] K. Burenina, *Zadushevnyi razgovor*, M, 2000, p. 45.
[60] Ol'ga Bocharova, 'Formula zhenskogo schast'ia: zametki o zhenskom liubovnom romane', *Novoe literaturnoe obozrenie*, 22, 1996, p. 292.
[61] N. Pod"iablonskaia, 'Kak voznikaiut zhenskie romany: Prakticheskie zametiki', *Oktiabr'*,12, 1998, p. 110.

This close relationship to everyday realia is something that RRF shares with women's glossy magazines. At the end of the twentieth century, these magazines began to transmit a myth of the 'new Russian woman'.[62] Given the lack of a native Russian tradition of romantic fiction, the writing in magazines such as *Liza, Dasha, Good Housekeeping* (*Domashnii ochag*) and *Mothers and Daughters* (*Dochki-materi*) was in a journalistic and reportorial vein. Advance publicity for the magazine *True Stories* (*Pravdivye istorii*) promised readers 'the things that concern all of us: love and betrayal, crime and punishment, money, inheritance, relations with your family. The authors and the heroes of their tales are not celebrities but the kind of ordinary people we live among. The distinctive feature of these stories is their absolute honesty, and for this reason they are closest to the genre of confession. Often the author tells us on the pages of the magazine about what has caused her most pain – the kind of things she wouldn't even tell her closest friends so as not to worry them. For this reason the reader will discover in many of our heroes something of her own, some part of herself'. As in the West, glossy magazines in Russia have started to play a crucial role in shaping women's self-image and aspirations. Advertisements, fiction and advice columns all tell women insistently that they should conform to a particular kind of beauty. Women's magazines are 'a machine for destroying individual and moral distinctions; a depersonalising force for conformism; an instrument for subjecting women to the standards of external appearance and attractiveness'.[63]

RRF contains numerous precise references to the world of objects. Beautiful furniture, a well-chosen wardrobe, cars and property are given prominence as in advertising copy. When outfits are described, the name of the designer rarely escapes mention. In the kitchen, the heroine is commended for her speed and excellence in cooking – and for producing dishes similar to those recommended in the latest cookbooks. The hero and heroine are images of ideal lovers transferred to the contemporary era. They resemble real people in so far as that is required by plot development, but they resemble more than anything else a typical selection of notions of what real life should be. It is not surprising that in the USA well-known women authors often have columns in fashionable magazines or appear in women's TV programmes, where they give all kinds of advice – from

---

[62] Nadezhda I. Azhgikhina, '"Zheleznaia ledi" ili Baba Iaga? "Zhenskaia tema" v sovremennoi rossiiskoi presse', *Materialy Pervoi Rossiiskoi letnei shkoly po zhenskim i gendernym issledovaniiam "Valdai-96"*, M, 1997, pp. 43-46.

[63] Zh. Lipovetskii, *Tret'ia zhenshchina: nezyblemost' i potriasenie osnov zhenstvennosti*, SPb, 2003, p. 240.

psychological to everyday. In Russia this practice has been initiated by Dilia Enikeeva, the author of 'sentimental detective novels' who is also a psychiatrist and a sexologist, and by Dar'ia Dontsova, who in 2003 published a *Cookbook for the Lazy Woman*.

It is not surprising, then, that the heroines of RRF are in thrall to the objects that surround them. 'Now she [Lika] was sitting on the sofa, examining the skirts, trousers and jackets strewn over the floor. This brightly coloured heap of things gave her a feeling of chaos ... She was on the point of snapping, rushing over to this heap of quite innocent things, and ripping them to pieces ... But at that moment a cold and unpleasant voice told her: "Stop!" Lika looked around and breathed out loudly. "You're rather keen on Mikhail Aleksandrovich", the voice continued, "so you must try to improve your appearance".'[64]

The connection between RRF and the world of things is confirmed by the frequently explicit references to consumer goods. Often romantic novels seem to be tied in with advertising campaigns. One of Dar'ia Dontsova's characters finds herself admiring the smooth and clear, and apparently natural, complexion of a woman in late middle age. But, she reflects, 'I used to work in a modelling studio and I know how much it costs to buy makeup that will give you that kind of natural effect. Her clothes too were perfect for her face ... Her hands were immaculately manicured and without the least signs of the pigmentation that older people get ... And the lady had the scent to match: simple but tasteful, a perfume that she had probably been using all her life – Chanel No. 5'.[65] Such up-to-date beauty tips are regularly dispensed, and gratefully received, on the pages of RRF. They contribute to the 'mystification' of woman diagnosed by Simone de Beauvoir: concern for one's appearance becomes an absolute fixation.[66]

Food is another crucial part of the material world that is brought to the fore in RRF. Some passages read like word-for-word extracts from cookery books. Recipes are often impressively elaborate, involving multiple stages and a range of exotic ingredients. They may culminate in a visual flourish: one character lovingly recommends a chicken dish which is finished by dousing the meat in brandy and setting it alight.[67]

Another indication of a character's endowment with essential life skills is her use of language. A novel by Ol'ga Sakredova brings together two characters who are

---

[64] Burenina, *Zadushevnyi razgovor*, p. 57.
[65] Dar'ia Dontsova, *Tri meshka khitrostei*, M, 2003, p. 78.
[66] Simon de Bovuar [de Beauvoir], *Vtoroi pol,* SPb, 2002, p. 145.
[67] Burenina, *Zadushevnyi razgovor*, p. 134.

both from small provincial towns, but who have used this background in very different ways. One of them, Asia, cultivates the speech style and manner of an *intelligent*; she makes a conscious effort to speak not only correctly but also elegantly. The other, Vera, plays up her provincial background, routinely mixes Ukrainianisms in with her Russian, and always chooses earthy language. When Asia meets up with Vera, she has to be careful afterwards that her speech is not invaded by 'worker and peasant turns of phrase that would be out of place in the vocabulary of an administrator and *intelligent*'.[68]

Much of the material discussed in this chapter would seem to show that women's mass culture is fixated on love, fashion, health, career, home, family, children and entertainment. But these key values do not quite explain the striking success of another female genre: 'women's detective fiction'. This type of writing challenges the trend whereby all women's mass culture is disparaged as melodrama and sinks to the bottom of the cultural hierarchy. As Tat'iana Tolstaia once observed, 'all good detective writers are women and English'. The women's detective genre, which is discussed in more detail in Marina Koreneva's chapter in this volume, provides heartening evidence that women can gain a strong position in that most 'male' of domains: crime-fighting. Women writing in this genre – Marinina, Dashkova, Dontsova, Malysheva, and many others – have achieved an interesting hybrid of detective and romantic fiction.

Romantic fiction in post-Soviet Russia offers a fascinating case study in cultural adaptation and appropriation.[69] Although this genre had shallow roots in Russia before the early 1990s, it was not simply transplanted in its entirety from Western to Russian soil. Certain key elements in the Harlequin formula could not easily be made to work in a post-Soviet setting. The glamorous and wealthy male protagonist could not be quite such a positive hero in a society where wealth was always dubiously acquired. Happy endings, similarly, were a more problematic form of plot resolution in Moscow than in Toronto, New York or London.

We should not underestimate, however, the extent to which the mere fact of a 'female' genre makes a difference in a society that is still much more patriarchal

---

[68] O. Sakredova, *Tarif na liubov'*, M, 2000, p. 45.
[69] In any case, it is possible to overstate the uniformity and formulaic nature of romance fiction in 'the West'. Harlequin novels may be an international genre par excellence, but it still makes sense to speak of the 'national' romance cultures of, say, North America and Britain. See G. Linke, *Populärliteratur als kulturelles Gedächtnis: Eine vergleichende Studie zu zeitgenössischen britischen und amerikanischen popular romances der Verlagsgruppe Harlequin Mills & Boon*, Heidelberg, 2003.

than many in Western Europe and North America.[70] In her study of Harlequin romances, Janice A. Radway argued that we are slightly missing the point of romantic fiction if we focus exclusively on its content. Although romances do not offer much in the way of ideological resistance to the values of a male-dominated society – they ultimately require their heroines to find a strong and charismatic man – they offer their audience an opportunity to reject (if only temporarily) the demands made on them by husbands, children, work and household duties. In other words, we need to give the act of reading its due as well as the substance of the reading matter itself.[71] The right to retreat into a corner with a book was particularly hard-won for ex-Soviet women, who were encumbered for decades with the 'double burden' of work and family and who lived in a culture that treated female preoccupations and aspirations very inadequately.

Nor should we forget that RRF has undergone significant development, and shown considerable diversity, in the first ten years of its existence.[72] From primitive Cinderella fictions it has grown to incorporate elements of adventure and irony. Through its presentation of social roles, its poetics of everyday life, and its interconnections with the other mass media, it has taken an important place in a complex system of social myths centring on relations between the sexes. Nietzsche's ironic words in *Beyond Good and Evil* that 'Where there is no room for love and hate, there can be no major role for women' suggest that romantic fiction is unlikely to come under threat in Russia in the near future.

(Translated by Stephen Lovell)

---

[70] In this light, a very interesting comparative case for the Russian reception of romantic fiction is that of India. See J. Puri, 'Reading Romance Novels in Postcolonial India', *Gender & Society,* 11, 1997, 4, pp. 434-452.

[71] Janice A. Radway, *Reading the Romance: Women, Patriarchy, and Popular Literature,* Chapel Hill, 1984.

[72] It should also not be forgotten that the romance genre in the West underwent considerable development in the twentieth century. One of the strengths of the Mills & Boon company (founded 1908) was its ability to keep in step with changing social mores (especially those pertaining to sex and personal relationships). See J. McAleer, *Fortune's Passion: The Story of Mills & Boon,* Oxford, 1999.

Boris Dubin

Russian Historical Fiction[1]

In the 1990s, historical novels based on Russian material were on prominent display in the bookshops, kiosks and street stalls of post-Soviet Russia. Part of this body of literature comprised prerevolutionary historical novels and émigré prose that was reprinted, or printed for the first time, in the glasnost' years or later. Names from the Tsarist period included Daniil Mordovtsev and Nikolai Geintse (who were rediscovered in the post-Soviet era), Mikhail Zagoskin, Ivan Lazhechnikov and Grigorii Danilevskii (who had been published in Soviet times); émigré historical fiction was represented by Mark Aldanov, Petr Krasnov, Ivan Lukash, and others. Historical prose written during the Soviet period was another component of the book market. But the major part of the literary Atlantis that emerged before the eyes of the mass reading public in the 1990s comprised new works by contemporary authors, and these will form the main subject of the present chapter.

The marketing of historical novels with mass appeal took off in the 1990s. Terra, one of the most powerful private publishing houses, launched its *Secrets of History in Novels* (*Tainy istorii v romanakh*). Its lead was soon followed by Moscow publishers such as Armada, Leksika, Tsentropoligraf, Astrel', Russkii mir, and many others: these firms released mini-libraries with titles such as *Russia: History in Novels* (*Rossiia. Istoriia v romanakh*), *Sovereigns of Rus' the Great* (*Gosudari Rusi Velikoi*), *The Romanovs: A Dynasty in Novels* (*Romanovy. Dinastiia v romanakh*), *Confederates and Favourites* (*Spodvizhniki i favority*), *The History of the Fatherland in Events and Destinies* (*Istoriia otechestva v*

---

[1] A complementary English translation of a text that overlaps in parts with the current chapter can be found in Boris Dubin's 'The Banality of the Past: A Sociological Perspective on Popular Russian Historical Novels of the 1990s', trans. Liv Bliss, *Russian Studies in Literature*, 40, Winter 2003-4, pp. 55-78. I used this text to correct a few errors and infelicities in my own first draft [translator's note].

sobytiiakh i sud'bakh), *Faith* (*Vera*), *Leaders* (*Vozhdi*), *The Greats* (*Velikie*), *Russia: Historical Investigations* (*Rossiia. Istoricheskie rassledovaniia*), *Soul of Russia* (*Dusha Rossii*), and many others. Historical novels quickly assumed a leading position in the popularity charts. According to a 2000 survey by VTsIOM (the All-Russian Centre for the Study of Public Opinion), 29 per cent of adult Russians preferred detective fiction to all other genres, 24 per cent opted for 'romance novels' and the same proportion for 'historical novels, books about history'. Moreover, the popularity rating for detective and romance fiction had slightly declined since 1997, when these genres were at their peak (from 32 to 29 per cent and from 27 to 24 per cent respectively), while historical prose had maintained a stable presence on the market.[2]

This was not the first time that Russian readers and writers had taken such a keen interest in the fictional representation of history, though in previous eras the extent and nature of their interest had been quite different. The historical novel enjoyed a massive upswing in its fortunes in the 1830s and the 1870s: both of these decades (the 'Pushkinian' and the 'Tolstoian') were key stages in the development of a national literature as a crucial part of the cultural heritage of the country. To take a more general sociological view, cultural elites in societies undergoing late and accelerated modernisation, with the radical shift in value systems that this process entails, are more than likely to refer back to an idealised society and culture of the past (just as they may also make reference to an equally idealised future). Karl Mannheim called the first of these strategies of cultural construction 'ideological' and the second 'utopian'.[3] A 'struggle for history', where the winners get to impose their own legendary version of the past, is a typical phenomenon among public intellectuals who are competing to build a new symbolic order for society by constructing symbols of national identity and even of the 'national character' itself. The importance of these issues for cultural elites is such that, in both the eras of nineteenth-century Russian history mentioned above, the greatest literary figures of the age played a leading role in establishing new narrative models for historical fiction.

My main concern in this chapter lies with the processes occurring in contemporary Russian society and culture. I will focus primarily on the patriotic historical novel of recent times. But I am interested in this kind of fiction as a form of epi-

---

[2] See M. Levina, 'Chitateli massovoi literatury v 1994-2000 gg.', *Monitoring obshchestvennogo mneniia*, 4, 2001, pp. 30-31.

[3] On this distinction, see K. Mannheim, *Ideology and Utopia: An Introduction to the Sociology of Knowledge*, New York, 1936.

gonism that draws together in its thematic, metaphorical and stylistic characteristics all the fundamental issues and themes raised by Soviet historical prose of the 1920s-30s and the 1970s.[4] Moreover, today's patriotic historical novel – and in particular its restorationist ideology – is closely tied to the Soviet era and incomprehensible in isolation from it. For this reason, if we are to provide a satisfactory explanation either of historical fiction itself or of the broad ideological movement of restoration of which it forms part, we must make at least a short excursus into the past – in particular, the past of the historical novel itself.

A Brief Historical Outline of the Genre

In various national literatures around the world, historical fiction is inextricably linked to the modern age: to the processes of social and cultural modernisation that have occurred in the West, and above all in Europe. A clear indication is given by the annotated reference guide compiled by Daniel D. McGarry and Sarah Harriman White, which includes 337 novels about the ancient world, 540 on the Middle Ages and the Renaissance, and 4,015 on the modern (post-1500) West (of which 2,052 are set in Europe and 1,579 in the United States). The historical novel is a conventional, fictionalised, and often even moralised narrative that deals with conflicts arising from the transition from a clan-based, status-dependent, hierarchical social structure with its traditional forms of relationship (primarily relationships of dominance and authority) and its strictly prescribed caste, clan, intergenerational, gender and familial ties, to the modern bourgeois order, with its individualist ethos, 'social contracts' of various kinds, and representative forms of elected government. Novels of this kind centre on the 'human cost' of this sort of transition: whether for men of power, for the upper aristocracy, for the elites of army and Church (who are, for the most part, representatives of the traditional ruling elite) or for the 'new' hero, the impoverished nobleman, the representative of the third estate, the 'little person', often a woman or a youth, who will usually be the first in the clan or family group to have a biography of her or his own and to have the opportunity to 'make' a life independent of that group. These new heroes find themselves at the very heart of the caste, dynastic, confessional or intergovernmental conflicts of their age. A later,

---

[4] On the important cultural phenomenon of epigonism, see H. Asbeck, *Das Problem der literarischen Abhängigkeit und der Begriff des Epigonalen*, Bonn, 1978, and B. Dubin, *Slovo – pis'mo – literatura. Ocherki po sotsiologiii sovremennoi kul'tury*, M, 2001, pp. 267-270.

and very popular, development of this biographical thrust of the historical novel is the *biographie romancée* of political leaders, literary or artistic geniuses or 'successful people' more generally (irrespective of the nature and causes of their success).[5]

Different members of different social groups vary in the moments at which they enter these historical processes. Consequently, they find themselves in a variety of social situations and historical circumstances and take differing attitudes to potential social 'partners' and 'addressees'. They also show significant variations in the ways they interpret the broad phenomenon of 'modernisation', and these variations are crucial in accounting for the manifest differences between national traditions of historical fiction in Western and Eastern Europe, North and South America.[6] The major peaks both in the production of historical fiction and in the popularity of such fiction with readers come at moments of social transformation when caste is transcended by the creation of a bourgeois national state.[7] At these times the best writers of the era are drawn to the historical novel, and the genre comes to dominate literary culture, to acquire high literary ambitions and to claim cultural authority.[8]

A different constellation of historical circumstances and factors (social crises, major challenges to the liberal bourgeois era and its world-view) lead to other varieties of the historical novel – for example, the novel of social criticism, often with elements of satire, allegory and parable, that we find in Germany in the 1930s-40s in the novels of Leon Feuchtwanger and Heinrich and Thomas Mann.[9]

---

[5] Prominent exponents of this genre include André Maurois, Stefan Zweig and Emil Ludwig.
[6] In Western Europe these traditions date back to the works of Mary Edgeworth, Walter Scott and Alessandro Manzoni in the first quarter of the nineteenth century. The first Russian historical novels known to me are Ivan Gur'ianov's *Bitva Zadonskaia, ili Porazhenie Mamaia na poliakh Kulikovskikh* (1825) and Ivan Telepnev's *Gosnitskii* (1827), which is about the Zaporozhian Cossacks. For an index of early Russian historical prose, see D. Rebekkini, 'Russkie istoricheskie romany 30-kh godov XIX veka', *Novoe literaturnoe obozrenie*, 34, 1998, pp. 416-433.
[7] Thus, for example, the Spanish sociologist of culture Juan Ferreras sees a direct connection between the rise of the romantic and adventure-orientated historical novel in Spain and the brief triumph of liberalism in the country's political life. See J.I. Ferreras, *El triunfo del liberalismo y de le novela historica, 1830-1870*, Madrid, 1976.
[8] Characteristically, the heyday of the historical novel came between 1850 and 1870; a canon of German literary classics on the national level was established in the same era. See G. Mülberger/K. Habitzel, 'The German Historical Novel (1870-1945)', *Reisende durch Zeit und Raum/ Travellers in Time and Space. Der deutschsprachige historische Roman*, Amsterdam, 1999.
[9] See K. Schrötter, 'Der historische Roman: Zur Kritik seiner spätbürgerlichen

Finally, at the turn of the nineteenth century, in the heyday of the decadent and symbolist historical novel, the *cultural* rupture between eras emerged as the key problem for historical fiction, while the collapse of an entire symbolic world, 'the end of faith', the advent of an age of heresy and a time of troubles in late antiquity or the Middle Ages, offered rich allegorical material for historical narratives.[10]

In eighteenth- and nineteenth-century Russia the initiative behind political and social modernisation lay, in Pushkin's famous formulation, with 'the government', and elite groups (in particular the intellectual strata and their journals) took shape by competing for the right to interpret the government's notions of modernisation. Characteristically, the 1830s, the decade when historical fiction became established in Russia through the novels of Mikhail Zagoskin, Ivan Glukharev, Ivan Lazhechnikov, Aleksei Moskvichin, Konstantin Masal'skii, Rafail Zotov and Nikolai Zriakhov, were marked by acute ideological and literary conflict between an aristocratic formula for the historical novel and historical drama (as represented by Pushkin) and the initiatives of third estate ideologues (as represented most notably by the entertaining and didactic novels of Faddei Bulgarin).[11] Superimposed on this conflict was the opposition between the intellectual independence of the nobility (which tended to manifest itself in restrained aristocratic criticism of the government and of the speed and direction of its half-hearted social and political reforms) and accommodation with the authorities (a kind of official populism), a contrast that was later complicated by the opposition between Slavophiles and Westernisers. Both sides, however, were united in their opposition to drastic social changes and radical methods of transforming the country. For the Slavophiles, unacceptable and disastrous radicalism was embodied by the Westernisers, while the bogeymen of the Westernisers were the nihilists and the revolutionaries of the People's Will. In this sense the nineteenth-century Russian historical novel articulates a rejection, on both gradualist liberal and hard-line conservative grounds, of the very idea of fundamental and massive reforms, let alone of social revolution. Prerevolutionary Russian writers sympathetic to revolutionary populism, and later to Marxism,

---

Erscheinung', in *Exil und innere Emigration*, Frankfurt am Main, 1972, pp. 111-151.

[10] In Russia the main writers in this vein were Dmitrii Merezhkovskii, Valerii Briusov and Vera Kryzhanovskaia (Rochester).

[11] See Vladimir F. Pereverzev, 'Pushkin v bor'be s russkim plutovskim romanom', *Pushkin. Vremennik Pushkinskoi komissii*, vol. 1, M/L, 1936, pp. 164-188.

often turned their attention to the utopian novel (as in the case of Aleksandr Bogdanov), but almost never worked in the genre of the historical novel.

By contrast, revolutionary situations and the heroes of revolutionary upheavals in Russian history (Sten'ka Razin, Emel'ian Pugachev, the Decembrists, the People's Will) were the key preoccupations of the Soviet historical novel in the 1920s, to a large extent in the 1930s, and in many respects in all subsequent decades. More precisely, this was one of the ideological trends in Soviet historical fiction – a trend that we might call 'liberal-democratic' or 'progressive'.

The Post-Revolutionary Period

The historical novel – and, more broadly, historical fiction in general – emerged in Soviet Russia at the very earliest stages of the creation of a 'new' literature whose primary task was to offer a symbolic summing up of the revolution and civil war. The first critical surveys of this literary phenomenon appeared hot on the heels of the first historical works.[12] Characteristically, all this was occurring at the very time that the authorities were announcing a demonstrative ideological 'break with the past'. In actual fact, this loudly proclaimed 'break' meant only one thing: that the victorious regime and its adherents were laying claim to a monopoly on interpreting the life of society – both in prerevolutionary history and in the Soviet present. The subsequent construction of 'the historical' – the selection of material, the interpretation of the behaviour of historical actors – would depend almost entirely on the character of the regime in a given period of the Soviet era. Shifts and new emphases in official rhetoric on the past followed closely transfers of power within the ruling clique.

To begin with, the past was understood only as a projection of the recently occurred revolution; all key moments and heroes were selected with this end in view. The only historical figures deemed worthy of attention were those who had violently criticised or simply rejected the past (i.e., 'Tsarism') and those who could be considered 'close to the people' or to the proletariat (by this method Soviet society could begin to establish its literary and artistic classics – a process that became systematic only later, in the 1930s). This was the context for the emergence of two of the main thematic trends in the genre of historical fiction.

---

[12] O. Nemerovskaia's article 'K probleme sovremennogo istoricheskogo romana' appeared as early as 1927 (in the October issue of *Znamia*); I. Nusinov's monograph *Problema istoricheskogo romana* was published in the same year.

The first was the 'progressive' theme of the struggle for civil liberties as fought by the intellectual precursors of 1917. Novels that fit this pattern include the following: Ol'ga Forsh's *Clad in Stone* (*Odety kamnem*, 1924-25), Iurii Tynianov's *Kiukhlia* (1925) and Mariia Marich's *Northern Lights* (*Severnoe siianie*, 1926).[13] A variation on this theme was the *biographie romancée* of heroes 'from the people' (Lomonosov, Taras Shevchenko, the artist Pavel Fedotov, and others) that adopted the narrative and stylistic motifs of the 'novel of social ascent'. The second trend was the theme of the popular revolt: Aleksei Chapygin's *Razin Stepan* (1925-26) and *The Wanderers* (*Guliashchie liudi*, 1934-37); Aleksei Altaev's *Stenka's Outlaws* (*Sten'kina vol'nitsa*, 1925) and *The Rebels* (*Buntari*, 1926); Stepan Zlobin's *Salavat Iulaev* (1929); and Artem Veselyi's *Stroll About, Volga!* (*Guliai, Volga!*, 1932). From now on the treatment of historical figures in fiction would depend heavily on Lenin's notion of the three stages of the revolutionary movement in Russia. In the thirties the first thematic trend – that of the precursors to revolution – was developed by Anatolii Vinogradov in his *Tale of the Turgenev Brothers* (*Povest' o brat'iakh Turgenevykh*, 1932), Ol'ga Forsh in her *Radishchev* (1935-39), Iurii Tynianov in his *Pushkin* (1935-43), and Ivan Novikov in his *Pushkin in Exile* (*Pushkin v izgnanii*, 1936-43). The second trend – the novel of popular revolt – was continued by Georgii Shtorm in his *Tale of Bolotnikov* (*Povest' o Bolotnikove*, 1930), Viacheslav Shishkov in *Emel'ian Pugachev* (1938-45) and (even later) Stepan Zlobin in *Stepan Razin* (1951).

In the 1920s, however, a third trend began to emerge – one that is extremely significant for my topic: historical fiction about the Emperor, his empire and his people. In this category belong Aleksei Tolstoi's *Peter the First* (*Petr Pervyi*, 1929-45),[14] Anatolii Mariengof's *Catherine* (1936), and others.[15] If the first two

---

[13] From the mid-1920s onwards we start to find historical fiction about the 1905 Revolution: V. Zalezhskii's *Na putiakh k revoliutsii* (1925), I. Evdokimov's *Kolokola* (1926), E. Zamyslovskaia's *Pervyi groznyi val* (1926), as well as novels about the Western precursors of the Russian revolution, such as the same Zamyslovskaia's *1848 god* and *1871 god* (both 1924).

[14] A play with the same title and author was launched in the country's theatres in 1934. In 1937-38 came a film in two instalments by V. Petrov with the screenplay by Tolstoi; here the imperial motifs were even stronger, which did not prevent the first half of the film winning a prize at the Paris International Exhibition of 1937.

[15] The antithesis of this kind of 'court' novel might be considered the satirical novel of social criticism or the allegorical fable of a dictator. Many examples can be found in Western and Eastern European literatures of the first half of the twentieth century, and later in the literatures of Latin America. In Soviet Russia this kind of literature hardly existed. The very few exceptions from a later era include Moris Simashko's books about Eastern despotisms:

trends could be dubbed respectively those of the revolutionary *intelligent* (a mutation of the classic Russian novel about the 'superfluous man') and of the popular rebel (a version of the 'bandit novel'), the third was firmly in the statist-autocratic mode. Eventually, in the 1930s, yet another trend would become established: that of the patriotic military novel. Fiction of this kind included Aleksei Novikov-Priboi's *Tsusima* (1932-35), Vissarion Saianov's *The Shield of Oleg* (*Olegov shchit*, 1934), Sergei Sergeev-Tsenskii's *Toil in Sevastopol* (*Sevastopol'skaia strada*, 1937-39), and Vasilii Ian's *Chingiz Khan* (1939). Patriotic military themes were prominent in the mass culture of the period, which reflected the militarist ideology of the time and the effort to mobilise the population, especially young people, for an imminent great war. Further evidence can be found in historical narrative poems and in historical plays (by Il'ia Sel'vinskii, Konstantin Simonov and Vladimir A. Solov'ev).[16] Moreover, the statist and military-patriotic trends in historical prose were picked up and amplified by cinema (in Eisenstein's *Aleksandr Nevskii* and *Ivan the Terrible*, and in numerous biopics), theatre (in, for example, a two-part play by Aleksei Tolstoi on Ivan the Terrible), and painting.[17]

Here, then, is the general ideological framework of historical fiction in the 1930s and the war years. The mass reader was presented with an account of the turning points in the creation of an all-powerful Russian military state: the historical moments when the Empire 'gathered together' and strengthened its territories, when it experienced and survived awesome ordeals thanks largely to the intervention of outstanding individuals (tsars, military commanders, and heroes from the people). In the second half of the 1930s the general interpretation of Russian history and of the whole course of the country's modernisation (which was late, coercive, centralised, expansionist and driven by the ideas of reforming tsars and a few sections of the ruling bureaucracy) broke with post-revolutionary euphoria, with all its utopian and internationalist thrust, and took a new turn. Now the officially promoted 'legend' of history dwelt above all on the rise of a

---

Khronika tsaria Kavada (1968) and *Mazdak* (1971).

[16] Writers specialising in military topics were called together for a meeting in Moscow in February 1937. But even before this date military-historical novels were appearing. Besides those already cited, we should also mention G. Butkovskii's *Port-Artur* (1935), A. Dmitriev's *Admiral Makarov* (1935), K. Levin's *Russkie soldaty* (1935) and K. Osipov's *Suvorov v Evrope*.

[17] For more on this, see R. Stites, *Russian Popular Culture: Entertainment and Society since 1900*, Cambridge, 1994, pp. 64-97; *Agitatsiia za schast'e: Sovetskoe iskusstvo stalinskoi epokhi*, Düsseldorf and Bremen, 1994; *Sotsrealisticheskii kanon*, SPb, 2000.

powerful national state and a centralised military Great Power, on the themes of 'heritage', cultural synthesis, and the classics. What this meant was a focus on heroes and episodes from imperial and pre-imperial periods of Russian history. Ivan the Terrible and Peter the Great accordingly took centre stage.

In the mid-1930s, the Soviet leadership applied to these historical figures the full force of its propaganda apparatus. The historical profession, and in particular the authors of school programmes and textbooks, instantly fell into line. In 1933 the Central Committee passed a resolution on 'stable' school textbooks, and in May 1934 followed a resolution 'On the Teaching of Civic History in the Schools of the USSR'. The Stalin Constitution drew a thick line under the recent past, announcing that the process of building a new social system in the country was now completed. Consequently, the directly preceding period was rapidly historicised and processed according to principles of ideological selectivity. In July 1931 appeared a CC resolution – on Gor'kii's initiative – concerning the creation of a 'History of the Civil War'.[18]

Volumes in the famous biographical series *Lives of Remarkable People* (*Zhizn' zamechatel'nykh liudei*) began appearing in 1932, again at Gor'kii's initiative. The journal *Oktiabr'* published an extended discussion on the theme of 'Socialist Realism and the Historical Novel'. An academic account came in Mark I. Serebrianskii's monograph *The Soviet Historical Novel* (*Sovetskii istoricheskii roman*, 1936); the renowned Marxist critic György Lukács was simultaneously working on a book on the same topic. In 1936 the Institute of History of the Soviet Academy of Sciences was founded. At the same time, the canon of the Russian literary classics was taking shape, and schools were starting to teach Russian literature according to a standard programme. In 1938 came Stalin's *Short Course*, a document that set the tone for the whole discourse on the past, and in November of the same year the Central Committee delivered its resolution 'On the Provision of Party Propaganda', which roundly condemned the interpretation of history as 'politics projected back into the past'. The Stalinist regime made it clear that the struggle for the interpretation of the past was now over.

---

[18] The first novels about the historical actors of the October Revolution and the Civil War appeared in the second half of the 1930s, in the period that called itself 'Stalinist': Marietta Shaginian's *Bilet po istorii* (1938, about Lenin) and others. Aleksei Tolstoi's *Khleb* and Mikhail Bulgakov's *Batum*, which both focus on Stalin himself, date from the same period.

The Stalin and Post-Stalin Eras

The 'winners' of the Revolution – the ruling elite, the bureaucracy, the more educated and qualified strata of society – set the tone and the ideological parameters of the historical novel in the 1930s-40s as well as those of contemporary prose on the Revolution and the subsequent era (it is worth emphasising that historical fiction in this period was regarded as a branch of 'modern' literature, and some of the very best literary talents of the era were drawn or pushed towards it).[19] The formula of the historical novel in the mature period of Soviet society drew heavily on the themes and values of 'government, 'people' and 'intelligentsia', of 'the West' and its dark shadow, the East.[20]

The Soviet regime was the only ideological institution that could confer legitimacy on the actions of fictional heroes. The behaviour of figures representing any other social forces, even if only in embryonic form, had to keep within strict limits: it had to be classified either as subordination to the Soviet state or as some form of deviation (ranging from revolt to treason). Any independent actions by a private individual were ipso facto suspect both to his surrounding characters and to the reader. Even the character himself might find them dubious: any person was liable to succumb to 'doubt', 'loss of bearings', 'temptation' or even 'treachery'. Like real citizens in that period, characters in novels might not even realise that they were assisting the enemy and turn out to be 'involuntary accessories'. The more complex, individual and ambivalent a character was, the more he left himself open to this kind of suspicion. The reverse was also true: only straightforwardness, artlessness and openness could serve as a guarantee of a character's pure motives and unswerving commitment to his duty.

The simplicity and transparency of fictional characters and their motives were designed to confirm in the mind of the mass reader that they were 'true to life', like 'the rest of us', recognisably human. In accordance with the postulates of

---

[19] Besides the already mentioned Tynianov, Bulgakov, Veselyi and Aleksei Tolstoi, we should also mention Andrei Platonov and his tale of the Petrine era 'Epifanskie shliuzy' (1927).

[20] The Near Eastern dimension of Soviet Russian geopolitics was reflected in various ways by Iurii Tynianov's *Smert' Vazir-Mukhtara* and Vasilii Ian's (Ianchevetskii) Tatar-Mongol trilogy; the Far Eastern dimension by the novels of Nikolai Zadornov, from *Amur-batiushka* (1944) to *Simoda* (1975). The North American dimension was developed in the years of the Cold War and the Stalinist campaign against cosmopolitanism by I. Kratt's novels about Russian colonists in North America *Ostrov Baranova* (1945) and *Koloniia Ross* (1950).

socialist realism (which were thrashed out in 1932-33, after the party decree on the liquidation of all literary organisations and just before the centralisation of the literary and artistic organisational apparatus, and given the force of law at the first Congress of Soviet Writers in 1934), this kind of literary anthropology was to be accepted by readers as 'life itself'.[21]

At the same time, however, the tradition of the progressive intelligentsia – of moderate liberal criticism – continued in the Soviet historical novel between the 1920s and the 1980s. Writers from Iurii Tynianov and Ol'ga Forsh through to Natan Eidel'man, Iurii Trifonov, Bulat Okudzhava, Iurii Davydov, and Mark Kharitonov spent most of their time on the human costs of the processes of forced modernisation. As a bulwark against the impersonal cruelty of the state and the isolationist official ideology of the 'new person' as espoused by socialist realist novels, they were able to put forward the 'eternal' Christian human being (in Bulgakov), the 'elemental' Russian (as in Veselyi), the 'private' individual (as in Okudzhava), or simply the 'historical being' (as in Tynianov, Trifonov and Davydov).

Novels of this kind often followed the model of the nineteenth-century classics by making the 'little person' – who has no choice but to fall under the wheels of history -- their main protagonist and the antithesis of state power. The system of values implied by this sort of narrative is reflected in its preference for the first person and derives from its key notion of the individual as the victim of history. Historical actors, conflicts and plot developments are seen from the point of view of those on the receiving end. The 'tsar and subject' formula adopted in this fictional formula has as one of its variants the pairing 'artist and government' (as in Tynianov's novels and stories, Lidiia Chukovskaia's *Tale of Taras Shevchenko* [*Povest' o Tarase Shevchenko*, 1930], and Bulgakov's *Life of Monsieur de Molière* [*Zhizn' gospodina de Mol'era*, 1932-33]). Another important aspect of these novels is their positive, or at least constructively neutral, assessment of 'the West', with all that implies for the depiction of individual characters. Only in this tradition was it possible to write a historical novel that drew exclusively on Western material (for example Vinogradov's *Condemnation of Paganini* [*Osuzhdenie Paganini*], 1936).

---

[21] In July 1933 *Pravda* published the editorial 'Literatura i stroitel'stvo sotsializma', and a few days later Gor'kii's programmatic 'O sotsialisticheskom realizme' appeared. Ideological and organisational preparations for the writers' congress proceeded apace, and at the beginning of 1936 an All-Union Committee on Artistic Affairs was created.

The other trend in historical fiction – let us call it conservative – dated back to Aleksei Tolstoi and concerned itself primarily with the patriotic themes of Russia as a Great Power (or later on, from the 1970s, Russia as readers' 'native soil' [*pochva*]), the country's unity, its military might and triumphs. It put the autocrat and his 'devoted servants' centre stage. The latter always acted with extreme cruelty in the interests of the nation as a whole, without giving a moment's thought to the social costs and human losses that these entailed. In this schema, the figure of the historical victim is again prominent, but is accorded a very different value. Naturalistic scenes of torture and death are frequent, and the victims are often the youngest heroes – a young girl or a youth estranged from his surroundings – who symbolise the immaturity, purity, vulnerability, even the doom of an entire people, homeland or country.

Later, in the 1970s, when the intelligentsia in the wake of the Thaw yet again split into pro-Western and conservative patriotic camps, narratives of state power often took the approach of 'going back to the origins' and seeking the historical 'roots' of a particular way of life or national character. These preoccupations – and also a rejection of the internationalist propaganda according to which 'the new historical human community is the Soviet people' – drew writers such as Dmitrii Balashov, Vladimir Lichutin, Oleg Mikhailov and Valentin Pikul' to adopt as their key symbols the 'native soil' and other, similarly 'organic' emblems of national identity such as 'kin' (*rod*) and 'blood'.[22] Alongside the imperial era of Russian history (above all the 'Petersburg' period of state-led centralising modernisation), more and more novelists of this variety were drawn to the early stages of Russian state formation – the Kievan and Muscovite periods – and to the final phase of the Russian monarchy (as in Solzhenitsyn's *August 1914* [*Avgust chetyrnadtsatogo*, 1971] and Pikul''s *At the Last Frontier* [*U poslednei cherty*, 1979]). Writers also took a heightened interest in the deepest roots of the fatherland: those that lay in the pre-state era – in 'the original Rus', to quote the title of a then well-known novel by Valentin Ivanov (*Rus' iznachal'naia*, 1961).

Pikul' added elements of adventure and even melodrama to the general pattern of novels about 'native soil' and 'the Russian character' (as, for example, in his *By the Pen and the Sword* [*Perom i shpagoi*, 1972]). He invited his readers to

---

[22] See E. Anisimov, '"Fenomen Pikulia" – glazami istorika', *Znamia*, 11, 1987, pp. 214-223. A national conference on the subject 'A new historical human community [*obshchnost' liudei*]: the Soviet people and socialist realist literature' was held in Moscow in October 1972.

interpret all plot lines connected with the West through a kind of filter: to apply to them the stereotypes of the picaresque novel with its 'low' heroes and their correspondingly base (egotistical, mercenary, lascivious, at any rate suspect and disreputable) motives. By contrast, historical fiction of the liberal variety (by the likes of Trifonov, Davydov and Okudzhava) tended to place emphasis on inhuman bureaucratic rule, social stagnation, 'hard times', and the severe reduction of the options available to the country and the 'thinking' part of its population. Novels from the series *Ardent Revolutionaries* (*Plamennye revoliutsionery*), by Vasilii Aksenov, Anatolii Gladilin and Aleksandr Borshchagovskii, and the *biographies romancées* of the series *Lives of Remarkable People* (*Zhizn' zamechatel'nykh liudei*), by Natan Eidel'man and others, make allegorical play with the theme of terror – as enforced both by the state and by its opponents (the People's Will, the Bolsheviks).

These terrorists of the revolutionary movement had, as I described above, entered Soviet historical fiction at its earliest stage, just after the Revolution, when, in the spirit of the age, they were treated as heroes. In the 1930s and 1940s such heroic depictions of the opponents and slayers of tyrants and tsars practically disappeared from historical fiction, for obvious reasons (the handful of exceptions include Valerii Iazvitskii's novel about the People's Will member Ippolit Myshkin, *The Unvanquished Prisoner* [*Nepobezhdennyi plennik*, 1933]). In the 1970s historical figures of this kind started to undergo subtle reassessment, in some cases serving an allegorical purpose in the 'dual consciousness' and 'Aesopian language' of the liberal intelligentsia. Views of the Russian revolutionaries took another strong negative turn in the second half of the 1990s and the start of the 2000s, this time on patriotic, statist and Orthodox grounds. This latest wave of re-evaluation included works such as V. Serdiuk's novel about Nechaev, *Without a Cross* (*Bez kresta*, 1997). The trend had been anticipated by Solzhenitsyn's historical novels about Bolshevism and by émigré historical prose of the interwar period such as P. Krasnov's *The Tsar-Killers* (*Tsareubiitsy*, 1938). It also relates back to the anti-nihilist novels of the 1860s: Pisemskii's *Troubled Sea* (*Vzbalamuchennoe more*), Leskov's *Nowhere to Go* (*Nekuda*), Kliushnikov's *The Mirage* (*Marevo*), and other examples of ideologically engaged prose about revolutionaries in the era following the Great Reforms. Novels on the theme of the revolutionary movement offered rich material for investigating issues of cardinal importance for the intelligentsia in both tsarist and Soviet eras, both within Russia and in emigration: the conflict between the individual and state power, the choice between adaptation and revolt, submission and violence.

Contemporary Russian Historical Fiction

The historiosophical and anthropological trends that I have identified in earlier Russian and Soviet historical fiction find their most obvious and routine continuation and onward development in the patriotic historical novel of the 1990s. As usual, it is the epigones who do most to illuminate – even to the point of caricature – more general cultural processes. Throughout the Soviet era, the main corpus of literature was always designed for a mass audience; more precisely, its role was to mobilise this audience. After assimilating the techniques of translated adventure fiction and 'studying' the Russian classics in the second half of the 1920s and the start of the 1930s, Soviet writers of the official mainstream used the standard patterns of a given genre (production novel or military novel, village novel or spy novel) to fulfil the propaganda tasks of the moment – but also in some ways to continue the traditions of the classic nineteenth-century Russian 'ideological novel'. After the collapse of the USSR and the (temporary) retreat of Soviet ideology, the genre system of Soviet literature was devalued and eroded in its turn. Characteristically, however, when a restoration period in Russian culture began in the mid-1990s, the mass historical novel was at its forefront. This genre met all the requirements of the time: it was both highly ideologised and politicised yet at the same time exciting and entertaining for the reader.[23]

In contemporary historical fiction, by comparison with the 1970s, and even more so with the 1930s, direct ideological declarations by authors and their characters are much more frequent and more categorical. Sometimes they even seem exaggerated and parodic, as I will discuss in more detail below. For the time being, let us identify the key points of the genre's currently dominant ideology.[24] The main unit of existence here is 'the people', and this expansive national

---

[23] The steep rise of formulaic fantasy literature in the guise of 'Slavic fantasy' dates from the same period. The same kind of synthesising tendencies appeared in the late 1990s even in 'artistic' prose: in the stylised detective novels of B. Akunin and L. Iuzefovich and in novels about empire written in the spirit of postmodernist 'alternative history' (Sergei Smirnov, S. Karpushchenko).

[24] The search for 'origins' and 'roots' in the past was, of course, under way in many other social and political domains at this time – for example in practical politics, with its public relations agencies and lobbying groups. This kind of enterprise has already been noted by specialists: see for example K. Aimermakher/F. Bomsdorf/G. Bordiugov (eds), Mify i mifologiia v sovremennoi Rossii, M, 2000.

collective serves as the main hero: particular dramatis personae are either the people's allegorical personification or else no less allegorical embodiments of unacceptable, threatening and potentially destructive human aspirations and qualities (as manifested by enemies and traitors). The 'path' of each people is absolutely predetermined: 'Every people must have a single goal. And a great people must have a great goal'.[25] At the outset of this pre-assigned historical path, the territory of the future Russia was inhabited only by isolated and widely dispersed tribes; by the culmination of its historical destiny, Russia is a united and mighty empire. 'The era of biological evolution had come to an end, and the age of historical development had begun. Rus' had taken its first step towards the Russian Empire'.[26] After the zenith of imperial power has been attained, a period of decline and weakening of creative potential sets in along the same organic lines: the curtain rises on the age of 'the single ideology'.

The national whole is embodied by its leader: 'Every people needs a guide on its historical path. The guide of a people can be a great leader [*vozhd'*] or a prophet'.[27] The motifs of earth (the soil, the native land), people, autocrat and individual hero are symbolically interchangeable. The semantic identity between them is a fundamental characteristic of the neo-traditional world-view of the patriotic historical novel. It offers the reader the opportunity to identify with everything that is represented in the narrative, with the full picture of the world it provides, and facilitates the transition from the more concrete levels of symbolic identification to the more general.

One other factor needs to be mentioned to explain the reception of this type of literature. The version of history it presents is predetermined; other versions are impossible. No space is offered for independent assessments and alternative interpretations. Subject-centred forms of narration, the subjunctive mood, humour, irony, the absurd, and other modes of authorial self-reflexivity are absolutely ruled out. The world depicted by these novels is just as categorical as their style of writing is authoritarian. History – contrary to Tynianov's principle of narrative uncertainty in *Kiukhlia* – is unquestionably and indisputably over. It is a monolithic whole that cannot be reworked or rethought. It can only be retrospectively presented as a kind of allegorical panorama or historical survey – and only as such must it be perceived and assimilated.

---

[25] V. Zima, *Istok*, M, 1996, p. 257.
[26] Ibid., p. 472.
[27] Ibid., p. 231.

The ups and downs in the life of an individual are, in this predetermined world, unfathomable for that individual and no different from those experienced by anyone else; they are side-effects of the ubiquitous forces of 'fate'. This kind of traditional, epic image of the world lies at the heart of the notion of causation employed by the patriotic historical novelist. It determines the actions of individual characters, who are not for the most part responsible for consequences and results, which are always unpredictable. 'Life is a river ... It carries some midstream, while others it runs aground'.[28] In the patriotic historical novel, as in the epic novels of Anatolii Ivanov, Petr Proskurin and other writers of similar mass appeal in the 1970s, 'life' – defined as the common, super-individual existence of all ('all' in the sense of all people who are identically akin to one another) – is equated to an unpredictable force of nature. This set of basic assumptions is usually conveyed by stereotyped metaphors of temporal 'currents' or 'rapids'.

The misfortunes of people and nations are linked to violent displays of power, to an aggressive striving for domination, to ambition and egocentrism. As a rule, such disasters for the country, people and individual hero come from without; they are brought about by outsiders who are alien in language, way of life, and faith. Human diversity, dissimilarity of individuals, nuances in social organisation, and gestures of autonomy by particular groups of people are all treated in this type of novel – as in traditionalist and neo-traditionalist thinking more generally – as illegitimate and inexplicable. Any kind of difference is suspect: it always carries a threat and ends in catastrophe. For this reason, both in the consciousness of the fictional heroes and in the historiosophical digressions by the author, the social and cultural diversity of existence has to be simplified and reduced to the usual opposition between 'one's own' and 'alien': 'The greatest of mysteries is the division of people into those who are our own and those who are alien'.[29] Yet Russians need to beware of 'their own' even more than of outsiders, since the former are motivated by envy. 'The name of the Russian Satan is envy.'[30]

This introduces into the mass patriotic novel a motif that is important for understanding the entire collective mythology of the Russians (otherwise known as 'the Russian fate' or 'the Russian path'): namely, the motif of schism. And this is schism not only on the 'external' social level (as in the already mentioned themes

---

[28] V. Bakhrevskii, *Strastoterptsy*, M, 1997, p. 12.
[29] Zima, *Istok*, p. 149.
[30] Bakhrevskii, *Strastoterptsy*, p. 235.

of 'betrayal', 'the turncoat' and the 'involuntary accessory') but also on the deeper level of human character, of anthropological patterns. Here we find a mass-cultural version of the theme of the inner dualism of the Russians that is so central to the work of writers from Dostoevskii to Sologub and beyond: 'There slumbers within us a warm love for the living alongside a bloodthirstiness; it drags us now into a rotting swamp, now into a sunny meadow'.[31] Individualism and ambition are similarly associated with treacherous and destructive dualism: 'the cause of all his troubles was the fact that he gave no thought to those close to him, had no concern for their happiness and benefit, but thought above all else only of his own advantage and considered himself – a man of ambition and soldier of fortune – the most important person in the world'.[32]

The ideal that is set against this deadly schism and strife, both in the collective consciousness and in the patriotic historical novel, is, by contrast, a combination of qualities of inner wholeness, equanimity and resistance to outside influence. All of these super-individual attributes are united and embodied in the Russian 'land', the homeland, the unified state power, the special Russian cast of mind and way of life (the part here being mythologically equal to the whole). According to this kind of fictionalised historiosophy and anthropology, only patriotic integrity offers a stability and continuity that cannot be undermined by change or wear and tear. Only the Whole, by definition unattainable and inaccessible to direct human understanding, can provide the individual with security and stability by making him, an individual particle, part of an eternal community: 'Beauty lies in unity, and pride in a recognition of your own beauty, not the kind that comes from over the seas ... above all it means the Russian person, the Russian land ... to look after and preserve and defend this land so richly endowed with beauty – this is happiness that cannot be equalled'.[33]

Characters in popular historical fiction offer 'patience' and 'service' as symbolic reciprocal gifts in exchange for the salvation the Whole offers them. The hero must be ready at all times for self-denial and self-sacrifice as part of the common cause: 'In order to emerge unbowed from constant warfare with the enemy, our state had to require of its fellow-countrymen as many sacrifices as were necessary ... This was how the foundations of what would later be called the enigmatic Slavic soul would be laid!'[34] Not only that, it is precisely at such moments

---

[31] V. Usov, *Tsari i skital'tsy*, M, 1998, p. 243.
[32] V. Baliazin, *Okhotnik za tronami*, M, 1997, p. 417.
[33] E. Zorin, *Ognennoe porubezh'e*, M, 1994, p. 125.
[34] Zima, *Istok*, p. 406.

of submission to fate and acceptance of any sacrifice that the hero experiences – in a characteristically passive and martyred way – a feeling of community with others and of belonging to the national whole. In this context, the meaning of 'conscience' lies not in the individual or in conventional ethics but in the collective: 'Who are we? The dust of time ... But dust with a conscience'.[35] Patience is here not an attribute of individual character but rather represents silent collective faithfulness to ancestral traditions, and a hero can only recover from his 'fall' and return to life by joining with the entire people. 'We have borne it ... for the truth of our fathers ... God willing, we shall be resurrected'.[36] This means that the novel's hero – like 'each one of us [readers]' – has a duty to restore the lost honour, glory and might of the empire. As one novelist characteristically opines, 'the life of a person or of an entire people is not easy ... but it must carry with it the dream of future greatness'.[37]

In the novels described here the antithesis of the might of, and universal recognition due to, a people, a country or a state – of the power and glory that are always experienced as lost and invariably lie in the past or the future but never in the present – is the state of mere 'survival'. Russia is plunged into this shameful condition century after century by 'antipopulist reformers': 'Did not Russia hold back a groan, through gritted teeth, when Peter the Great reared her up ... did she not grit her teeth ... under the yoke of the so-called Marxist-Leninists ... is not the Russian suppressing a groan nowadays, realising that Russia has been brought to the edge of a precipice and that the Great People of this Great Power are now turned not to glory and might but to survival?'[38]

In the patriotic historical novel the limits and dimensions of human existence are presented on two separate levels. The 'higher', more general level has already been discussed: this is the thematic cluster of land, people and leader as the embodiment of a predestined and immutable whole. The 'lower' level (roughly speaking, the 'popular' or folkloric dimension of the nationalist vision) contains the minimal diversity of human types that is available to the patriotic novelist, who cannot look beyond the fixed models of behaviour laid down in a closed, clan- or caste-based society. This rudimentary level of social differentiation is reflected in the speech styles of the characters, which correspond to a linguistic 'table of ranks' and contain clumsy admixtures of 'low' and 'high' registers.

---

[35] Bakhrevskii, *Strastoterptsy*, p. 537.
[36] Ibid, p. 536.
[37] Usov, *Tsari*, p. 11.
[38] G. Anan'ev, *Kniaz' Vorotynskii*, M, 1998, p. 451.

Heroes have a narrow range of social attributes. In fact, there are really only two that are worth speaking about. The first is a character's position in the hierarchy of power or in the system of traditional authority (sometimes this position is not stated directly but suggested, in true archaic fashion, by the minimal indicators of sex and age: man or woman; underage, mature or old). The second is the fact of belonging to a clan, a people, or a faith ('one of us, baptised in the faith' or 'an outsider, a non-Christian'). The basic character types in patriotic historical fiction are therefore placed on the axis of domination. The key character types, who bear the greatest ideological burden, are the following: the adolescent whose path in life is still undefined but who shows signs of saintliness or the inexperienced young girl who is yet to know love; the married woman (usually depicted as a faithful, understanding and obedient wife); and the exemplary executor – the ideal servant, the ruler's Doppelgänger, a subject but not a courtier, a 'simple man' not an 'intriguer', who has no power of his own and no aspiration to acquire any.

This kind of executor is usually a fighter or military commander. He is entirely subordinate to the higher values of national integrity, might and glory; his duty is 'to serve sovereign and fatherland according to honour and conscience'.[39] This military chief can be permitted a basic minimum of socially acceptable calculation, cunning and even 'deception' (since it is at the expense of the enemy and assists 'our own' cause). But much more important than foresight and calculation is the hero's 'faithfulness to the glorious martial traditions of the fatherland'.[40] It is quite clear why this should be so. The hero is an idealised embodiment of the dedication to the whole that is so crucial to a militarised society and forms part of its entire mythological structure and legitimation. Of course, he also represents a sublimation of the illicit and suppressed aggression of a 'little man' without rights and autonomy. But this is just the anthropological aspect of the hero motif; there is more to it than that. It is crucial that the image of the commander brings to a focus popular understandings of social order: only the military model can serve to impose order, whether in the home, the country or the world. In other words, the strict military organisation of the premodern era (the *druzhina*) or other similarly archaic political institutions offers an ideal model of state-society relations – a recognisable and acknowledged means of regulating the life of the community. Any deviations from this kind of political structure are

---

[39] Ibid., p. 436.
[40] Ibid., p. 452.

presented to the mass consciousness in catastrophic terms – as being synonymous with chaos and destruction.[41]

The Sociocultural Context of Soviet Historical Fiction

The ideological and symbolic structures I have described above were not articulated in so detailed a manner, passing with the constancy of stereotype from one novel to another, in the patriotic historical prose of the Stalin era or even in the statist 'native soil' oeuvre of the 1970s and early 1980s. And there are good reasons for this. The recent intensification of the ideological elements in this kind of historical fiction has two main causes.

The first, and the simpler, of these is the transfer of a literary model into the hands of epigones: by ratcheting up the ideology, these mass-market authors are able to compensate for the hackneyed means they employ to interpret the past and their equally pedestrian symbolic repertoire. The second cause is of a more general social-historical kind, and reflects the functions and operations of ideological systems at various stages of a society's existence. In the 1920s and 1930s, when new social strata were coming to the fore in Soviet Russia, the official ideology sought above all to mobilise the masses by directing them to strive for social goals that were presented as achievable, near, and comprehensible to all. The authorities proclaimed their confidence in the possibility of rapid, voluntarist, 'political' (as was then said) solutions to all problems (a confidence that was shared by many people, especially the younger generation). Official rhetoric gave enormous prominence to planning and technology in the broad sense of any rational standardised techniques developed in the early stages of modernisation, industrialisation or civilisation, whether they concerned machinery or linguistic competence (i.e. literacy). Rhetoric on the past similarly emphasised 'decisive' images and motifs, moments of successful political, social or economic transformation and rapid achievement, at any price, of the goal of general welfare. The main paradigmatic hero of historical prose in this period (and of cinema and art more generally) was, characteristically, Peter I. A close textual analysis would reveal that the rationale of human behaviour, the principles of fictionalised anthropology, implied in Aleksei Tolstoi's novel about Peter were

---

[41] Similar attitudes have been revealed by recent public opinion surveys: see B. Dubin, 'Model'nye instituty i simvolicheskii poriadok: elementarnye formy sotsial'nosti v sovremennom rossiiskom obshchestve', *Monitoring obshchestvennogo mneniia*, 1, 2002, pp. 14-19.

strikingly similar to those of such socialist realist classics as Nikolai Ostrovskii's *How the Steel Was Tempered* (*Kak zakalialas' stal'*) and Boris Polevoi's *The Story of a Real Man* (*Povest' o nastoiashchem cheloveke*).

A new sociocultural situation emerged between the end of the 1960s and the start of the 1980s, as the Soviet sociopolitical system entered a period of deepening crisis and its principal ideological myths began to erode and fragment. The official rhetoric of the Soviet people as 'the new historical human community' had now lost all its vigour and could do no more than sketch out the fictional contours of a communal whole that no longer existed. The mobilising spark was gone. At the same time, and as a form of ideological compensation, the ideological resources of the unofficial sphere came to the fore: the humanist values of the liberal-minded reformist intelligentsia that had adapted to the Soviet system; the defence of civil rights and the quest for a non-falsified history pursued by the dissidents and a section of the cultural underground; the 'native soil' quest for 'roots' and 'origins', along with the statist nationalist ideas, of the journals *Molodaia gvardiia* and (later) *Nash sovremennik* and *Moskva*.

Neither the official ideology nor the communo-nationalist alternatives were interested in looking for new universal values and goals of sociocultural development; the question of a new anthropology for the modern world barely came on the agenda. The only ways to hold together a collapsing moral universe were, first, to opt for the symbols of the traditionalist, particularist national community (such as homeland, national uniqueness, national character, 'special path', and so on) and, second, to focus on images of internal and external enemies (from the USA to 'non-Russians' and the 'non-Orthodox'). Both of these approaches no longer had the positive charge of ideological mobilisation. Instead, their role was passive and defensive: they were a desperate attempt to shore up the symbolic boundaries of a disintegrating social and ideological whole. The most effective way to carry out this rearguard action was to shift the coordinates of the community as far back in historical time as possible (if possible, to the 'origins') or else to raise the ideological stakes, and thus conceal the absence of a coherent identity, by demonising and scapegoating 'enemies' who had apparently obstructed the emergence of the desired harmonious and stable national community. Historical myths of this kind are redolent above all of a closed society with a particularist notion of national community. It is no surprise, therefore, that the motif of the secure defensive barrier against the outside world, of immunity to 'alien' influence, figures large in patriotic fiction.[42]

The myth of the past constructed in Soviet patriotic historical fiction derives from collectivist and de-individualised ideological postulates and plot structures; its language is correspondingly unremarkable – to the point of banality.[43] These features became exceptionally marked from the mid-1990s onwards, as the failure of attempts to reform the country 'from above' in the late 1980s and early 1990s became clear to all sections of the population. Yet the patriotic novel of recent times has features that distinguish it from all its earlier Soviet counterparts. For the first time since the Revolution, books are now sold to readers as a purely commercial product, and not as part of the state propaganda machine. They are written, distributed, purchased and consumed beyond the zone of state control without depending on its financial subsidies. In other words, the former state 'legend' of history has now been assimilated by the mass reader and forms part of his world-view. The other new feature of the late 1990s was that, unlike the booms in historical fiction in the 1930s and 1970s, the dominance of the patriotic conservative camp is completely undisputed. This version of the national past, for the first time in Russian cultural history of the nineteenth and twentieth centuries, has no intellectual or artistic rival.[44] Another novelty is that most authors of these novels were yesterday's newspaper journalists – run-of-the-mill members of the Union of Journalists or the Union of Writers. These were people without an established name, reputation or literary biography. This was precisely the kind of anonymous interchangeable fiction that is characteristic of mass literary production in other genres as well.

---

[42] On this point, see my article, 'Zapad, granitsa, osobyi put': simvolika "drugogo" v politicheskoi mifologii sovremennoi Rossii', *Monitoring obshchestvennogo mneniia*, 6, 2000, pp. 25-35.

[43] On this, see Boris Dubin, 'O banal'nosti proshlogo: opyt sotsiologicheskogo prochteniia rossiiskikh istoriko-patrioticheskikh romanov 1990-kh godov', in idem, *Slovo – pis'mo – literatura: Ocherki po sotsiologii sovremennoi kul'tury*, M, 2001, pp. 256-258.

[44] Towards the end of the 1990s, so-called postmodernist writers began to produce works in the vein of 'alternative' history (Pavel Krusanov and others). Their readership was largely restricted to the student population of the major cities and seems not to have overlapped at all either with the audience for historical novels in the liberal intelligentsia tradition (the readers of the 'thick journals', for the sake of argument) or with the mass audience of patriotic historical fiction. Readers in this last category pick up their books at street stalls: the novels they consume are not advertised in thick journals or glossy magazines or on literary websites.

The production, mass marketing and reader reception of the patriotic historical novel have all been profoundly affected by the changes at work in Russian society in the 1990s. The end of the 1980s saw the symbolic self-abasement for Soviet people (who were pejoratively dubbed *sovki* in those years), and the early 1990s were a time of enormous uncertainty and bitter frustration for any sense of social and national identity. By 1994-95, however, Russians showed increasing signs of positive self-image and a willingness to identify themselves as belonging to the national whole of Russia – its 'land and territory', but especially 'its past and history'. By the mid-1990s, Russian citizens were starting to mention as national characteristics not only negative features (such as degradation, reliance on protection 'from above', lack of practical sense, idleness) but also positive features such as energy, hard work, hospitality, religious feeling, and readiness to help others. The basis for a renewed sense of identity among Russians was above all the production of symbols of collective belonging to the broadest possible whole: a national community. And the symbols that took pride of place were those that related either to an imagined past of shared ordeals and triumphs or to a traditional society with 'archaic' features such as social passivity ('patience', readiness to make sacrifices), cultural unsophistication and straightforwardness.[45] The contrasting background for all these shifts in mentality during the 1990s was a mass crisis of trust with regard to all social and state institutions in Russia except the army and the Orthodox Church (in other words, a crisis of trust in precisely the institutions that were identified as modern, democratic, held in common with the rest of the world). The population at large became convinced that everything in Russia was 'being run by the mafia', that 'everything is completely corrupt', that the state was not working, and that anarchy, theft and discord held sway. By contrast with the mindset of the Soviet period, and with the expectations of the early perestroika era, middle-aged and elderly Russians lost their confidence in what tomorrow might bring and looked instead for someone to take a 'firm hand'. This popular mood was seized on not only by the small-circulation communist or nationalist press. It was also whipped up by the populist tabloid press, which wasted no opportunity to sensationalise cases of crime and corruption.

In the second half of the 1990s – after the first Chechen war, the events in Yugoslavia, and then Russia's involvement in a second Chechen war whose end

---

[45] For more detail, see Lev Gudkov, 'Pobeda v voine', *Monitoring obshchestvennogo mneniia*, 5, 1997, pp. 12-19, and idem, 'Kompleks "zhertvy"', *Monitoring obshchestvennogo mneniia*, 3, 1999, pp. 47-60.

is still not in sight – Russia became more isolated in the world both economically and politically. But within the country the outcome was quite different. The government, the population and the greater part of the media independently of one another all chose to focus on the significance and symbolic prestige of the national whole and its special historical path and destiny. This phantom wholeness, like the imaginary prestige that bolstered it, found most of its symbolic support in the past. Thus, the 'best' period in the living memory of Russian citizens was deemed to be the Brezhnev era, and the favourite subject for historical idealisation by the intelligentsia in literature and film (in the work of Eduard Radzinskii, Nikita Mikhalkov, Gleb Panfilov and others) was the last phase of the Romanov dynasty. This powerful wave of cultural expression added momentum to the steep ascent of the patriotic historical novel, which enticingly combined elements of costume melodrama, crime fiction, and spy novel.

(Translated by Stephen Lovell)

Birgit Menzel

A Selected Bibliography of Works on Post-Soviet Popular Literature

This list of further reading is limited to the publications most directly relating to Russian popular fiction (as opposed to Russian cultural history more generally). For more detailed references, both on the broader context and on individual genres, see the footnotes to each chapter.

Amusin, Mark, 'Strugatskie i fantastika teksta', *Zvezda,* 7, 2000, p. 208-216.

Apenko, Elena, 'Transcultural Modes and Myths of Mass Literature', *Trans: Internet-Zeitschrift für Kulturwissenschaften,* 2002, 14 December, no pagination.

Arbitman, Roman, 'Nauchnaia fantastika v odinochestve: Zametki o sovremennom sostoianii zhanra', *Voprosy literatury,* 1996, 1, pp. 308-316.

Baraban, Elena V., Russia in the Prism of Popular Culture: Russian and American Detective Fiction and Thrillers of the 1990s, *Dissertation Abstracts International, Section A: The Humanities and Social Sciences,* 64, 2004, 12 (June), U of British Columbia.

Borisova, Ol'ga, '"Damskii roman" i ego chitateli', *Zvezda,* 12, 1993, pp. 198-200.

Brintlinger, Angela, 'The Hero in the Madhouse: The Post-Soviet Novel Confronts the Soviet Past', *Slavic Review,* 63, 2004, 1 (Spring), pp. 43-65.

Cardullo, Bert (ed.), 'American and Russian, or Gangsters, Tyrants, and Bombshells', *Popular Culture Review,* 13, 2002, 1 (January), pp. 89-99.

Dark, Oleg, 'Rukovodstvo po ekspluatatsii deistvitel'nosti. Griadushchie nepriiatnosti luchshe vstrechat' s pistoletom v rukakh – schitaiut avtory 'zhenskikh' detektivov', *Nezavisimaia gazeta,* 13 August 1998, p. 11.

Dubin, Boris, 'Ispytanie na sostoiatel'nost': K sotsiologicheskoi poetike russkogo romana-boevika', *Novoe literaturnoe obozrenie,* 22, 1996, pp. 252-274.

Dubin, Boris, 'Semantika, ritorika i sotsial'nye funktsii "proshlogo". K sotsiologii sovetskogo i postsovetskogo istoricheskogo romana', in idem, *Intellektual'nye gruppy i simvolicheskie formy. Ocherki sotsiologii sovremennoi kul'tury,* M, 2004, pp. 74-100.

Filippov, Leonid, 'Umnyi ne skazhet...O proizvedeniiakh Strugatskikh voobshche i o fantastike v chastnosti', *Neva,* 8, 1998, pp 188-198.

Filiushkina, S.N., 'Detektiv', *Russkaia slovesnost',* 5, 1998, pp. 13-18.

Galina, Maria, 'Outside the Law: Russian Detective Stories', *Russian Social Science Review: A Journal of Translations,* 36, 2000, 2, (Spring), pp. 86-92; 42, 2001, 2, (March-April), pp. 93-99.

Givens, Laura, 'The Bestseller: The Russian Accent', *Social Science Review: A Journal of Translations,* 39, 1998, 3, p. 87-95.

Gomel, Elana, 'The Poetics of Censorship: Allegory as Form and Ideology in the Novels of Arkady and Boris Strugatsky', *Science Fiction Studies,* 22, 1995, 1 (March), pp. 87-105.

Hägi, Sara, ‚Aleksandra Marinina und ihre Krimis', *Osteuropa,* 3, 2000, pp. 304-310.

Hänsgen, Sabine, 'Kommerzialisierung der Literatur/Literarisierung des Kommerzes', in Forschungsstelle Osteuropa (ed.), *Kommerz, Kunst und Unterhaltung. Die neue Popularkultur in Zentral- und Osteuropa,* Bremen, 2002, pp. 109-124.

Khlebnikov, Boris, 'The Secret of the Bestseller', *Russian Studies in Literature,* 1, 1998, pp. 64-72.

McReynolds, Louise, 'Reading the Russian Romance: What Did the Keys to Happiness Unlock?' *Journal of Popular Culture,* 31,1998, 4 (Spring), pp. 95-108.

Mela, Elen, 'Igra chuzhimi maskami: Detektivy Aleksandry Marininoi', *Nauchnye doklady vysshei shkoly: Filologicheskie nauki*, 3, 2000, pp. 93-103.

Mélat, Hélène, 'Nasilie versus rasskaz 'Zmeinye detektivy' Evgeniia Mironova', *Welt der Slaven*, 48, 2003, 2, pp. 303-312.

Mokrusov, Aleksei, 'The Bestseller. The Russian Accent', *Russian Studies in Literature: A Journal of Translations*, 1, 1998, pp. 73-81.

Nakhimovsky, Alice Stone, 'Soviet Anti-Utopias in the Works of Arkady and Boris Strugatsky', in Gribble, Charles (ed.), *Alexander Lipson: In Memoriam*, Columbus, OH, 1994, pp. 143-153.

'Na rande-vu s Marininoi: Kruglyi stol',, *Neprikosnovennyi zapas*, 1, 1998, pp. 39-44.

Nepomnyashchy, Catharine Theimer, 'Televising Aleksandra Marinina: The Representation of Crime in Post-Soviet Russia', *Welt der Slaven*, 48, 2003, 2, pp. 313-320.

Nepomnyashchy, Catharine Theimer, 'Markets, Mirrors, and Mayhem: Aleksandra Marinina and the Rise of the New Russian Detektiv', in Barker, Adele Marie (ed.), *Consuming Russia: Popular Culture, Sex, and Society Since Gorbachev*, Durham, ND, 1999, pp. 161-191.

Olcott, Anthony, *Russian Pulp. The Detektiv and the Russian Way of Crime*, Oxford, 2001.

'O massovoi literature, ee chitateliakh i avtorakh', *Znamia*, 12, 1998, pp.157-162. (Dark, Oleg, Ol'ga Slavnikova, Tat'iana Sotnikova).

Peterson, Nadya, 'Science Fiction and Fantasy: A Prelude to the Literature of Glasnost', *Slavic Review*, 48, 1989, 2 (Summer), pp. 254-268.

Pogacar, Timothy, 'The Theme of Culture in the Soviet Detective Novel', López Criado, Fidel (ed.), *Studies in Modern and Classical Languages and Literature*, I, Madrid, 1988, pp. 127-134.

Populiarnaia literatura. Opyt kul'turnogo mifotvorchestva v Amerike i v Rossii. Materialy V Fulbraitovskoi gumanitarnoi letnei shkoly, Moskva, 30 maia – 8 iiunia 2002 goda, Moscow, 2003.

Ponomareva, Mariia, 'Zhenskie detektivnye dela ...', *Nash sovremennik*, 4, 1999, pp. 280-283.

Rogatchevski, Andrei, 'May the (Police) Force Be with You: The Television Adaptations of Alexandra Marinina's Detective Novels: With Special Reference to The Coincidence of Circumstances', *Russian Studies in Literature: A Journal of Translations*, 40, 2004, 3 (Summer), pp. 79-94.

Rybakov, Viacheslav, 'Nauchnaia fantastika kak zerkalo russkoi revoliutsii', *Neva*, 4, 1996, pp. 146-162.

Smyrniw, Walter, 'From 'Ulla, Ulla' to 'Cosmic Linguistics': Alien Languages and Cultures in Western and Russian Science Fiction', *Germano-Slavica*, 12, 2000-2001, pp. 29-49.

Sotnikova, Tat'iana, 'The Karaoke Function', *Russian Studies in Literature: A Journal of Translations*, 2000, 36, 4 (Fall), pp. 62-69; 'Funktsiia karaoke', *Znamia*, 12, 1998, pp. 168-172.

Stel'makh, Valeria D., 'Reading in Post-Soviet Russia', *Libraries & Culture*, 33, 1998, 1 (Winter), pp. 105-112.

Stolyarov, Andrey, 'The Red Dawn', *New York Review of Science Fiction*, 8, 1996 (90), pp. 8-12.

Trepper, Hartmute, 'Aleksandra Marinina: Pionierin auf dem bekannten Feld des russischen Milizromans', in Forschungsstelle Osteuropa (ed.), *Kommerz, Kunst, Unterhaltung*, pp. 143-160.

Tsiplakov, Georgii, 'Evil Arising on the Road and the Tao of Erast Fandorin', *Russian Studies in Literature: A Journal of Translations,* 38, 2002, 3 (Summer), pp. 25-61; 'Zlo, voznikaiushchee v doroge, i dao Erasta Fandorina', *Novyi Mir*, 11, 2001, pp. 159-181.

Velthues, Christoph, 'Ein Fall von Perestrojka-Opportunismus: Ideologische Wendungen in zwei 'politischen Romanen' Julian S. Semenovs [1979] / [1988]', in Eimermacher, Karl/Kretzschmar, Dirk/Waschik, Klaus (eds), *Russland, wohin eilst du? Perestrojka und Kultur*, Bochum, 1994, pp. 249-263.

Zorkaya, Natal'ja, 'Problemy izucheniia detektiva: opyt nemetskogo literaturovedeniia', *Novoe literaturnoe obozrenie,* 22, 1996, pp. 65-78.

Notes on Contributors

Stephen Lovell is a Lecturer in Modern European History at King's College London. He is the author of *The Russian Reading Revolution: Print Culture in the Soviet and Post-Soviet Eras* (2000) and *Summerfolk: A History of the Dacha 1710-2000* (2003) and co-editor of *Bribery and Blat in Russia: Negotiating Reciprocity from the Middle Ages to the 1990s* (2000) and *Russian Literature, Modernism and the Visual Arts* (2000).

Birgit Menzel is Professor of Russian Literature and Culture at the University of Mainz, Germersheim. Her publications include *V.V. Majakovskij und seine Rezeption in der Sowjetunion 1930-1954* (1992), *Bürgerkrieg um Worte. Die russische Literaturkritik der Perestrojka* (2003), *Umbruch in Osteuropa – alte und neue Mythen* (co-edited with Clemens Friedrich, 1994), and *Kulturelle Konstanten im Wandel. Zur Situation der russischen Kultur heute* (editor, 2004).

Marina Koreneva is a Research Fellow for Russian-German comparative literatures at the Russian Academy of Sciences, Pushkinskii Dom, St Petersburg. She is also a prize-winning translator and screen-writer, and an interpreter. Besides numerous publications and editions she has translated the works of E.T.A. Hoffmann, Keller, Broch, Nietzsche, Rilke, Hesse, Nadolny, Sebald and Genazino.

Boris Dubin is a Senior Research Fellow at the All-Russian Centre for Public Opinion Research (VTsIOM), Moscow. He has published extensively in the fields of sociology and literary history; he is also a renowned translator from Spanish. His books include *Literatura kak sotsial'nyi institut* (with Lev Gudkov, 1994), *Slovo-pis'mo-literatura. Ocherki po sotsiologiii sovremennoi kul'tury* (2001) and *Intellektual'nye gruppy i simvolicheskie formy. Ocherki sotsiologii sovremennoi kul'tury* (2004).

Mariia Cherniak teaches in the Department of Modern Russian Literature at the Herzen State Pedagogical University, St Petersburg. Her main interests are Soviet literature in the 1920s, twentieth-century mass culture, and post-Soviet literature and criticism, and she has published extensively in all these areas. Her latest study, *Fenomen massovoi literatury XX veka*, is forthcoming in 2005.

ARBEITEN UND TEXTE ZUR SLAVISTIK
BEGRÜNDET VON WOLFGANG KASACK (Herausgeber der Bände 1-71)
HERAUSGEGEBEN VON FRANK GÖBLER UND RAINER GOLDT
München (Verlag Otto Sagner) 1973 ff.

1. Sabine Appel: Jurij Oleša. „Zavist'" und „Zagovor čuvstv". Ein Vergleich des Romans mit seiner dramatisierten Fassung. 1973. 234 S.
2. Renate Menge-Verbeeck: Nullsuffix und Nullsuffigierung im Russischen. Zur Theorie der Wortbildung. 1973. IV, 178 S.
3. Josef Mistrík: Exakte Typologie von Texten. 1973. 157 S.
4. Andrea Hermann: Zum Deutschlandbild der nichtmarxistischen Sozialisten. Analyse der Zeitschrift „Russkoe Bogatstvo" von 1800 bis 1904. 1974. 198 S.
5. Aleksandr Vvedenskij: Izbrannoe. Herausgegeben und eingeleitet von Wolfgang Kasack. 1975. 158 S.
6. Volker Levin: Das Groteske in Michail Bulgakovs Prosa mit einem Exkurs zu A. Sinjavskij. 1975. 214 S.
7. Геннадий Айги: Стихи 1954-1971. Редакция и вступительная статья В. Казака. 1975. 214 S.
8. Владидмир Казаков: Ошибка живых. Роман. 1976. 201 S.
9. Hans-Joachim Dreyer: Petr Veršigora. „Ljudi s čistoj sovest'ju". Veränderungen eines Partisanenromans unter dem Einfluß der Politik. 1976. 101 S.
10. Николай Эрдман: Мандат. Пьеса в трех действиях. Редакция и вступительная статья В. Казака. 1976. 109 S.
11. Karl-Dieter van Ackern: Bulat Okudžava und die kritische Literatur über den Krieg. 1976. 196 S.
12. Михаил Булгаков: Ранняя неизданная проза. Составление и предисловие Ф. Левина. 1976. 215 S.
13. Eva-Maria Fiedler-Stolz: Ol'ga Berggol'c. Aspekte ihres lyrischen Werkes. 1977. 207 S.
14. Christine Scholle: Das Duell in der russischen Literatur. Wandlung und Verfall eines Ritus. 1977. 194 S.
15. Aleksandr Vvedenskij: Minin i Požarskij. Herausgegeben von Felix Philipp Ingold. Vorwort Bertram Müller. 1978. 49 S.
16. Irmgard Lorenz: Russische Jagdterminologie. Analyse des Sprachgebrauchs der Jäger. 1978. 558 S.
17. Владимир Казаков: Случайный воин: Стихотворения 1961-1976. Поэмы. Драмы. Очерк «Зудесник». 1978. 214 S.
18. Angela Martini: Erzähltechniken Leonid Nikolaevič Andreevs. 1978. 322 S.
19. Bertram Müller: Absurde Literatur in Rußland. Entstehung und Entwicklung. 1978. 210 S.
20. Михаил Булгаков: Ранняя несобранная проза. Составление Ф. Левина и Л. В Светина. Предисловие Ф. Левина. 1978. 250 S.
21. Die Russische Orthodoxe Kirche in der Gegenwart. Beiträge zu einem Symposium der Deutschen Gesellschaft für Osteuropakunde. Hrsg. von Wolfgang Kasack. 1979. 86 S.
22. Георгий Оболдуев: Устойчивое неравновесие. Стихи 1923-1949. Составление и подготовка текста А. Н. Терёзина [Г. Айги]. Предисловие А. Н. Терёзина. Послесловие В. Казака. 1979. 176 S.
23. Wolfgang Kasack: Die russische Literatur 1945-1976. 1980. 72 S. [ersetzt durch ATS 28 und ATS 46].
24. Михаил Булгаков: Ранняя неизвестная проза. Составление, послесловие и примечания Ф. Левина. 1981. 254 S.

25. Поэт-переводчик Константин Богатырёв. Друг немецкой литературы. Редактор-составитель Вольфганг Казак с участием Льва Копелева и Ефима Эткинда. 1982. 316 S.
26. Константин Вагинов: Собрание стихотворений. Составление, послесловие и примечания Леонида Черткова. Предисловие В. Казака. 1982. 240 S.
27. Михаил Булгаков: Белая гвардия. Пьеса в четырёх действиях. Вторая редакция пьесы «Дни Турбиных». Подготовка текста, предисловие и примечания Лесли Милн. 1983. 152 S.
28. Wolfgang Kasack: Die russische Literatur 1945-1982. Mit einem Verzeichnis der Übersetzungen ins Deutsche. 1983. 120 S.
29. Михаил Булгаков: Забытое. Ранняя проза. Составление и предисловие Ф. Левина 1983. 140 S.
30. Лев Лунц: Завещание Царя. Неопубликованный киносценарий. Рассказы. Статьи. Рецензии. Письма. Составление и предисловие Вольфганга Шрика. 1983. 214 S.
31. Lev Loseff: On the Beneficence of Censorship. Aesopian Language in Modern Russian Literature. 1984. 278 S.
32. Gernot Seide: Die Klöster der Russischen Orthodoxen Kirche im Ausland in Vergangenheit und Gegenwart. 1984. 196 S.
33. Андрей Платонов: Старик и старуха. Потерянная проза. Составление и предисловие Фолькера Левина. 1984. 216 S.
34. Luise Wangler: Vasilij Belov. Menschliche und gesellschaftliche Probleme in seiner Prosa. 1985. 70 S.
35. Wolfgang Kasack: Russische Literatur des 20. Jahrhunderts in deutscher Sprache. [1. Band:] 350 Kurzrezensionen von Übersetzungen 1976-1983. 1985. 160 S. [siehe ATS 50].
36. Владимир Линденберг (Челищев): Три дома. Автобиография 1912-1918 гг., написанная в 1920 году. Подготовка текста и послесловие Вольфганга Казака. 1985. 92 S. 16 Abb.
37. Renate Schäper: Die Prosa V.G. Rasputins. Erzählverfahren und ethisch-religiöse Problematik. 1985. 294 S.
38. Wolfgang Kasack: Lexikon der russischen Literatur ab 1917. Ergänzungsband. 1986. 228 S. [ersetzt durch ATS 52].
39. Wolfgang Schriek: Ivan Šmelev. Die religiöse Weltsicht und ihre dichterische Umsetzung. 1987. 321 S., 10 Abb. ISBN 3-87690-319-X. 19,43 €.
40. Wolfgang Kasack: Bücher – Aufsätze – Rezensionen. Vollständige Bibliographie 1952-1987. Anläßlich des sechzigsten Geburtstages zusammengestellt von Irmgard Lorenz. 1987. 102 S.
41. Barbara Göbler: A. Adamov und A. und G. Vajner. Aspekte des sowjetischen Kriminalromans. 1987. 104 S. ISBN 3-87690-321-1. 7,67 €.
42. Fritz Wanner: Leserlenkung, Ästhetik und Sinn in Dostoevskijs Roman „Die Brüder Karamazov". 1988. 274 S. ISBN 3-87690-322-X. 19,43 €.
43. Frank Göbler: Vladislav F. Chodasevič. Dualität und Distanz als Grundzüge seiner Lyrik. 1988. 304 S. ISBN 3-87690-371-8. 19,43 €.
44. Tausend Jahre Russische Orthodoxe Kirche. Beiträge von Geistlichen der Russischen Orthodoxen Kirche im Ausland und Wissenschaftlern verschiedener Disziplinen. Herausgegeben von Wolfgang Kasack. 1988. 200 S. ISBN 3-87690-372-6. 14,32 €.
45. Die geistlichen Grundlagen der Ikone. Herausgegeben von Wolfgang Kasack. 1989. 204 S., 23 Abb. ISBN 3-87690-373-4. 14,32 €.
46. Wolfgang Kasack: Russian Literature 1945-1988. Translated by Carol Sandison. 1989. 160 S., 35 Abb. ISBN 3-87690-374-2. 12,27 €.
47. Иван Ахметьев: Миниатюры. 1990. 76 S. ISBN 3-87690-375-0. 10,23 €.
48. Christopher Hüllen: Der Tod im Werk Vladimir Nabokovs. Terra Incognita. 1990. 252 S. ISBN 3-87690-376-9. 18,41 €.
49. Michaela Böhmig: Das russische Theater in Berlin 1919-1931. 1990. 328 S. ISBN 3-87690-457-9. 26,59 €.

50. Wolfgang Kasack: Russische Literatur des 20. Jahrhunderts in deutscher Sprache. 2. Band: 450 Kurzrezensionen von Übersetzungen 1984-1990. 1991. 286 S. ISBN 3-87690-458-7. 23,01 €.
51. Birgit Fuchs: Mensch, Gesellschaft und Religion im Werk Timur Pulatovs. 1992. 100 S. ISBN 3-87690-460-9. 9,20 €.
52. Wolfgang Kasack: Lexikon der russischen Literatur des 20. Jahrhunderts. Vom Beginn des Jahrhunderts bis zum Ende der Sowjetära. 2., neu bearbeitete und wesentlich erweiterte Auflage. 1992. XVIII S., 1508 Sp. ISBN 3-87690-459-5. 50,11 €.
53. Frank Göbler: Das Werk Aleksej Konstantinovič Tolstojs. 1992. 461 S. ISBN 3-87690-511-7. 44,99 €.
54. Сергей М. Сухопаров: Алексей Кручёных. Судьба будетлянина. Редакция и предисловие В. Казака. 1992. 166 S., 30 Abb. ISBN 3-87690-512-5. 12,78 €.
55. Jan Paul Hinrichs: Verbannte Muse. Zehn Essays über russische Literatur der Emigration. A. Nesmelov, G. Ivanov, V. Lebedev, D. Knut, V. Lourié, B. Poplavskij, A. Štejger, V. Perelešin, N. Moršen, I. Elagin. Aus dem Niederländischen übersetzt von Thomas Hauth. 1992. 144 S. ISBN 3-87690-513-3. 12,27 €.
56. Eberhard Reißner: Das russische Drama der achtziger Jahre. Schmerzvoller Abschied von der großen Illusion. 1992. 342 S. ISBN 3-87690-514-1. 26,59 €.
57. Daniela von Heyl: Die Prosa Konstantin Vaginovs. 1993. 111 S. ISBN 3-87690-510-9. 10,23 €.
58. Ян Сатуновский: Рубленая проза. Собрание стихотворений. Составление, подготовка текста и предисловие В. Казака. Послесловие Геннадия Айги. 1994. 328 S., 5 Abb. ISBN 3-87690-548-6. 25,56 €.
59. Marion Munz: Boris Chazanov. Erzählstrukturen und thematische Aspekte. 1994. 122 S. ISBN 3-87690-549-4. 10,23 €.
60. Annette Julius: Lidija Čukovskaja. Leben und Werk. 1995. 272 S., 2 Abb. ISBN 3-87690-551-6. 23,01 €.
61. Olaf Irlenkäuser: Die russischen Literaturzeitschriften seit 1985. Kontinuität und Neubeginn. 1994. 116 S. ISBN 3-87690-550-8. 10,23 €.
62. Wolfgang Kasack: Die russische Schriftsteller-Emigration im 20. Jahrhundert. Beiträge zur Geschichte, den Autoren und ihren Werken. 1996. 360 S. ISBN 3-87690-552-4. 29,65 €.
63. Kirchen und Gläubige im postsowjetischen Osteuropa. Herausgegeben von Wolfgang Kasack. 1996. 234 S. ISBN 3-87690-553-2. 21,47 €.
64. Jan Paul Hinrichs: In Search of Another St. Petersburg. Venice in Russian Poetry (1823-1997). 1997. 112 S. ISBN 3-87690-602-4. 10,23 €.
65. Pia-Susan Berger-Bügel: Andrej Platonov. Der Roman Sčastlivaja Moskva im Kontext seines Schaffens und seiner Philosophie. 1999. 240 S. ISBN 3-87690-603-2. 21,47 €.
66. Vsevolod Setschkareff: Russische Literatur des 20. Jahrhunderts. Beiträge zu Aldanov, Annenskij, Brjusov, Gumilëv, Moršen, Muratov, Nabokov, Osorgin. Herausgegeben von Wolfgang Kasack 1999, 286 S. ISBN 3-87690-604-0. 24,54 €.
67. Wolfgang Kasack: Christus in der russischen Literatur. Ein Gang durch die Literaturgeschichte von ihren Anfängen bis zum Ende des 20. Jahrhunderts. Wissenschaftliche Ausgabe mit Anthologie in russischer Sprache. 1999, 296 S. ISBN 3-87690-758-6. 28,12 €.
68. Wolfgang Kasack: Lexikon der russischen Literatur des 20. Jahrhunderts. Bibliographische und biographische Ergänzungen. 2000, 88 S.
69. Amory Burchard: Klubs der russischen Dichter in Berlin 1920-1941. Institutionen des literarischen Lebens im Exil. 2001, 349 S. ISBN 3-87690-759-4. 29,60 €.
70. Бронислав Кодзис [Bronisław Kodzis]: Литературные центры русского зарубежья 1918-1939. Писатели. Творческие объединения. Периодика. Книгопечатание. 2002, 318 S. ISBN 3-87690-760-8. 32,00 €.
71. Wolfgang Kasack: Dmitri Klenowski. Geheimnis des Seins. Gedichte zu Tod, Transzendenz und Schutzengel. Mit 123 Gedichten in russischer Sprache. 2002, 223 S., 4 Abb. ISBN 3-87690-762-4. 22,00 €.

72. Birgit Fuchs: Natal'ja Baranskaja als Zeitzeugin des Sowjetregimes. 2005, 250 S. ISBN 3-87690-900-7. 32,00 €.
73. Wolfgang Kasack: Der Tod in der russischen Literatur. Aufsätze und Materialien aus dem Nachlaß. Herausgegeben von Frank Göbler. 2005, 353 S. ISBN 3-87690-907-4. 39,80 €.
74. Irmgard Lorenz: Jagdwörterbuch Russisch-Deutsch. 2005, 181 S. ISBN 3-87690-908-2. 22,80 €.
75. Benjamin Specht: Die Lyrik Bella Achmadulinas. 2005, 220 S. ISBN 3-87690-911-2. 29,80 €.
76. Frank Göbler (Hrsg.) unter Mitarbeit vom Ulrike Lange: Russische Emigration im 20. Jahrhundert. Literatur – Sprache – Kultur. 2005, 412 S. ISBN 3-87690-909-0. 39,80 €.
77. Frank Göbler (Hrsg.): Polnische Literatur im europäischen Kontext. Festschrift für Brigitte Schultze zum 65. Geburtstag. 2005, 289 S. ISBN 3-87690-910-4. 36,- €.
78. Stephen Lovell, Birgit Menzel (ed.): Russian Popular Literature. Post-Soviet Trends in Historical Perspective. 2005, 206 S. ISBN 3-87690-912-0. 32,- €.